Food Security in Iran

Edareh-ye Arzaq, 1910–1935

Willem Floor

MAGE PUBLISHERS

MAGE PUBLISHERS INC
WWW.MAGE.COM

LIBRARY OF CONGRESS CATALOGING-IN-PUBLICATION DATA
Available at the Library of Congress

FIRST HARDCOVER EDITION
ISBN: 978-1-949445-37-4

VISIT MAGE ONLINE: WWW.MAGE.COM
EMAIL: AS@MAGE.COM

CONTENTS

TABLES

ILLUSTRATIONS

IRANIAN CURRENCY

Late Qajar period

One *tuman* is 10,000 dinars

200 *shahi*s equal 1 *qran*

10 *qran*s equal 1 *tuman*

Nickel coins

1 and 2 *shahi*s

Silver coins

1, 2, and 5 *qran*s

Pahlavi period

As of 1925, one *tuman* equals 1,000 dinars

Nickel coins
1 *shahi* 20 equal to 1 *qran*
2 *shahi*s 10 equal to 1 *qran*

Silver coins
3 *shahi*s
5 *shahi*s 4 equal to 1 *qran*
10 *shahi*s 2 equal to 1 *qran*
1 *qran*
2 *qran*s
5 *qran*s

In 1932 the *qran* was replaced by the *rial* and divided into 100 dinars or 20 *shahi*s.

Nickel coins

1, 2, 5, and 10 dinars

Silver coins

0.5, 1, 2, and 5 *rial*s

Weights

1 *mesqal* equal to 5 *derham*s or 5 grams

1 *sir* equal to 75 *derham*s or 75 grams

1 *man* equal to 3,000 *derham*s or 3 kg

1 *kharvar* equal to 300,000 *derham*s or 300 kg

FOREWORD

Until recent times, Iran was a subsistence agricultural society that due to the vagaries of the weather regularly had to cope with local or national famines. Prior to the second decade of the 20th century, the government had neither a policy nor institutional arrangements to deal with grain shortages, artificial or not, and the resulting famines. In severe cases of famine and in case of urban riots it might intervene temporarily in the market, but the government usually left the care for the hungry to private philanthropy. Invariably, this private effort was inadequate.

As of 1909, isolated government measures were taken to secure the food supply of Tehran. However, it was only after 1918 that a beginning was made for more permanent and structural pro-active measures to prevent rather than to combat famine. Such measures were also taken in Tabriz, at least until 1920, but not in other major cities, where (except for 1925-27) any intervention continued to be left to the local government and private initiatives. It is surprising that, given the regularity of famine, bread rings and other means of creating artificial grain shortages in urban markets, the activities by the Alimentation Service/*Edareh-ye Arzaq*, which saved thousands of lives, has been almost totally ignored. No encyclopedia has an article on the Service and information about its performance is scarce. Even those most involved with the urban bread question issue, such as as Arthur Millspaugh, only mention it in passing. Ja`far Shahri in his two monumental works on the social history of Tehran does not mention it at all.[1] Therefore, it is high time that the work of the Alimentation Service be brought back from oblivion, so that those interested in the social history of Iran may learn about this important chapter in Iran's history.

In this book, I discuss the early efforts to combat famine and the beginning of a more targeted and structural approach developed by Lambert Molitor in Tabriz in 1917-18. After an Introduction to the underlying issues of the bread problem, I review in chapter 1, the execution of the food programs in Tehran from 1911 to 1917-18. In chapter two, the situation in Tabriz is analyzed; first, the early efforts started by Emile Ransquin in 1913-14, and then the program that was improved upon by Molitor in 1917-18. After 1919 we have no further information on food security activities in Tabriz. In the third chapter the situation in Tehran is examined during 1918-22. This was the period when Molitor established the basic structure, scope, and guidelines for the Alimentation Service in Tehran. Chapter four offers the reproduction of two reports assessing the food situation in Tabriz in 1923 and the policy proposals to improve existing operations. Unfortunately, no further data are available about the situation in Tabriz. In chapter five the activities of the Alimentation Service of Tehran under the management of the Millspaugh mission (1922-27) are discussed. This is followed by an examination of the Service under Iranian leadership (1928-35), although not much information is available on its activities during that time. After 1935, the tasks of the Alimentation Service were taken over by the Grain Price Stabilization Company and thus, a new chapter in food policy in Iran began, and therefore, this study stops there.

I thank Dr. Shahram Gholami (Farhangian University, Tehran) for his comments as well as for making available the documents reproduced in Appendix III.

---

1. Shahri 1368; Idem 1371.

INTRODUCTION

Throughout the history of Iran until the 1930s, its grain markets were small, i.e. there was no national market, but only regional markets. This was because the trade in grain was urban and regional in nature, due to the high cost and the limited capacity of transportation.[2] This situation was graphically described by the Iranian economist Mohammad Fateh as follows: "Persia is like a hungry person who has plenty of food in another part of the house but is unable to partake of it because of his physical inability to walk."[3]

Members of the elite, the middle class as well as anybody with sufficient means, acquired grain from their village[s] or in the market after the harvest and stored a year's supply. The same was done with regard to flour, beans, oil, and other products. Foodstuffs like butter, cheese, fruit, vegetables, and meat were usually bought daily in the market.[4] This grain and other food stuffs were used for their

---

2. On this issue in general, see Floor 2015.
3. Fateh 1926, p. 44; see also Molkara 1325, p. 56; Curzon 1892, vol. 1, p. 638.
4. Amir Khizi 1339, p. 320; Polak 1865, vol. 1, p. 111; Wilbraham 1838, pp. 42-43 ("The greater portion of the higher classes possess villages, within a day or two's journey of the capital, and draw from thence their supplies of wheat and barley and straw: they keep their fifteen or twenty mules; and, when they do not themselves require them, they either let them out, or send them to the provinces bordering upon the Caspian to

households, which not only consisted of their own extended families, but also of their retainers, followers and other dependents. The grain owners sold what they did not need for their own consumption in the market; the major grain owners often tried to manipulate the market to their advantage. Thus, it was only the urban lower classes, who represented more than 70 percent of the urban population (their numbers increased towards the end of the nineteenth century), who had to make daily visits to the market, not only for fruit, vegetables, dairy, and other products, but also to bakeries (which had to buy their flour from wholesale dealers).[5]

Notwithstanding the importance of this grain supply , the government was never able to effectively deal with the problem, and, until 1950, bread scarcity and even famine was one of the structural problems facing many Iranian consumers. The bread supply issue was aggravated by three main factors: (i) inadequate transportation system due to unsafe, bad or non-existent roads, the scarcity of pack animals, and inefficient organization of transport; (ii) the irresponsible system of government, which allowed individuals to manipulate the market, while ineffectively and weakly using its own position to positively influence the grain market; and (iii) the deficient taxation system, where the government quickly sold its taxes paid in kind via conversion (*tas`ir*) into cash at fixed low rates, which weakened its position in the grain market. Also, the sale of Crown lands (*khaleseh*) after 1885 further weakened the already ineffectual capacity of the government to influence the grain market.[6]

After the severe famine of 1871-72,[7] Naser al-Din Shah took steps to prevent similar calamities. Orders were issued to establish large state granaries that together would hold reserves sufficient to feed the population of Tehran for at least six months. To implement the new bread policy Naser al-Din Shah built a big new granary in

---

fetch rice or fuel- a part of which they can sell for sufficient to cover all expense of that which they retain for their own use.")

5. Issawi 1971, chapter two; Kasravi 1319, vol. 1, p. 196.

6. Floor 1999, pp. 265, 342.

7. Okazaki 1986.

Shah `Abdol-`Azim to store wheat from the rural areas around Tehran. Within the Ministry of Finance a new office was created to serve as the granary office of Tehran (*edareh-ye anbar-e ghalleh-ye dar al-khelafeh*) and was placed under the direction of a court official.[8] Government grain was to remain in storage until the next harvest, when it was sold to the bakers and replaced with newly harvested grain. This new policy was not only intended as a hedge against calamities of an unforeseen nature such as droughts, but also to act as a check on bread rings. An adequate reserve of grain in the state granaries would deter major landowners from driving up grain prices in a bad year, for the government would sell grain at normal prices, and thus act as a stabilizing factor in the grain market. Although in principle it was a well-intentioned policy, it was difficult to implement with a corrupt bureaucracy. Col. Kosogovski, the commander of the Cossack Brigade, knowingly remarked: "On the one hand this policy seemed an advantage; on the other hand it was a source of income."[9]

How was the new system supposed to work? The big cities had a government granary (*ambar-e dowlati*) where the grain (wheat and barley) was stored that the government received in kind as tax payment and as income in grain from its so-called Crown lands or Domains (*khaleseh*) as well as grain that the government might buy from private landowners. Normally, the government converted tax payments as well as income in kind into cash, ideally at a price fixed in accordance with the situation of the grain market. However, under the new system, based on an estimate of annual bread consumption in the city, the local governor would not convert the estimated equivalent of grain needed for bread consumption into cash. To counter speculation by grain owners, the government sold part of the grain stored in the government granary to licensed bakers, at a moderate price; bakers

---

8. Millspaugh 1925, p. 77 ("The huge ambar or granary with a capacity of four hundred thousand bushels."), which is about 11,000 tons; Sani` al-Dowleh 1306, appendix, p. 27.
9. Kosogovski 1341, p. 171; Mostowfi 1324, vol. 2, p. 43.

buying the rest of their grain needs in the market at daily market prices. This ensured a reasonable price for regular bread, because only some bakers, who did not receive government grain, baked 'luxury' bread. This system worked well in normal years, but things would totally go wrong when the governor and his officials as well as the big landlords took advantage of their control over the grain market and drove up the price by artificially creating a grain shortage, if such a deficit situation had not arisen by natural means.[10]

To address weak elements in government grain policy, the *Majles* made a good start by abolishing the application of conversion rates (*tas`ir*) on grain produced by crown lands in 1907. The objective of this decision was to increase the government income both in cash and kind. However, the leaseholders of these crown lands refused to pay the higher taxes. A compromise was eventually reached.[11] Other measures taken by the *Majles* were extensions of Naser al-Din Shah's decree of 1303 (1885), which, like the law concerning the Organization of the Provinces (*Qavanin-e Tashkilat-e Eyalat va Velayat*) of 4 Dhu'l-Qa`deh 1325 (9 December 1907), was aimed at strengthening central government control over the grain market. Articles 1, 6 and 4.48 of this law stipulated that above all, governors had to take the necessary steps to ensure the food security of their province. Article 42 defined the task of governors more specifically. Governors were ordered to promote the development of agriculture, especially in those areas where scarcity and famine could be expected. They were also charged with regulating the price of grain and other life necessities. Together with municipal and police authorities, governors had to take strong action against the use of false weights and manipulation of the market. However, this law did not contain any punitive measures that could be taken against fraudulent or negligent governors. But, even if such measures had been provided, the central government

10. On bread speculation in Iran, see Floor 2015, pp. 119-33.
11. Kasravi 1319, vol. 1, p. 227; Mostowfi 1325, vol. 2, p. 353.

could not have applied them, because it had neither the power nor the means to do so.[12]

Nevertheless, the members of the *Majles* continued to try taking the right steps to improve the food supply of Tehran, to keep the bread price down and to prevent grain price speculation. In December 1910, the report by the Parliamentary Bread Oversight Commission (*komisiyun-e taftish-e nan*) was discussed. The report informed the members that the Minister of Interior wanted the price of wheat to be free and the price of bread to be fixed. The report argued that to achieve access to bread at a reasonable price for the consumers of Tehran the government had to supply 150 *kharvar*s of wheat daily to the bakers. Furthermore, this meant that during a period of eight months a total of 36,000 *kharvar*s of wheat were needed. Of this quantity, 30,000 *kharvar*s had been or were in the process of being obtained, but the remaining 6,000 *kharvar*s had to be bought in the market. Therefore, the Ministry of Interior requested that the government agree to sell its grain at a price that would be one *tuman* cheaper than the prevailing market rate. Also, that the government had to be ready to always sell its grain below the market price. To that end a commission had to be formed within the Ministry to discuss the price of wheat and of bread, while the government also had to approve the purchase of the 6,000 *kharvar*s of wheat. The said commission had to consult with merchants and bakers concerning the bread situation. The daily supply of 150 *kharvar*s to the bakers was necessary to prevent price speculation (*ehtekari*), but this required the approval of the Ministry of Finance, which was also needed for the financing of 36,000 *tuman*s, if the government would sell its grain at one *tuman* below the market price. Although the *Majles* committee endorsed the report's recommendations it concluded that approval by the full *Majles* was required. The Budget Committee also agreed with the report, but some of its members submitted that the Ministry of Interior should have control over the market price to prevent price speculation. Other members worried about the question: Who would be in charge of the

12. Demorgny 1913, p. 96. See, for example, the inclusive discussions about the bread issue between *Majles* deputies and members of the government in 1907 and 1908. Sharaf al-Dowleh 1377, pp. 102, 154.

entire process of the food supply chain. The Committee did not want to repeat the disaster that had occurred in 1909, when the *Majles* had agreed to pay Hajj Vakil al-Ra`aya 80,000 *tumans* for providing 20,000 *kharvars* of wheat. However, he had only supplied 3,000 *kharvars* of wheat and nobody knew what happened with the remaining 17,000 *kharvars* or with the 80,000 *tumans*. The same members wanted to know where the wheat was coming from. Although no immediate decision was taken, the committee members were very much worried about the danger of price speculation.[13]

Despite the worries expressed about price speculation, and even the discussion about a draft law to ban it (*qanun-e man`-e ehtekari*) altogether,[14] members of the *Majles* were not always working for the benefit of the population. The accusation that some interest groups in the *Majles* or in the provincial councils fixed prices that were advantageous to themselves, was justified. Through pamphlets, secret societies attacked the deputies and the authorities, drawing attention to their dubious activities. But these and other protests did not have any effect either on the authorities or on the food situation.[15] People wrote poems and satirical prose decrying the speculation with the grain market. E.G. Browne quotes one such poem dealing with "*Ihtikar* or *Anbar-dari* (*i.e.* cornering the wheat or bread markets)" by Mirza Hoseyn Tabib-zadeh a.k.a. Kamal of Tabriz, which was recited for him by Mirza Mohammad Khan Ashrafzadeh from memory.

> So long as the fingers of the bread-cornerers are on the bread
> There is unrest in the world and ruin in the age.
> That fair ascendant star of Justice is eclipsed;
> That beauteous face of Equality is hidden.

---

13. *Ruznameh-ye Majles* 1376, vol. 4, p. 154 (no. 39, 14 Dhu'l-Qa`deh 1328/16 December 1910); for the worries expressed about price speculation, see also *Ruznameh-ye Majles* 1376, vol. 4 (nos. 40, p. 158 and 41, p. 162).

14. *Ruznameh-ye Majles* 1376, vol. 4, pp. 290 (no. 72- 13Rabi` I 1329/10 March 1911), 318 (no. 79 – 16 Rabi` II 1329/16 April 1911).

15. Kasravi 1319, vol. 1, p. 320; RMM 15/1911, pp. 176-79; de Lorey 1910, pp. 21, 25 (November 1906 bread riot by starving people).

> O hungry child, cry not thus, or else
> There will be a slap on thy face from the
> hands of the bread cornerers!
> O mother, surrender that ornament of thy embrace to the earth,
> For a human life is cheaper than a mouthful of bread!
> The pen is wearied of talking so much of bread;
> The pages of the *Kamal* are dyed with
> blood: what hurt is there in this?[16]

Neither Naser al-Din Shah's measures to have a government stock of grain to control the grain market nor the laws passed by the *Majles* making governors responsible for implementing an effective food supply program had the desired impact, because famines and 'bread corners' continued to be a regular phenomenon, for food shortages continued to bedevil the population of Iran as if there had been no laws passed or granaries built. However, as of 1911 the authorities in Tehran began to take temporary institutional steps to resolve the food supply problem. Moreover, as of 1917 in Tabriz and as of 1918 in Tehran, measures were taken to establish a permanent institutional response to the recurring problem of food supply deficits, mainly caused by bad harvests and grain speculation by landowners. This led to the permanent establishment of the so-called *edareh-ye arzaq*, an organization led by Lambert Molitor, a Belgian Customs official.[17] Although initially a stand-alone organization or even a municipal one, at Molitor's suggestion it became an office of the Ministry of Finance with national responsibility. Although its jurisdiction was national, the Alimentation Service initially only operated in Tehran and Tabriz. Although, as of 1925 a large number of provincial branches were opened these were all closed in 1927 and, thereafter, the Alimentation Service seems to have been mainly active in the province of Tehran.

---

16. Browne 1914, pp. 108, 299-300.

17. The Persian term used for the Alimentation Service mostly is *edareh-ye arzaq*, although often the term *servis-e arzaq* is also used, especially in the reports by Millspaugh. In 1917, in Tabriz, the official term used was *edareh-ye baladiyeh-ye ta'min-e adhuqeh-ye markazi-ye Azerbaijan*, i.e. the municipal central food security office of Azerbaijan.

In 1935, the task of the Alimentation Service was taken over by the *Sherkat-e sahami-ye tasbiyat-e ghalleh-ye Iran*, which operated throughout Iran Therefore, in this study, I only discuss the activities of the Alimentation Service in Tabriz (1917-23) and Tehran (1911-35). What's more, the limited information available is only about these two cities during those periods.

CHAPTER ONE

THE SITUATION IN TEHRAN 1912-1917

The growth of Tehran since 1870 led to an increase in its demand for food beyond the productive capacity of its traditional food supply districts, which "rendered its supplies precarious and expensive, owing to the heavy cost of transport from distant centres."[1] In the 19th century and in a normal year Tehran's grain needs were supplied by Varamin, Sauj Bulagh, Khar (Garmsar), Shahriyar and to a much lesser extent Khar and Fashafuyeh. Tehran began importing grain immediately after the harvest of barley in July and of wheat a month later, and the bulk of the harvest was brought into the government Granary by the end of December before the inclement winter weather. The import of grain, however, continued during the winter, be it in smaller quantities, until the spring. Grain brought into the government Granary was collected:

1. From the Crown lands (*khaleseh*) in the districts of Tehran.

1. IOR/L/MIL/17/15/23, p. 112.

2. From the land tax (*maliyat*), in kind.
3. By purchase from landlords.

By 1918, Tehran's population had doubled in size since 1870. Because there was no change in production methods (better cultivation and irrigation methods, repairs of the *qanat*s), its traditional neighboring supply districts were unable to satisfy Tehran's growing demand for food. Moreover, after 1885, the government sold much of its Crown lands or Domains, thus reducing its leverage in the Tehran grain market. As a result, by the second decade of the 20th century, when annual demand had reached more than 110,000 *kharvar*s, the traditional wheat growing districts were only able to supply 90,000 *kharvar*s of wheat. The remaining 20,000 *kharvar*s of wheat had to be obtained from Saveh, Arak (Soltanabad), Qazvin, and in bad crop years from as far a field as Damghan, Hamadan and Malayer. These additional grain supply districts also had to deliver Tehran's entire demand for 70,000 *kharvar*s of barley. These districts still had a small surplus of barley to supply Qom, while there was scope for increased barley production, in particular in Saveh. Needless to say that the greater distance that grain had to travel caused transportation problems and increased the cost of grain in the market.[2]

The bread crisis of 1912

In the fall of 1911 the food situation was critical not only in Tabriz, but in northern Iran in general, and in Tehran in particular, where there was a severe bread scarcity. The harvest had been poor partially due to drought and partially due to destruction of crops caused by disorders in 1910, mainly due to the incursion of Mohammad Ali, the ex-shah. The government asked Morgan Shuster, the American Treasurer-General, to supervise the provisioning of Tehran. In the execution of his task, Shuster was obstructed by reactionary grandees, who were already making a bread ring to enrich themselves and embarrass the

2. IOR/L/MIL/17/15/23, p. 113. On the sale of Crown lands, see Floor 1998, pp. 340-45.

government, and it "was only by the most extraordinary means that I was able to gather five thousand to six thousand tons of wheat and barley." The assassination at the end of November 1911 of the head of the bakers' guild, one of the leading grain speculators, eased some of the difficulties in supplying food.[3]

The temporary improvement brought about by Shuster's brisk policy reverted, after his departure, to its former condition of wheat cornering. The winter of 1911-12 had been cold and the spring was rather dry. On New Year's Day, 21 March 1912, bread was scarce and the governor of Tehran ordered that the supply of Tehran be put under the supervision of Joseph Mornard, the Belgian Director of Customs, who succeeded Shuster as Treasurer-General. Mornard created a new office in the Treasury department and appointed Matin al-Saltaneh as its head. Because, according to Mostowfi, this official knew nothing about the problem at hand, he asked the heads of the bakers' guild Mashhadi Hoseyn Nanva and Hajji Mohammad Hoseyn Razzaz, to advise him. Grain remained scarce throughout the harvest period and people were afraid that new supplies would not reach the city. There were riots, and a stream of pamphlets was published accusing the authorities of causing a willful and orchestrated famine. One pamphlet stated that this

> The famine is not natural, it is provoked. In fact, from 21 July until 8 August [1912], six to ten hundred loads of grain entered Tehran regularly. After 8 August, in addition to the loads for the government, about 1,600 loads were brought in daily for private persons. It is interesting to note that in the second half of July one could buy bread without difficulty. However, during the first half of August, where there was plenty of grain in the market and prices should have fallen, they increased enormously, and bread was scarce and of inferior quality.[4]

---

3. Shuster 1912, pp. 170-72, 206, 288.

4. Demorgny 1913, p. 102. It is probably at this time that new regulations were proposed to improve the bread situation of Tehran, of which certain parts were later implemented, see Afshar 1389, pp. 489-91.

The heads of the bakers' guild and Matin al-Saltaneh wanted to sell wheat from the state granary at harvest time, although these reserves were to have been kept until the end of the Iranian year (March), when stocks were very low, awaiting the new harvest. The bread at harvest time had to be prepared from grain bought in the market, because bakers had mostly used up their entire stocks by then. Mornard, however, hesitated to sell the government grain so early in the year. Therefore, the leaders of the bakers' guild created an artificial shortage of bread by closing their granaries. Mornard was deceived by this stratagem and gave orders to collect wheat from the districts around Tehran and to supply the two leaders of the bakers' guild daily with 300 *kharvar*s or 9 tons of wheat from the state granary at low prices. This measure brought an end to the bread shortage. Mornard wanted to isolate the grain merchants by refusing to buy grain from them and forcing them to leave their grain to rot in their granaries. Abdollah Mostowfi, then head of the Treasury Department within the Ministry of Finance and our main, if not only, source of information for this period, pointed out that the state granary just did not have enough in storage to last until the next harvest. Mornard countered that according to the *omana-ye maliyeh* (fiscal agents in charge of a district)[5] there was enough grain for two years. Mostowfi told him that these officials did not know the difference between wheat and barley and that what was actually available was 30,000 *kharvar*s from Crown lands and 45,000 *kharvar*s from tax payments in kind. This quantity was insufficient to provide a four-month supply of bread for Tehran. "Moreover, now that the sale of government grain at harvest time has become known, things will get worse. Those who have grain will now hide their grain and will not give even one seed. They will wait until the end of the year when you will have to go to them. Then they will sell to you at whatever price they dictate. You will not make their wheat rot, but they will empty the Treasury."[6]

5. Mostowfi 1324, vol. 2, p. 385. On the *omana-ye maliyeh*, see Floor 1998, pp. 299, 343.

6. Mostowfi 1324, vol. 2, p. 386.

From the beginning of October 1912 the bread situation in Tehran became serious. It had become very difficult to provide the bakers with 300 *kharvar*s of wheat. About one-third of the city remained without bread most of the time. The greater part of *tafton* bread was now prepared mainly with barley. Gradually barley was also used for preparing *sangak* bread that was like a thick quilt and inedible. The bakers did not only prepare bread of unsifted wheat and barley flour, but added old bran, which usually was sold to cattle owners. The wheat price had risen from 17 to 35 *tuman*s per *kharvar* and the price of barley from 10 to 25 *tuman*s. Under growing pressure of public opposition to his policy, Mornard sent armed wheat buyers to the villages around Tehran to procure wheat and barley. The grain owners, however, were alarmed by this action; they were afraid that they would lose control over the market and refused to sell at prices even higher than the prevailing ones. It was then decided that Russian wheat would be imported. Because sweetmeat-sellers (*shirini forush*) were prepared to buy this wheat at high prices, the bakery office (*edareh-ye nanva'i*) ruled that bakers should be given a mixture consisting of one-fourth Russian wheat, one fourth-Iranian wheat and one half barley. However, bread prepared from this mixture was bad and inedible. The bakers separated the better quality mixture from the inferior, baked good bread and sold it for high prices. They baked bread of poor quality from the inferior mixture and sold it at 32 *shahi*s per *man* (3 kg). In this way the Treasury lost five to six thousand *tuman*s each day on the sale of grain to the bakers, or about one day of the operating cost of the Ministry of Finance.[7]

In November 1912, the bread situation deteriorated daily and Mornard asked Mostowfi to take charge of the bakery office. At that time there were four thousand *kharvar*s of Russian flour, three thousand *kharvar*s of barley and one thousand *kharvar*s of wheat in the government granary. This quantity was sufficient to provide a 40-day supply of bread. Mornard, who had arranged for the construction of a large Granary in Tehran, was able to buy and organize the delivery in two weeks time of 23,000 *kharvar*s or 6,900 tons of Russian flour, which

7. Mostowfi 1324, vol. 2, pp. 392-93; Destrée 1976, p. 264.

was shipped with great difficulty due to weather conditions via Enzeli to Tehran, while wheat and barley would arrive from areas around Tehran. Already around 1906, Mornard had taken steps to begin with the drawing up of a land register of Varamin, the main grain supplier of Tehran. Lambert Molitor, supervised by the Belgian engineer de Brucq, drew the plans for 15 villages. These registry records were used by Mohammad Ali's followers in June 1908 to set fire to the furniture of the *Majles* after their attack on the building.[8]

To assist him in performing his task, Mostowfi formed a committee of five people called the bread committee (*kumiteh-ye nan*). They divided the city into the following four areas, each of which was placed under the control of a different person.

Area	Person in charge
Mahalleh-ye Dowlat al-Dowleh	Mirza Hasan Khan Baqa
Majalleh-ye Sangalaj and Darvazeh Qazvin	Mirza Homayun Khan Sayyah
Mahalleh-ye `Udlajan	Mirza Ali Akbar Khan
Mahalleh-ye Bazar	Fathollah Mostowfi

After approval by Mornard the committee adopted various measures. First, it did not attempt to regulate the price of grain. Second, to improve the quality of bread it changed the mixture sold to the bakers so that it consisted of: Russian flour (50%), local wheat (25%) and barley (25%). Furthermore, the committee decided that for every six shops there should be one inspector (*mofattesh*) in whose presence dough had to be prepared to avoid adulteration of the bread. The wages of the inspectors did not cost the Treasury more than about 300 *tumans* per month. Regulations for the supervision of the bakers and a code of conduct for them were drawn up. Permits (*javaz*) stating amount, quantity, and name of the baker, his area, date of issue

8. MA, Delcorde and Molitor, pp. 20-21 (at that time, the documents were being examined by a Parliamentary commission). Mornard also championed the extension of the railway line from Shah `Abdol-`Azim to Varamin and later to Khar (the main suppliers of surplus grain), but this plan was torpedoed by the Russians. Idem, p. 23.

and duration were issued. The committee did nothing to control the financial relations between the government granary and the bakers who had to deal with the state granary by themselves.

The inspectors were in charge of controlling the incoming and outgoing quantities of flour, fuel, salt and bran of the bakery shops. They also sealed the bakeries' granary and coal bin. The baking of very crispy (*du atesheh*) bread was prohibited as were under-weight selling (*kam forushi*), half baked bread, foul water in the reservoir, and not sending away people queuing at the shop; each of these offenses had a specific fine , which was raised in case of repeat offenses. The chief inspector's office was located in the areas of which he was in charge. He had two police officers at his disposal to carry out his orders. Each night he would take a sample of bread from all the bakers in his area, on which a paper was pinned recording the name of the shop owner and would hand these to the chief of his area.

At an informal meeting with the bakers, Abdollah Mostowfi (our only source for this episode) told them that they no longer had a guild chief - *nanva bashi*. "I am your guild chief (*rish safid va kadkhuda*)," he said. He explained that they would do business with the government granary and pay for the flour, which they would receive on showing their permit or *javaz*. He explained the new mixture and acquainted them with the new supervisory measures and also bluntly informed them that he wanted bread on the counters.

According to Abdollah Mostowfi, the bread situation improved considerably. The inspectors were so effective that there was no more under-weight selling. Also, under their supervision, faulty scales were checked, patched-up flour sacks replaced with new ones, while hygienic conditions strictly observed. Flour and water were mixed in the presence of the inspectors, who also checked the morning dough (*khamir-e sobh*). In each area there was also a designated bakery that the chief inspector himself inspected. Two weeks after the new rules were implemented the bread price had stabilized to such an extent that the income of a baker had dropped from four to five *tumans* to two *tumans* per day.[9]

As the supply of grain offered in the market increased daily the wheat price fell. This trend was encouraged because the bakers were not allowed to buy grain, while the government did not buy any because there was enough grain in the state granary to satisfy 40 days of consumption. Mostowfi proposed to begin buying when wheat and barley prices had fallen respectively to 20 and 15 *tumans* per *kharvar*. His proposal was accepted because, as he pointed out, if prices fell lower, imports from Khamseh and Arak districts would not find buyers. He estimated the amount that the government lost on the price of bread was 12 *tumans* per *kharvar*. The flour mixture cost 30 *tumans* per *kharvar* and was sold for 18 *tumans* to the bakers, who in turn sold bread at 32 *shahis*. This loss would decrease by six *tumans* when wheat prices fell and the price for bakers would go up by two to three *tumans*, thus reducing their profit. His proposal was accepted by the government and the committee took steps accordingly. The result was that prices remained at the level of 22 and 15 *tumans* for wheat and barley respectively until the beginning of the following year. When wheat from Varamin finally arrived in July 1913, the import of Russian flour was discontinued and prices fell to 15 and 20 *tumans* for barley and wheat, which was less expensive than it had been two years previously.[10]

When the bread situation returned to normal by the summer of 1913, Abdollah Mostowfi wanted to return to his old job. His did not like Mornard and their collaboration was marred by strained relations. Moreover, allegedly Mornard didn't understand anything about the operation of the bread market and even after Mostowfi had explained matters to him he did not know enough to interfere in the work of the Bread Committee. Moreover, his interference was done in a high-handed manner. Mostowfi perceived this as a sign that Mornard and his Belgian collaborators were unhappy with an independent-thinking

9. Mostowfi 1324, vol. 2, pp. 396-401.

10. Mostowfi 1324, vol. 2, pp. 402-08.

Iranian, who moreover had solved the bread crisis, and wanted him to be a *mirza benevis* (a 'yes-man'). According to Mostowfi, the Belgians mistakenly believed that they were sufficiently informed to do the job, especially after he had told them that the harvest was good that year and production was one and half time the wheat needed by the country. Thus, they no longer needed the Bread Committee. The government accepted both his resignation and his suggestion to make bread baking free, so that villagers could bring bread into Tehran and sell it. This last measure would act as a check on bakers who cheated.[11]

The 1917-18 Famine

At the end of 1916 and the beginning of 1917 crops failed in many parts of Iran due to drought. As a result, famine conditions would prevail, unless the government took steps to ensure sufficient supplies of grain to the urban population and control the price of bread. Although this narrative of this section is focused on Tehran, famine conditions also prevailed in western Iran, in particular in Tabriz, Ormiyeh, Salmas, Khoy, Hamadan and Kermanshah. This was due to the fact that, in addition to the failed harvest, the people of that area also suffered from what is nowadays euphemistically called 'collateral damage' from the ongoing warfare between Ottoman and Russian troops. This situation worsened when after the February 1917 Revolution Russian troops in Hamadan and Azerbaijan lost discipline and began plundering the areas they passed through.[12]

---

11. Mostowfi 1324, vol. 2, pp. 430-32.

12. Sadr 1364, p. 229; Mostowfi 1324, vol. 3, p. 743. See, e.g. Floor 2018, pp. 75, 102-06 for a description of the situation in the Kermanshah area; IOR/L/MIL/17/15/23, pp. 43, 112. For the situation elsewhere in Iran, such as in central Iran, Semnan, Isfahan, and Ardabil, see Kuhestani-nezhad 1381, p. 43.

Fig. 1. Stamps benefiting the Alimentation Service (credit: Behruz Nassre)

Consequently, during the winter of 1917/18, thousands of people in Iran died of hunger and cold. This situation was further aggravated by hoarding and short-weight selling to customers by the bakers as well as the outbreak of the influenza pandemic.[13] To help the poor and destitute,

13. Chaqueri 1978, pp. 7, 20. For a very biased and, in my view, misleading analysis of the 1917-18 famine, see Majd 2003. For a critical review of this book, see Floor 2005. Kuhestani-nezhad 1381, p. 40 also blames Russia and Great Britain for the various food crises between 1912 and 1918, without providing any factual evidence. Major hoarders and/or participants in wheat corners during the famine winter

Iranians had organized some small relief operations (*kheyriyeh*) in various towns, such as in Tabriz.[14] To raise money for these activities in Tehran, the local relief committee organized the performance of a number of theater pieces in the Grand Hotel the proceeds of which were donated for relief activities. Also, special stamps were issued with the overprint of "Alimentation Service (*edareh-ye arzaq*)" in cities such as Tabriz and Khoy, the proceeds of which likewise served to raise funds for the poor.[15] Unfortunately, these local actions fell far short of the needs, often serving not more than a few score of the poor.[16] Fortunately, much larger foreign aid efforts helped to alleviate the famine conditions of the poor. In 1917, in addition to the American Food Relief,[17] which had been active in Azerbaijan already since 1915 (see chapter two), the British government also provided much food aid to reduce the distress caused by famine conditions in the winter of 1916-17 in e.g., Hamadan, Mashhad, and Shiraz.[18] Despite the food aid given the British were still suspected or falsely accused of buying local food stores, thus worsening local conditions. For example, in December 1916, the British consul Shiraz gave 12,000 *tumans* per month to the local Bread Committee to subsidize bakers to reduce the price of bread. Because supplies were short, and had to be brought from faraway places at high transportation cost, 1,000 tons of flour were imported from India by the British in the spring of 1917. Although the landed Indian flour was cheaper than local Iranian flour, it was decided to continue the monthly subsidy to bakers. Therefore, part of

---

of 1917-18 were Mohammad Taqi Khan Amir-e Jang Bakhtiyari, Akbar Mirza Sardar Mofakhkham and Mirza Ali Naqi Asaf-e A`zam. IOR/L/MIL/17/15/11/3, pp. 51, 370, 416.

14. Post 1920, p. 71.

15. Kuhestani-nezhad 1381, p. 42; see Fig. 1.

16. Sadr 1364, p. 229.

17. American Relief gave 35,000 *tumans* in Tehran, thus helping 35,000 people. Eyn al-Saltaneh 1376, vol. 7, p. 5282.

18. The British government contributed £5,000 for Mashhad as of July 1917. IOR/L/PS/10/646, Robert Chalmers/Treasury to FO, 08/07/1917 (Mashhad –where 600 people were fed daily); Robert Chalmers/Treasury to FO, 15/02/1917 (1,000 rupees/month for Mashhad).

the proceeds of the sale of flour (some 120,000 *tumans*) was given to the governor of Shiraz to continue to be used to reduce the price of bread of the poor. The local olama thanked the British consul for this assistance.[19] Although people were saved from starvation suspicion as to British activities remained among certain groups. In October 1917, the British consul reported that

> The condition of Shiraz this year is even worse than during the preceding year 1916-17, owing to the lack of rain, combined with the ravages of locusts. Moreover, the people, having but little to eat, are inclined to associate—with however little reason—the fact of the shortage of food with the presence of Indian troops, and the fact that large numbers of transport animals are kept at the headquarters of the South Persian Rifles at Shiraz, eating barley which would otherwise go towards feeding the nearly starving populace. Ill-feeling is therefore not too unnatural, and as starving persons are more inclined to give trouble than those who are well fed, unless something can he done at an early date, it may prove difficult to control the people and prevent trouble.[20]

A similar problem existed in Hamadan, where the British government made £20,000 available for Hamadan (March 1918), after having contributed 1,000 rupees monthly during four months, until harvest time. Nevertheless, the British consul reported that "Sufficient grain with other foods can probably be obtained to carry through till harvest but lower classes cannot buy at (? pay) present price which is seven times normal and rising owing to rumours of purchase for British troops spread by Governors gang to cause anti-British riot."[21] Col. Fortescue

19. IOR/L/PS/10/646, Lt. Col. Gough to Government of India, Shiraz 17/10/1917.

20. IOR/L/PS/10/646, Lt. Col. H. Gough to the Secretary to the Government of India in the Foreign and Political Department. Shiraz, 17th October 1917.

21. IOR/L/PS/10/646, Robert Chalmers/Treasury to FO, 08/06/1917 (Hamadan); Idem, Marling to FO, tel. 252, 26 March 1918. For a description of the famine at Hamadan and the activities undertaken by the British to deal with people's starvation, see Dunsterville 1932, pp.

reported that: "In Hamadan in the spring of 1918 (it started on June 10) from 160 to 200 persons daily were reckoned to be perishing from hunger."[22]

The situation in Tehran was as bad as in Hamadan. According to the author of an undated Persian report,[23] about the situation before the Alimentation Service in Tehran was established (in June 1918), thus referring to the situation 1916,

> The traditional system worked well in a normal year. The governor of Tehran had control over the bakeries, but hardly intervened when bakers behaved in an irregular manner. The bakers themselves took care of the preparation of wheat supply in relation to the baking needs of their shops. The government also supplied them with wheat at reduced cost, while the bakers did not pay any taxes to government. However, this changed

---

62, 102-14.

22. IOR/L/MIL/17/15/23, p 168. In 1923, a figure of 150,000 deaths was given. Government of Iran 1304 a, p. 18. In February 1918, there was hunger in the Rudbar area as well as elsewhere such as in Qom, Hamadan and in and around Qazvin. Eyn al-Saltaneh 1376, vol. 7, pp. 5093, 5111, 5114, 5215, 5227, 5271 (June 1918).

23. MA, Farde 41, 4102.pdf, Yaddasht, see Appendix II. The author probably was Mirza Eshaq Khan Haqiqi, inspector-general of the services, who was also known as Mirza Eshaq Khan Baha'i. Qodsi 1342, vol. 1, p. 511. The anonymous author was much upset by the undeserved criticism and intrigue against the Alimentation Service. He was outraged that despite all the trouble taken the staff of the Alimentation Service "are accused, cursed, and criticized in an intolerable manner, by those who have a stake in the business. It has an impact on everyone." Therefore, he had written his Note to inform the public that the Alimentation Service "has done a decent job, has done its duty, in conformity with its great responsibility. The Alimentation Service has worked in the interest of government of people and took steps against those who wanted to personally benefit from the famine in the capital. Continuation of the intrigues will free the Alimentation Service from all responsibility and will have a terrible consequence for the capital's bread supply that will no longer be assured." MA, Farde 41, 4102.pdf, Yaddasht, see Appendix II, p. 228.

> when the Law of 23 Jowzeh[24] was annulled[25] and replaced by the law on the Reorganization of Finance.[26] At that time, the Granary was filled with wheat, barley and under Minister Amir-e Nezam, then Minister of Finance[27] the salaries of the employees of the Ministries were drawn from and charged to the grain in the Granary. Its price was fixed at 6 *tuman*s per *kharvar*, so that there were buyers of the grains, only the *`allaf*s (traders in fodder and grain, etc.) bought the wheat and at very low prices, and by speculation they became the first 'grabbers' of the capital. The economic crisis began when the quantity of supplies in the Granary ran out and the city's only income was from its tithe (*`oshriyyeh*) of the brick kilns, so that [most of the staff of the Ministries, who were paid in kind] received their salary in the form of bricks. The Granary unfortunately ran empty in the year thereafter the harvest was not very good.[28]

Consequently, a dangerous food crisis came into being in the province of Tehran, where, moreover, the grain crop at Varamin, an important grain producing village near Tehran, had suffered from an insect pest (*senn*). The bakers benefited from this state of affairs by 'cornering' the grain. Also, some time thereafter, subterraneous granaries were discovered in Khar and Varamin where they had hidden grain two years before.[29] The price of wheat in Tehran that had been

---

24. Meaning the *qanun-e tashkil-e tartibat-e maliyati*, which was passed on 23 Jowzeh 1290/13 June 1911, see *Majmu`eh-ye Qavanin*, p. 398.
25. On 26 Hut 1293/17 March 1915, see *Majmu`eh-ye Qavanin*, p. 492 and `Aqeli 1370, p, 157.
26. The *qanun-e tashkilat-e edarat-e vezarat-e maliyeh* of 15 Jowzeh 1294/4 June 1915, see *Majmu`eh-ye Qavanin*, p. 497f.
27. Amir Nezam Hamadani was Minister of Finance in the short-lived government of Eyn al-Dowleh (1 May-18 August 1925). `Aqeli 1370, p. 171.
28. MA, Farde 41, 4102.pdf, Yaddasht, see Appendix II, p. 228. The author further commented: "Instead of controlling the grain of the Crown lands etc. the authorities let it be removed due to their weakness and the untrustworthiness of the agents and the rapacity of the landlords, who preferred to keep grain and only sell it at high price."
29. MA, Farde 41, 4102.pdf, Yaddasht, see Appendix II, p. 228

20 *tumans* per *kharvar* in the spring of 1916 rose to 25 *tumans* in the fall of 1916. The wheat price rose even more in the spring of 1917 and reached 30 *tumans* per *kharvar*. When harvest time arrived wheat became even more expensive. Seham al-Dowleh was appointed *ra'is-e nanva* (chief of the bakery office). To assist him in his task a so-called *kumiteh-ye arzaq* (Alimentation Committee) was appointed; this Committee, which met daily, consisted of seven or eight of the most important merchants. Due to World War I and the Russian Revolution, wheat could not be imported from Russia. The Committee advised the government to sell bread at two *qrans* and two *abbasis* per *man* (3 kg), which meant that it would suffer a daily loss of 32 *tumans* per *kharvar*.[30] The situation in Tehran worsened due to the arrival of peasants from neighboring villages, who, because of the drought had neither food nor fodder. They either killed or sold their animals and fled to the capital hoping to find relief given either by the government or their landlords.[31] The British government had offered aid, but

> The Cabinet of Ala-es-Sultaneh [5 June – 21 November 1917] had proved to be one of the most feeble and impotent that Persian democracy had yet seen. It had certainly come into office at a time when prospects throughout the country were most gloomy. For Tehran was not only in the throes of a campaign of political assassination, but was afraid of famine; the Treasury was empty and a large portion of the grain-producing areas were occupied by Russian troops, whose necessities practically forced them to pillage, while the province of Resht was in the hands of the Jangalis; and many of the

---

Concerning the *senn* plague, see also Eyn al-Saltaneh 1376, pp. 4771-72 (April 1917), 4849 (June 1917).

30. Mostowfi 1324, vol. 2, pp. 495-96; Idem, vol. 3, p. 34 (the real cost of bread was 4-5 *qrans*, but it was sold at 2 *hazars* and 2 *`abbasis* until April 1918, when the price was raised to 4 *qrans* and 3 *`abbasis*); Shahri 1368, vol. 2, p. 396; Eyn al-Saltaneh 1376, vol. 6, pp. 4651 (November 1916), 4717 (March 1917), 4771, 4777 (April 1917), 4860-61, 4889 (with price and other data concerning the Qazvin area); Idem, vol. 7, pp. 4919-21, 4925, 4928, 4936 (prices).

31. Eyn al-Saltaneh 1376, vol. 6, p. 3895.

> roads were infested by brigands. But Ministers, who had come into power on a wave of journalistic patriotism—preaching the elimination of foreign interference— and of an artificially created Anglophobia, preferred the risk of famine to acceptance of financial assistance at our hands; and in many other ways proved that they were actuated only by self-interest. The result was that everywhere but in the south their authority became negligible, while lawlessness and misery increased.[32]

In October 1917, Abdollah Mostowfi was again appointed chief of the Alimentation Service (*ra'is-e edareh-ye arzaq*), which was part of the Ministry of Finance. At that time nine months remained until the next harvest and Tehran needed 80,000 *kharvar*s or 24,000 tons of wheat during that period. Not even one-tenth of that quantity was available in Tehran or its vicinity, while the provinces had no grain surplus to send to Tehran. However, the rice harvest had been very good that year in Mazandaran. Because of the Russian Revolution, rice that normally would have been exported to Russia now remained in the hands of the farmers. Mostowfi, therefore, proposed to bring 30 to 40,000 *kharvar*s or 9,000 to 12,000 tons of rice to Tehran to prevent starvation of the capital's inhabitants. The government agreed to this proposal. By that time it had become extremely difficult to secure 300 *kharvar*s or 90 tons of wheat and barley, the daily quantity of grain needed to feed Tehran's population. The food crisis was intensified by the fact that in Tehran bread cost two *qran*s and two *`abbasi*s per *man*, while outside the city it rose to three to four *qran*s. This led to the export of bread from Tehran, thus worsening the food situation in the capital. One of the members of the Alimentation Committee was the Armenian merchant Alexander Toumaniantz, who had agents all over Mazandaran.[33] He undertook to buy and transport 30,000 *kharvar*s of 9,000 tons of rice to Tehran. Consequently, at the beginning of the winter of 1917/18 this quantity of rice was safely stored in the government granary and the danger of famine was prevented.

---

32. IOR/L/MIL/17/15/28, p. 260.

33. His main rice seller probably was Sepahsalar, see Eyn al-Saltaneh 1376, vol. 7, p. 5234.

As he had done in 1912, Mostowfi requested a few friends to supervise the implementation of the Alimentation Service's policy. The city of Tehran was now divided into the following three areas:

Area	Supervisor
Mahalleh-ye Chaleh Meydan	Ali Mansur
Mahalleh-ye Dowlat	Ali Dehkhoda
Mahalleh-ye Bazaar va Darvazeh-ye Qazvin	Fathollah Mostowfi

In addition to the three area chiefs, four chief inspectors and one inspector per six shops were appointed. Each day they checked the preparation of dough in the bakeries and the work of bakers in general. This led to a fall in under-weight selling, although the crowds made it impossible to prevent it altogether. Under-weight selling was very profitable for the bakers and they even sold half-baked bread, for in this way they could increase their income by 20 percent.[34]

Eyn al-Dowleh, who had been scheming to become grand vizier, finally achieved his objective on 28 December 1917. Under pressure from the bazaaris,[35] Ala al-Saltaneh resigned and Eyn al-Dowleh was appointed in his stead, who was heavily indebted and intended to take advantage of the food situation to improve his financial situation, according to Mostowfi. As a result, Mostowfi gradually had to close

34. Mostowfi 1324, vol. 2, pp. 498-500; Kuhestani-nezhad 1381, p. 42. According to Eyn al-Saltaneh 1376, vol. 6, p. 4904, writing in mid-October 1917, due to drought throughout Iran wheat had doubled in price (to 70 *tumans/kharvar*) in Tehran, while the authorities were unable to resolve the food shortage problem. He accused the Russian army of collecting provisions and storing it for its own use. He made the same accusation concerning the British, who had no troops in Qazvin at that time, as he asserts. In May 1918, he made the same point (Eyn al-Saltaneh 1376, vol. 7, p. 5236), when the British army was indeed at Qazvin. However, it was very careful to see to it that it did not worsen the local food situation, if only for political and public relations reasons, see above and Floor 2018, pp. 103-04, 106-09; Dunsterville 1932, p. 62.

35. According to Eyn al-Saltaneh 1376, vol. 7, pp. 4941-42, the British had engineered a bread demonstration to topple the government, which, given the new government's anti-British policy stance, seems highly unlikely.

bakeries and instead of the normal 300 *kharvar*s only 150 *kharvar*s and on some days only 100 *kharvar*s or 3 tons per day were supplied to the city. Each day, based on the state granary's stock, the price was fixed as were the number of shops that had to be open the next day in the various city quarters. Both the granary' stock and the number of working shops decreased; the latter were open by rotation. It was then decided to open the *dampokht pazi* kitchens and the people had no choice but to eat rice. With Mostowfi's agreement, Mokhber al-Saltaneh, who was the Minister of Alimentation (*vazir-e arzaq*), decided to fix the price of a dish of steamed rice mixed with fava beans (*dampokht pazi*) at 32 *shahi*s per *man* of 3 kg and readied the public kitchens. In November 1917 the food crisis worsened and more bakeries were closed. The preparation of *dampokht* was started, but the people preferred bread, despite the problems of obtaining it. Among the population this year of famine, therefore, was known as 'the year of steamed rice with fava beans' or *sal-e dampokhtak*.[36] The already strained relations between Mostowfi and Eyn al-Dowleh broke down when the latter ordered the state granary to discontinue selling grain to the bakers. During the subsequent discussion between the two men, Eyn al-Dowleh ordered one of his servants to strike Mostowfi, who then resigned from his post as chief of the Alimentation Service. The next day, on 16 January, Eyn al-Dowleh was dismissed. Mostowfi does not attribute his fall to their dispute, but he adds, "if it is coincidental it is strange."[37] Shortly thereafter, a Poor-House (*Dar al-Masakin*) was opened in Shahr-e Now and many people, including Ahmad Shah, gave much money, but apparently most of the poor fled the institution.[38]

Mostowfi al-Mamalek became the new prime minister. He limited the bakeries in Tehran to four and increased the price of bread to 4 *qran*s and 6,000 *dinar*s. Because there was not enough wheat to feed

36. Kuhestani-nezhad 1382, p. 40; Mostowfi 1324, vol. 2, p. 504; Idem, vol. 3, p. 34. As a result, the price of rice as well as local poverty rose in Tonakebun. Eyn al-Saltaneh 1376, vol. 7, pp. 4965, 4975 (in January 1918 life was still expensive).

37. Mostowfi 1324, vol. 2, pp. 504-06.

38. Eyn al-Saltaneh 1376, vol. 7, p. 5008.

the city's population, therefore, *dampokht* continued to be sold at 32 *shahi*s per 3 kg to make up for the shortfall. The *dampokht* was rather watery, but it was food. Cooked rice (*berenj-e polow*) was not very expensive either, but still cost two to three times more than in normal years.[39] Mokhber al-Saltaneh remained Minister of Food Supply.[40] According to an anonymous author, "wheat was almost unfindable and then at a price of 150 *tuman*s per *kharvar*. Some 20,000 persons died in Tehran; contrariwise a small number of greedy speculators enriched themselves. The government to address the famine had recourse to *dampokht*. Most of those who ate that dish died."[41] The same anonymous author submits that, "the government suffered a big financial loss as is clear from the reports by the Ministry of Finance if they are read. The bakeries instead of yielding some income to the government caused a loss of 700 to 1,500 *tuman*s per month. People's spirits were so down that they did not see a way out. All the misery was mainly due to the negligence and lack of care by the authorities and the lack of any well run organization, which nobody can deny."[42] This author is supported by Mr. Judson of American Relief, according to whom: "The year before, famine situation was 'shameful.'" as thousands of people died.[43]

According to Abdollah Mostowfi, during this period no one died of hunger in Tehran. Those who died, about 100 to 200 per day, were victims of influenza.[44] Contrariwise, Marling, the British Minister in

39. Mostowfi 1324, vol. 2, pp. 512-14; Idem vol. 3, p. 34.

40. Eyn al-Saltaneh 1376, vol. 7, pp. 5057, 5061 (wheat price in Tehran was 100 *tuman*s).

41. MA, Farde 41, 4102.pdf, Yaddasht, see Appendix II, p. 229. See also Sadr 1365, p. 229, who also argues that the government's response was ineffectual.

42. MA, Farde 41, 4102.pdf, Yaddasht, see Appendix II, p. 229.

43. MA, Farde 38, 3801.pdf. Alimentation, p. 7.

44. Mostowfi 1324, vol. 2, p. 513; Tafazzoli 1340, p. 534. However, according to Eyn al-Saltaneh 1376, vol. 7, p. 5063, the usual death rate in Tehran was 300 per week, while during the famine this figure had risen to 520. He also reports that, according to the newspaper *Ra`d*, that the Democrats were very critical of the bread situation in Tehran when

Tehran reported that 20-30 people daily died of starvation in Tehran in February 1918. He commented: "Government effort and charity of individuals is doing something but not adequate." Therefore, Marling asked for 5,000 *tumans* per month [£ 1,923] for famine relief; his wife was already feeding 750 per day; the amount asked would feed another 2,000 persons per day. As the political effect was considered to be valuable the request was approved with the proviso that the Foreign Office would pay 300 *tumans* for four months and the IETD would contribute 200 *tumans* per month.[45] Other Iranian sources were also less positive about Mostowfi's efforts to address the bread question. The newspaper *Ra`d* no. 61 reported that there were only 32 bakeries open (*barbari*, *saji*, *taftuni*, and *lavashi*) in Tehran. The paper severely criticized the government, and in particular the Alimentation Service, of mishandling the bread crisis, which latter only cost money, without having any value added.[46] Indeed, the situation for most people was not as positive as depicted by Mostowfi. On 21 Jomadi I 1336/4 March 1918, Sepahsalar Tonakaboni wrote in his diary:

> At present, since a few months that due to drought in Tehran high prices prevail; wheat costs 110 *tumans* per *kharvar*, at which price, the day before yesterday, the Shah sold grain from his granary to the poor people. Rice costs 100 to 120 *tumans* per *kharvar*. Barley costs 80 *tumans* per *kharvar*. All bakeries are closed. Hungry people bring bread from the villages. Since two days they buy bread at 12 *qrans* per Tabriz-*man*. Until then it had been one *tuman* and nine *hazar*. Each day I give food to 400 poor and each day one *qran* per person to 100 people. As God is my witness, I gave this year 200,000 *tumans* to those in need. I myself sold wheat and barley at a price of 30 to 40 *tumans* [per

---

their opponents were in power, but that they remained silent after they had taken over. He also made the point that people often died from the combination of hunger and disease. Eyn al-Saltaneh 1376, vol. 7, p. 5215.

45. IOR/L/PS/10/646, Marling to FO, tel, no. 118, 18 February 1918; Idem, FO to India Office 23/2/1918.

46. Eyn al-Saltaneh 1376, vol. 7, p. 5064.

> *kharvar*]. ... Each day at least 50 people die of hunger. This is mostly the government's fault. We have no government. The child Shah has fled the city and resides now at Farahabad.[47]

In March 1918, according to Mostowfi, the price of wheat in Tehran was 120 *tumans* per *kharvar*; all bakeries were closed and people had to get bread from the villages. Because rain had been plentiful during winter time, the harvest was satisfactory and consequently the price of wheat fell to 36 *tumans* per *kharvar* in July 1918.[48] However, in April 1918, in Tehran bakeries were free to open again and their number rose from 30 to 100, who sold bread from 6 to 8 *hazar* (6 to 8,000 dinars) per Tabriz *man*.[49] As to Mostowfi's optimistic assessment of the 1918 crop, other sources report that due to the 1917-18 famine one-third of animals, men, tools and necessaries for production had perished, which had negative consequences for next year's crop output.[50]

Also, for many of the poor hunger was still a daily burden. Moreover, after having survived the famine people were ravaged by the outbreak of disease; first malaria, followed by typhus, and finally by the influenza pandemic, which in Tehran broke out at the end of September 1918.[51] In Tehran, the mortality from famine and disease, chiefly influenza, was said to have totaled 100,000 people.[52]

---

47. Tafazzoli 1340, p. 534; see also Eyn al-Saltaneh 1376, vol. 7, pp. 5171, 5811-12.
48. Mostowfi 1324, vol. 2, pp. 512-14.
49. Eyn al-Saltaneh 1376, vol. 7, p. 5062.
50. MA, Farde 38, 3801.pdf. Alimentation, p. 6; see also, IOR/L/MIL/17/15/23, p 168.
51. Floor 2018, p. 99.
52. IOR/L/MIL/17/15/23, p. 168. In 1923, a figure of 150,000 deaths was given, Government of Iran 1304 a, p. 18. In February 1918, there was hunger in the Rudbar area as well as elsewhere such as in Qom, Hamadan and in and around Qazvin. Eyn al-Saltaneh 1376, vol. 7, pp. 5093, 5111, 5114, 5215, 5227, 5271 (June 1918). In 1918, a malaria outbreak was followed by a typhus epidemic, on top of which came the influenza pandemic, which coincided with famine in many parts of Iran. For details, see Floor 2018, pp. 93-105 and Idem 2021, pp. 305-07.

Because disease had broken out the government decided to provide assistance to the Poor-House (*Dar al-Masakin*), the House for the Disabled (*Dar al-Mo`jezeh*) and the Work-House (*Dar al-Sanaye`*) in the following way:

> i. From incoming government and private grain 2 *qran*s.
> ii. Seal of 1 *shahi* per telegram.
> iii. From domestic mail 1 *shahi.*
> iv. From passports (*tadhkereh*s) issued in Tehran 1 *qran.*
> v. From transport of goods entering Tehran 1 *qran.*
> except in case of grain, beans, and dairy products.
> vi. From cinemas and theaters 5% [of ticket price].[53]

There is no information available whether the revenues that these new fees yielded were sufficient to address the needs of these groups of poor, let alone to what extent they were actually used for that purpose. A fact is that the food supply situation of Tehran remained worrisome, which is the subject of chapter three.

53. Eyn al-Saltaneh 1376, vol. 7, p. 5115.

CHAPTER TWO

THE SITUATION IN TABRIZ 1917-1918

In 1917, the city of Tabriz, the second largest city of Iran, with an estimated population of 170,000 inhabitants, experienced famine conditions. Although the situation was worse in some places than in others, the cause, whether in Tabriz or elsewhere, was the same. Disappointing rainfall in November 1916 and subsequent drought were harbingers of a bad harvest. Drought impacted all cultivation, for man and beast, especially those crops that like in Azerbaijan were mostly rain-fed, especially in the hills. Collection of taxes (in kind) as well as reaction to resolve food problems was not effective, due to the disorganization of the financial administration everywhere. In all large towns land taxes or *maliyat*, paid in kind (grains), were an essential element to secure urban bread consumption. These grain payments in kind were brought into the city's granary (*ambar*) and constituted the stock to regulate the grain price to prevent malversation by major landowners. However, increasing corruption by government agents as of mid-1915 had led to the complete disorganization of the transport of grains to the state granaries.[1]

The main grain growing districts in Azerbaijan were Sarab, Hashtrud, Garmarud, Maragheh, Marand as well as Qaramalik and Hokmabad in the intermediate suburbs of Tabriz. In normal years the average agricultural yield was 10 percent, meaning 1 bushel of seed would yield one quarter two bushels of wheat. The main tax (*maliyat*) levied was paid in cash and kind, or a total of 750,000 *tumans* in 1887. Much of Azerbaijan's revenue was used to pay government officials, both military and civil, and relatively little was remitted to Tehran.[2] Taxes (*maliyat*) in kind were paid with *ghalleh*, i.e. grain consisting of 2/3 wheat and 1/3 barley. It was called *bar kardeh*, when the tax payer had the obligation to bring the grain into the government Granary, which existed in Tabriz, and *na bar kardeh*, when the state had to transport it. To enrich themselves, the Treasury agents used low rates to convert tax payments in kind into a cash value (*tas`ir*).[3]

In 1908 the city of Tabriz had risen up against the coup d'etat by Mohammad Ali Shah. The local Constitutional forces battled the royalist army, which was supported by the governor of Maragheh, Shoja` al-Dowleh, and the Shahseven robber chief Rahim Khan Chalibianlu. . The latter was arrested by the Russians, but after exacting a large sum of money from him they let him go, thus enabling him to continue causing much havoc. In 1910 he sacked Ardabil after which he placed himself under Russian protection.[4] At the end of December 1911, the Russians, who had troops near Tabriz, occupied the city and also took control over other parts of the province.

In 1910, the most important Domains or Crown Lands (*khaleseh*) in Azerbaijan were those of Alan Baraghush (near Sarab), which were properties that had belonged to Rahim Khan Chalibianlu , which, like many other villages previously owned by him, had been declared

1. MA, Farde 38, 3801.pdf, Alimenation, p. 1.
2. DCR 423, p. 3.
3. RP, Dossier 2, Aperçu, p. vii.
4. Browne 1966, pp. 141-42, 441, 446, 256, 269, 296, 347, 349.

khaleseh or Crown land by the *Majles*. However, he was under Russian protection and thus, the parliamentary decision could not be implemented. In 1912, the Russian Consul General appeared to want to use Rahim Khan's properties to compensate Russian subjects, who had suffered damage due to his marauding. In early 1912, to increase tax revenues, Ransquin, the Belgian provincial director of Customs and Finance, asked one of his collaborators, Asadollah Khan, to make a complete inventory of the Crown lands, as well as an analysis of the situation of the peasants, of the crops, and what needed to be done to improve both; in short, to submit any proposals that he believed would be useful.[5]

In May 1912, Ransquin decided to renew the leases of the Crown lands for one year as well as to establish clear accounting rules (monthly reporting) and an effective administration for the Crown lands (*khaleseh*) and the government Granary (*ambar*) to enable Khuy, Urmiyeh, Ardabil, and other towns to receive sufficient taxes in kind and sell the surplus grain to generate cash revenue.[6] This decision caused problems, because Shoja` al-Dowleh, the governor-general of Azerbaijan, did not like this as it cut into his illicit profits. Through the Russian Consul Préobragensky he demanded payment of more than 1,700 *tumans* for the service of transporting grain that he allegedly had rendered. Ransquin asked Préobragensky to tell Shoja` al-Dowleh to stop this kind of annoying hassle.[7] Ransquin also alerted Mornard in Tehran about this problem. In August 1912, Mornard informed him that, on the same day, Anastasinsky of the Russian Legation in Tehran would telegraph Shoja` al-Dowleh not to collect the revenues of the Crown lands and *maliyat*, because this was the exclusive domain of the Belgian officials.[8]

---

5. RP, Dossier 2, Aperçu, p. vii.
6. RP, Dossier 1, p. 159, Ransquin, Tauris to Quinet, Brussels, 10/05/1912.
7. RP, Dossier 1, p. 164, Ransquin to Préobragensky, n.d.
8. RP, Dossier 1, pp. 169-70, Mornard to Ransquin, Tauris, 14/08/1912. The Russians opposed all efforts by the Belgian officials to reinforce the authority of the central government. MA, Delcorde and Molitor, p. 25. On this issue, see the many letters in RP, Dossier 1, pp. 161-73, 178.

Land taxes or *maliyat*, which accounted in 1913 for 11 million *qran*s, were paid roughly half in kind and half in cash. In addition, the Crown lands yielded 1.5 million *qran*s. In that year, Ransquin introduced changes to increase government revenue. He sold the grain paid to the government at an average price of 10 *tuman*s per *kharvar*, while his predecessor allegedly had sold it at the same or a higher rate, but in reality it had been sold at only 5 to 6 *tuman*s. In 1913, Ransquin was able to collect more revenue by also obliging the Khan of Maku to pay. As a result, Azerbaijan became self-supporting and he expected to remit 0.5 million *tuman*s to Tehran the following year, if expenditures did not increase. This was an excellent result, given that the proceeds did not include taxes due from the area occupied by Turkish troops,[9] while expenditures had been higher.

Ransquin also made a difference as to the bread question.[10] Despite fierce opposition from the landowners and transport problems he brought almost all taxes in kind into the government granary. He established a special department, selected its staff, and designated the regions that had to supply the government granary (*ambar*) with *maliyat* in kind. This department or the Alimentation Service (*edareh-ye arzaq*) had to supply a certain number of bakeries with grain, based on a service contract. Ransquin intended to extend the operations of the Alimentation Service to all major towns in Azerbaijan to prevent hunger to occur again. In this way, he kept control over the grain stock, which he sold gradually to prevent landowners from driving up the price, while also supervising the bakeries. As a result, bread was cheaper and of better quality than in the preceding years. Ransquin intended the Alimentation Service to become a steady source of income for the government. The landowners were in uproar, because they had

---

9. On the Turkish occupation of parts of Western Azerbaijan, see RP, Dossier 2, Récit de l'invasion turque dans la région d'Ourmiah. 1907.

10. Ransquin was praised for his work by the newspaper *Towfiq*. It reported that on 9 Jomadi II 1330/5 June 1912, Ransquin in person made a surprise inspection of the bakeries and fined several of them. Thereafter, inspectors supervised the bakeries and Ransquin earned the gratitude of the paper and the people of Tabriz. RP, Dossier 2.

to pay taxes and were prevented from grain speculation. This led to an anti-Belgian campaign that failed to rouse the public, because, what's not to like about cheaper and better bread?[11]

A few months later, in April 1913, Ransquin was replaced by Lambert Molitor, who then served as Director of Customs and Finance of the province until May 1915. Ransquin was furious about Molitor's appointment and in protest resigned on 24 April 1913. He blamed Mornard, who had not even informed him of Molitor's appointment, in fact, he heard about it from others in Tabriz. Ransquin wrote Mornard that he had ruined his health, working hard for 14 months, and now being replaced without recognition was too much. Moreover, in Tabriz "in the eyes of the public [it was seen as] a disgrace, which my feelings of dignity cannot accept, also considering that a recent fact shows that no account is taken in Persia of the respective circumstances of Belgian officials. … I will deal with current affairs, pending the arrival of Molitor to whom I will provide all services"[12]

Before leaving Tabriz,[13] Ransquin who was still furious, vented his feelings to Quinet, his former superior in Tabriz, who had proposed Ransquin as his successor, to let him know, how much aggrieved he was by his treatment.

> For more than a year, I work hard, I spend my days and most of my nights building up organizations in the midst of incredible difficulties; I am looking for all kinds of expedients to deal with the lack of money and meet a thousand needs that

11. Government of Great Britain 1914, N. Patrick Cowan to Sir Walter Townley. Tabriz 24/02/1913 (enclosure in no. 141). pp. 56-57.

12. RP, Dossier 1, p. 181, Ransquin to Quinet, 13/04/1913. However, Ransquin already knew about Molitor's appointment in January 1912, see RP, Dossier 1, pp. 152, 156. According to MA, Mémoires, p. 276 and Idem, Delcorde and Molitor n.d., p. 25, n. 1, the Russians had ordered Ransquin to be transferred after he had protested against a blatant case of Russian usurpation of Iranian sovereign rights.

13. Ransquin left Tabriz in September, after having handed over of his work to Molitor, and went to Enzeli where he was Director of Customs and Finance of Gilan until July 1914, when he left Iran.

> politics likes to create to stop my work. Despite everything, without any instructions from the Central Administration, I succeed, the money comes in, my receipts exceed expenses, the administration takes shape and when the difficulties decrease, when my work becomes less hectic, less tense, easier, the administration designates another, who has done nothing in another province, to come quietly to enjoy the fruits of my efforts; better, I am put under his orders knowing that, in fact, it is I who will continue to do the work, without getting the credit. Faced with this injustice, of this theft, I protest; they send me back the holy water of the court, believing that I will be satisfied. I send in my resignation, they ask me - something incredible - not to raise questions of self-esteem. I persist in my intentions and Tehran is playing dead, I have given [the Administration] until 1 July to make a prompt decision and I leave if they continue, following the usual tactic, neither wishing to answer me nor to give me satisfaction.[14]

Despite the resentment that Ransquin felt, a sentiment shared by his Belgian collaborators in Azerbaijan, the latter expressed their surprise that Lambert Molitor was a totally different person than they had expected or had been led to believe. One of them, Lejeune, wrote to Mrs. Ransquin that Lambert Molitor "was a calm man, a very hard worker and not an intrigant at all." Moreover, Molitor was surprised by all the work that Ransquin had done and he expressed his admiration for his predecessor.[15] Molitor continued Ransquin's policy of ensuring the collection of taxes in kind (grain), as this was essential to city's food supply. Therefore, during Molitor's tenure of this office the government granary in Tabriz was always well-stocked with grain. This had not been an easy task due to difficulties created by the Russian Consul-General Orlow, who interfered with the execution of Molitor's function, i.e. the collection of taxes. In addition, there was the occupation of the province by the Russian army, which led to abuse, intimidation and even demoralization of Molitor's fiscal

14. RP, Dossier 1, pp. 181-85, Ransquin, Tauris to Quinet (Belgium), 13/07/1913.

15. RP, Dossier 1, p. 189, Lejeune to Juliette Ransquin, 09/11/1913.

agents, whose task it was to arrange for the transport of government grain (taxes paid in kind) to the granary in Tabriz.[16] His conflict with Orlow was the subject of discussion by the British Consul Shipley in June 1914.

> Even with reference to the Government taxes properly so called, the cost of collection, was in his, M. Orlofs opinion, entirely out of proportion to the amount collected and, though his remarks in this connection had no reference to the Belgian officials upon whom he had no desire to whatever to cast any reflections, there was, he maintained, as much peculation going on among the subordinate Persian collectors as under the old system, while the conduct of these latter had given rise to continual complaints. As far as Russian subjects, however, were concerned, he was glad to say that this had now been put an end to. The latter would henceforth pay their taxes directly to the Russian consulate and would consequently be free from this particular form of vexation. In reply, and without entering into a discussion as to how far abuses might be said to exist or not on the part of these subordinate collectors, I said that as far as the Belgian officials themselves were concerned the duty for which they had been appointed, viz., to account for and exercise control over such funds as were received on behalf of the State was, I had always understood, being efficiently performed by them and from this my colleague did not dissent.[17]

Although Shipley pointed out that Molitor was in his legal right, Orlow made all kinds of spurious arguments to continue to undercut Molitor's activities. To give his agents moral and physical backing Molitor wanted to arm them so as to reduce the incidence of

---

16. MA, Mémoires, pp. 286-88. According to MA, Delcorde and Molitor, p. 25, in August 1912, one of the Russian consuls told the Belgian official in charge of the financial affairs of one of the Caspian regions: "I will do anything to obstruct your financial activities. You will find me everywhere on your path opposing any organization that might ensure new revenues to this country."
17. IOR/L/PS/10/450, Consul Shipley to Sir Walter Townley, Tabriz 10/06/1914.

intimidation. This led to an exchange of frank letters between Orlow and Molitor. The former flatly refused to allow Molitor's fiscal agents to be armed.[18] In reply Molitor called into question Orlow's objectivity and respect for the rule of law.

> Concerning your refusal that officials of the Finance Department carry arms, I protest that you qualify them as being chosen from among elements that were part of the revolution two years ago. You always make vague accusations, but never offer anything factual or proof concerning these officials. They are ma'murs [officials] to collect taxes; I find your argument specious, when you write that Russian authorities collect these taxes without help from Cossacks armed horsemen. Apart from the fact that this is illegal, I wish to point out that there is a difference between my authority in Azerbaijan and any Russian organization that directly or indirectly relies on the protection by the use of force, i.e. many regiments. Russian protected subjects can simply pay my administration if you tell them to. The Government of Iran has not yet informed me that it acknowledges that Russian consular authorities in Azerbaijan have the right to demand a permit to carry arms by Iranian officials. I only asked you, because I thought you would not make any difficulty and approve it. I report this illegal intervention to my superiors.[19]

Orlow's behavior was typical for Russian officials in northern Iran. Since the occupation of much of Azerbaijan in December 1911, Russian officials increasingly had tried to put the administration of Azerbaijan in disarray.[20] A case in point was the situation in Urmiyeh, where there was a strong Russian garrison and about 500 Russian subjects and protected persons. According to Capt. A. T. Wilson:

---

18. MA, Farde 34, 3402 and 3403.pdf, Molitor to Consul General, Tabriz 5 July 1914/13 Saratan 1332; Orlow to Molitor 30/13 July 1914.
19. MA, Farde 34, 3404.pdf, Molitor to Orlow 20/07/191; Idem, Farde 34, 3405.pdf, Molitor to Mornard, 21 July 1914; Idem, Mémoires, p. 285.
20. Some Russian officers openly stated that the province would be annexed. Demorgny 1916, p. 73; Siassi, 1971, p. 74.

I found no difficulty in crediting [vice-consul] M. Vedensky's assertion that he had more than enough to do collecting taxes from his subjects and protégés, but known facts give the lie to his protestations that he had no concern with the taxes of genuine Persian subjects. Part of the Russian vice-consulate at Urmia has been set apart as a revenue office, and three busy clerks, besieged by a crowd of would-be taxpayers were proudly pointed out to me in support of the complaint of overwork referred to above. On my mentioning to M. Vedensky that I had seen a proclamation at Ushnu requiring all taxpayers to remit Government dues through the Russian vice-consulate he disclaimed any knowledge of it, and stated that the collection of taxes in Urmia was governed by the provisions of the proclamation of which I attach a translation, i.e., was limited to Russian subjects and protégés.

Enclosure 5 in 1. (Translation.)
In pursuance of the orders of the administration of His Excellency the Farman Farma and the wishes of the Russian consulate; and in accordance with the instructions of the officials of his honour the Governor of Urmia, it is hereby made known to all burghers and taxpayers that, hereafter, all tax payers will transmit their taxes through the Governor of the Russian consulate for deposit in the Banque d'Escomptes; the taxes on slaughter animals, intestines and opium, which were administered by the local Government and will in future be administered by the municipality, should be paid in like manner. All burghers who are desirous of being members of the municipality are requested to submit their names to the local Government. Those approved of by the inhabitants of the township will be elected members.
Kawam-es-Sultan.
Ushnu, 17th Shaban, 1332 (June 10, 1914).

Enclosure 6 in 1. (Translation.)
The following copy of instructions for the collection of revenue which has been received from the administration of his Excellency the Farman Farma is hereby published for the information of the people of Urmia :—

> "To the Governors of the districts of Azerbaijan.
> "It has come to my knowledge that revenue officials are in the habit of collecting taxes from individuals who are under the protection of the Russian Government and who should, according to a notification received from the Imperial Russian consul-general, pay their taxes to Russian officials. You are, therefore, requested to instruct all revenue officers in your respective administrative areas not to collect taxes from the above-mentioned persons. In the event of their acting contrary to these orders they will be required to refund such amounts as they may have recovered, even though they should have paid them into the provincial Treasury.
> Shuja-ed-Dowleh."
> 3rd Ramazan, 1148 (July 26, 1914).
>
> On the authority of the above telegram it is binding on all persons who are under the protection of the Russian Government to pay all taxes to Russian officials through the Russian consulate. Should they have paid the said taxes to any one else they will, nevertheless, be called on to pay a second time.
> Itimad-ed-Dowleh.[21]

The fact that Russia prevented that the Iranian finance administration, through its Belgian director, collected taxes from Russian subjects and from Iranians who were under Russian protection, was unacceptable to Joseph Mornard, the Treasurer-General. The British Foreign Secretary Sir A. Grey also expressed his concern about this matter and informed the Russian chargé d'affaires that the fact that Russian consuls took over the financial administration of Iran was contrary to the 1907 Agreement. Russia took the view that it was only helping the Iranian government and its Belgian administrators.[22]

---

21. IOR/L/PS/10/451/1, Capt. Wilson to Townley, Camp Mawana, August 15, 1914; see also, MA, Mémoires, pp. 286-87.

22. In 1914, Korostovetz became the new Russian Minister in Tehran. He was transferred from Peking, where he had tried to have Manchuria separated from China. Now in Tehran, he tried to do the same with regards to Azerbaijan. Under the guise of 'the pacific military

However, when the Ottomans began making claims that it might do like what Russia was doing for its subjects in Iran, Great Britain demanded that Russia stop its collection of taxes. To break the deadlock between the parties concerned the Iranian government proposed that Russia would instruct its Consuls to no longer collect taxes and that Iran would deposit the taxes collected in Northern Iran in the Russian Bank instead of the (British) Imperial Bank of Persia. Russia, with some changes accepted this proposal, but this did not mean that Mornard's life became easier. He was beset by the Russian and the Iranian government as well as by Shoja` al-Dowleh, the governor-general of Azerbaijan, who wanted to replace all Belgians with Russians. As a result of the growing pressure, Mornard and many other Belgians working in northern Iran considered that their working conditions had become intolerable. Therefore, out of protest and in solidarity with his compatriots, Mornard resigned from his function as Treasurer-General, which was not accepted by the government; a few months later he resigned as Administrator-General of Customs, but continued working as Treasurer-General in which function he died in Tehran in September 1916, just when he had stepped down from this post. Mornard was succeeded by his compatriot Heynssens.[23]

At the same time, there was an ongoing discussion between Russia and Great Britain to replace Shoja` al-Dowleh as governor-general of Azerbaijan. Russia wanted to keep him, but it was willing to replace him, be it on its terms. In July 1914, Russia agreed to replace Shoja` al-Dowleh with the *Vali `Ahd* or Crown Prince, on condition that the Crown Prince would not come to Tabriz, but only would be nominally governor-general of Azerbaijan. Also, it insisted that Shoja` al-Dowleh's henchman Rashid al-Molk had to have a suitable role in

---

occupation' of the province he increased the number of Russian troops in Azerbaijan and used them to collect taxes for the account of the Russian Consulate." MA, Mémoires, p. 277; Idem, Delcourt and Molitor, p. 26.

23.. MA, Delcourt and Molitor, p. 26. For a detailed discussion of the tax collection conflict, see Nazem 1975, pp. 139-44. For the reason of the exodus of Belgian officials, see Destrée 1976, pp. 281-88; Laureys 1996, pp. 48-49.

the provincial government (which was unacceptable to Great Britain), while an acceptable Iranian official could be the prince's *pishkar* (provincial chief executive) and actual governor. However, the two sides were unable to reach an agreement on this issue; meanwhile WW I had broken out relegating the issue to the background. It was only because of the Turkish invasion of Azerbaijan that Shoja` al-Dowleh had to step down (March 1915) and Russia allowed the *Vali `Ahd* to take up his post in Tabriz.[24]

In early January 1915, the Turks forced the Russians to retreat to Jolfa and entered Tabriz on 8 January. However, by month's end, the Russians defeated the Turks at Sofian and led by General Tshernozubov re-entered Tabriz on 30 January 1915. It was announced that Consul Orlow would soon return from Tiflis. Molitor returned to work after having sought refuge in the American mission during the Turkish occupation.[25]

On 19 March 1915, the *Vali `Ahd* arrived in Tabriz with Sharif al-Dowleh as governor-general, who had been *kargozar* there in 1912-13, thus replacing Shoja` al-Dowleh, the reactionary Russophile. Molitor was astonished by the Crown Prince's arrival, because not the Iranian governor-general, but Orlow was the law in Azerbaijan! On 22 Apil 1915, Heynssens, who had succeeded Mornard, informed the Ministry of Finance that Molitor resigned from all his functions except those of Customs.[26] This was due to the many resignations by Belgians officials in the wake of Mornard's departure, because many tasks that Belgian officials had managed (such as Finance reform; collection of Taxes, Crown lands, Public Works) were taken away from them.[27] Therefore, in May 1915/25 March, Lambert Molitor became Director of Customs of Azerbaijan.[28] As director of Finance

24. For a discussion of Shoja` al-Dowleh's position and the tug-of-war about his activities and who should be his successor, see Nazem 1975, pp. 163-71.

25. On this episode and Molitor's contacts with the Turkish occupation force, see Destrée 1976, p. 280; Laureys 1996, pp. 45-48.

26. MA, Farde 35, 3502.pdf, Memorandum.

27. Laureys 1996, pp. 48-49.

28. Laureys 1996, p. 49.

and Taxes he was replaced by an Iranian official. Thereafter, the central granary in Tabriz was emptied due to carelessness, greed and unscrupulousness of Molitor's successor.[29] Such development was facilitated by the absence of any meaningful control by the central government in Tehran over the province. Moreover, as a result of the outbreak of WW I, Ottoman and Russian forces fought each other in the occupied parts of Azerbaijan with varying degrees of success, causing much collateral damage to humans, animals, and crops.

In fact, the bread situation of West Azerbaijan had become critical as a result of the Ottoman invasion. The main relief came from outside, in particular from the USA, where already in 1915 a committee was formed to provide relief, which was officially named Near East Relief in 1919.[30] In Urmiyeh, Armenian and Assyrian refugees suffered starvation and only with the help given by American missionaries was their lives saved. The latter, financed by the American Committee of Armenian and Assyrian Relief, had organized a bread distribution as follows: until noon bread was sold, thereafter one sheet of thin bread was distributed to each needy person who had no money to buy bread or nothing to eat. To distribute the bread required 20-30 men over seven hours each day. In May 1915, demand was overwhelming; more than 3,000 bread tickets were issued and re-issued and these were updated regularly. On one day more than five tons of bread were distributed, but thereafter the need became less; fortunately bread was cheap at that time. An amount of $10,000 was sent from the USA and received in the fall of 1915. This kept 10,000 Assyrians and Armenians alive on rations of bread and salt only. In 1916, the situation did not change and hundreds of people had only one dry scrap of bread to eat. Even well-to-do people were begging bread, while bread became more expensive.[31]

---

29. MA, Farde 38, 3801.pdf, Almentation, p. 1.

30. Barton 1930; Jackson, 1920.

31. Rockwell 1916, pp. 17-18, 24-25, 35, 47, 67. For pictures of the American compound in Urmiyeh, the breadline, and refugees. In general, see Hellot-Bellier 2002, p. 339; Zirinsky 2002, pp. 359f; Shedd 1922.

I

In 1917, due to hoarding by landowners and mismanagement of the grain stocks by the leading Iranian authorities in Azerbaijan,[32] who exported foodstuffs, while, due to lack of rain, there had been only a small spring crop of wheat (only one-third of normal), famine occurred. The same authorities also exported many cattle by train to Tiflis to supply the Russian army at Qars and elsewhere with meat. In May 1915, a large slaughter-house was built at Sharaf-Khaneh, the head of the railway line connecting Tabriz with Tiflis.[33] Between 21 March 1916 and 20 March 1918 more than 150,000 cows and about 320,000 sheep were exported from Azerbaijan to Russia (see Table 2.1). The worsening food situation was reinforced by the presence and plunder of Russian and Turkish troops in Azerbaijan, which were rapidly losing all semblance of discipline as well as by a grain deficit caused by drought that had begun in the summer of 1916. Therefore, serious steps needed to be taken to avoid a catastrophe in Tabriz and other towns. Every day there were about 100 deaths due to hunger, while children died in the streets. The main supply problem was that the large landowners kept their stock of grain hidden or was exported across the border, so that grain was sold at very high prices. The price of bread in Tabriz had risen with 500%, while rice had become impossibly expensive. In many villages people had no food and therefore, many peasants came to the cities, where most of them died of hunger. Bodies of people (men, women, and children) and animals littered the roads. In Tabriz the situation was not so bad for the last 2-3 months of 1916 as bread was available in the bakeries. However, that situation did not last and the effect of the drought was felt there too.

32. It was said that Mo`addel al-Dowleh, the *pishkar* of Azerbaijan had sold all government grain and emptied its granary. Kasravi 1350, p. 688; Adhari 1354, p. 122; MA, Mémoires, pp. 361-62.

33. MA, Mémoires, pp. 360-61; Laureys 1996, p. 62. Kasravi 1350, p. 698 writes that the conditions leading to famine were worse than he had ever had imagined.

As a result, there also was a shortage of pack animals due to scarcity of fodder. Moreover, the roads were closed due to cold weather and insecurity, so that grain could not reach the city, and thus, the price of bread rose and grain speculators took advantage of this situation. The authorities did nothing to address this problem. The police had a difficult time, because of attacks on bakeries.[34]

Table 2.1: Export of cows and sheep to Russia (1916-1918)

21/03/14-20/03/15	Cows	Value *qrans*	Sheep	Value *qrans*
	16,348	2,771,190	149,167	5,761,458
21/03/15-20/03/16	10,229	1,589,495	74,874	2,720, 831
21/3/1916 – 20/03/1917	66,390	14,076,055	61,243	1,769,056
21/03/1917 – 20/03/1918	116,445	27,553,620	37,778	1,181,284
Total	209,521	45,990,360	323,062	11,423,629

Source: MA, Farde 38, 3804.pdf, Renseignements de la statistique douanière persane (handwritten note of 02/07/1958 in reply to a request from Mr. Sawiz of the Customs Administration, Tehran, 30/03/1958), see MA, Farde 38, 3805.pdf.

Although Sharif al-Dowleh, governor-general of Azerbaijan, had established an Alimentation Commission (*Komisiyun-e adhuqeh*),[35] it was not really operational. At the end of February 1917, Sharif al-Dowleh invited Molitor to participate in the Alimentation Commission with full powers. He informed Molitor that this was a government decision and therefore, he would have all the help he needed.[36] Like the Democrats later in the year, Sharif al-Dowleh probably asked Molitor, because of his excellent track-record of keeping the government granary filled during his tenure as director of Finance until May 1915. Molitor

34. Bahrami 1344, vol. 1, p. 549; MA, Mémoires, p. 361; Majd 2003, pp. 30-32; Kasravi 1350, p. 288; Laureys 1996, p. 61; Adhari 1354, pp. 122-23.

35. Kasravi 1350, p. 688. It seems that in other cities similar organizations existed, such as in Khuy where in 1917 an Alimentation Commission (*kumisiyun-e arzaq*) was created. Aghasi 1350, p. 425.

36. MA, Mémoires, p. 363; Idem, Farde 38, 3802.pdf, Note-Resumé, p. 1; Idem, Farde 36, 3603.pdf, Sharif al-Dowleh to Molitor, 29/02/1917.

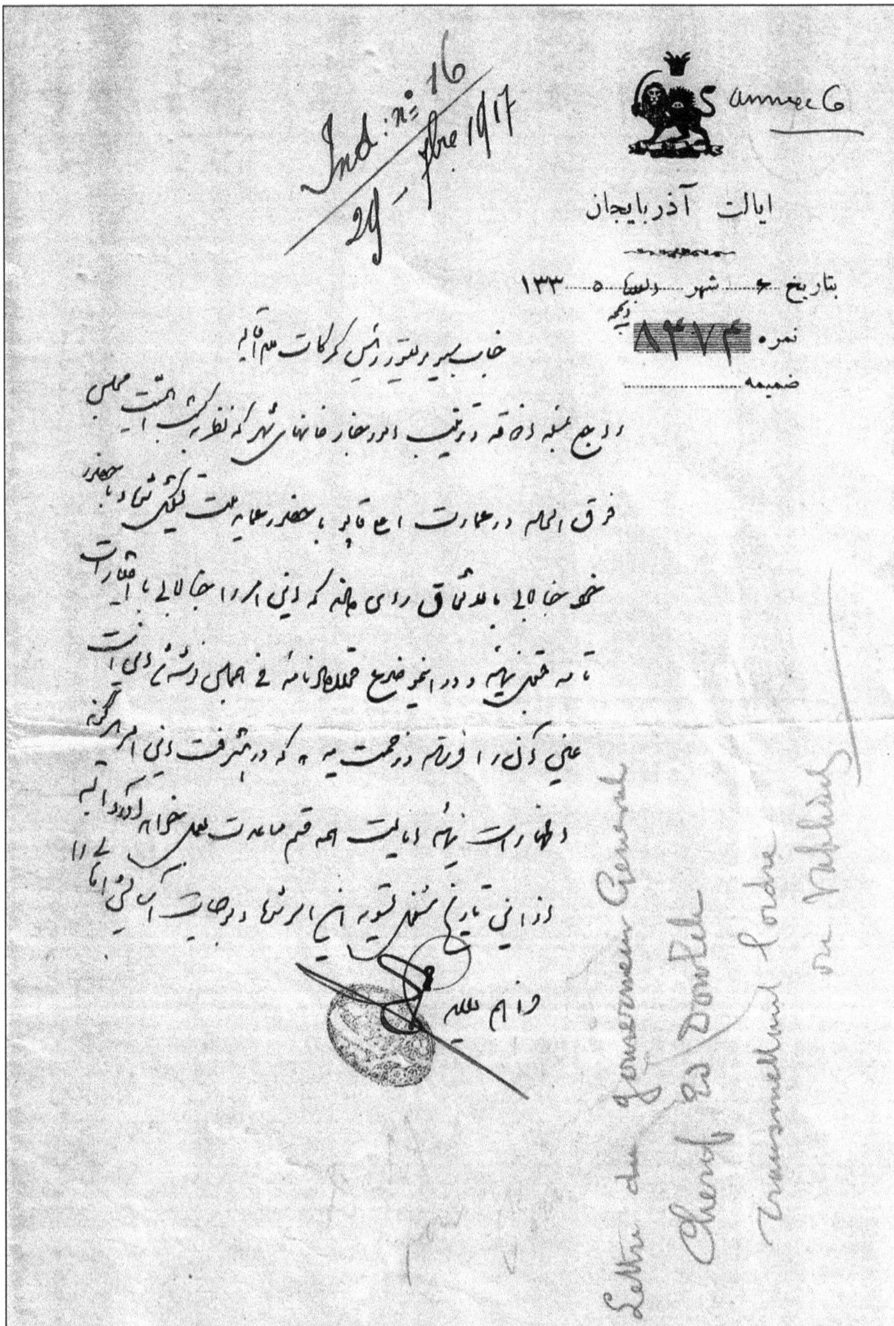

Fig. 2. Sharif al-Dowleh, governor-general of Azerbaijan, to Molitor appointing him director of the Alimentation Service of Tabriz, date 6 Sonboleh 1335/29 September 1917.

refused and repeated his refusal several times thereafter, when Sharif al-Dowleh repeated his invitation. However, probably in March or April 1917, Heynssens allowed him to participate in meetings with the *Vali `Ahd* to examine important questions concerning the city and province. Heynssens only agreed if he would merely participate as an advisor to the Alimentation Commission in Tabriz. Thus, at the prince's repeated insistence, Molitor attended the meetings of the Alimentation Service since that time. Molitor would have preferred to stick to his work at the Customs Administration, but he noted that it was difficult to refuse the *Vali `Ahd*. Molitor noted that the discussions by the Committee produced a lot of hot air, while drinking tea, but it took no relevant decisions, such as how to get grain to the city and supply flour to the bakeries. Therefore, Molitor gave the Committee the revised regulations for bakeries and mills drawn up by his predecessor Ransquin. His February appointment had a calming impact on the bazaaris, the more so, since on the day of his appointment it rained for the first time since months.[37]

Because of the political upheaval and changes in Russia (the February Revolution), Heynssens was worried that these events might have consequences for Iran as well as for Belgian officials working there. Therefore, in July 1917, he sent a telegram to all Belgian officials in Iran in which he "strongly urge you to be prudent and circumstancial about intervening in matters that are not directly related to Customs and its agents."[38] Heynssens was clearly concerned about this matter,

---

37. MA, Farde 36, 3602.pdf, Heynssens, Admin. Gen. Customs to Molitor, Dir. Prov. Customs (31/08/1917); Idem, Mémoires, pp. 358-60; Idem, Farde 36, 3617.pdf, Note Camille. The 17-year old Crown prince was not in favor of Iran's Constitutional freedoms. When Molitor referred to the advantages of these freedoms, the prince said: "Bègàv o khar éguèr àzadi midèhid, miravend bâghtchè khérab mi konend." (If you give freedom to a cow or donkey they go into your garden and destroy it). This answer by the young prince made such an impression of Molitor that he recorded his answer in Persian. MA, Mémoires, p. 324.
38. MA, Farde 36, 3601.pdf, Telegram Heynssens to all Belgian officials (04/07/1917).

because six weeks later he wrote to Molitor that Belgian officials were too much attacked and not sufficiently defended by the [Iranian] government, when they involved themselves in matters outside of Customs, in accordance with their contract. Molitor commented in a marginal note on this letter that these "attacks were made by factions and 'komitehs' of the so-called patriots in which individuals reside, who want to take the place of the Belgians – they attack the Belgians as much as the government. Parliament stopped working as of 14/12/1916." Heynssens was very much worried about these criticisms and asked Molitor to submit an official request for the indemnity he claimed "for your good offices in Tabriz unrelated to your post as Director of Customs."[39]

Given Heynssens' letter not to get involved in anything outside Customs, Molitor withdrew from the Alimentation Service Commission in September 1917. Molitor allegedly was pleased that he was no longer involved in the work of the Alimentation Service. By that time, the bread situation had gotten worse, and the inhabitants of Tabriz panicked. People who owned animals released them into the streets where they died. On 24 September 1917 (24/09/17 = 6 Zu'lHijja 1335) the city was in turmoil. The bazaar was closed and groups of people threatened to riot, because of the worrisome bread issue. Finally, the Democrats, led by Mirza Esma`il Nowbari, and some other outspoken local politicians decided to form an Alimentation Association (*anjoman-e arzaq*).[40] They demanded a competent and energetic director; in fact, they demanded Molitor to be appointed as its director with unlimited powers and authority. When on that day, Molitor arrived at his office there was a message from the prince-governor for him. Molitor sent a message that he was engaged otherwise. However, the prince had

39. MA, Farde 36, 3602.pdf, Heynssens, Admin. Gen. Customs to Molitor, Dir. Prov. Customs (31/08/1917). Molitor was right as to the sources of these attacks, see e.g., Mostashar al-Dowleh Sadeq 1367, pp. 19, 24, 29, 31, 34, 47-49, 51, 58, 60, 69, 74, 81; Destrée 1976, pp. 284-85. The remark concerning the *Majles* refers to the move of many deputies to Qom, see, e.g. Floor 2018, pp. 407-08.

40. Bahrami 1344, vol. 1, pp. 549-550. The Democrats used the bread shortage to drum up support for their ideas and party. Adhari 1354, pp. 122-24.

him called by phone to say that it was an order. When Molitor arrived at the *Ala Qapu* palace he found there was a meeting that had been called by the prince. The meeting was presided by Sharif al-Dowleh and attended by the city's notables and representatives of the political parties. Sharif al-Dowleh told Molitor that the people in the mosque demanded that he had to take charge of the Alimentation Service, otherwise they would riot. Molitor said that he was unable to do so, since this was a local political matter. However, those attending the meeting told Molitor that he was mistaken and that if he would not accept the job terrible things would happen. Molitor later informed Heynssens that he had made the point about the lack of government support in the case of attacks on Belgians to the prince and Sharif al-Dowleh. However, they replied that the fact that they as well as the entire population of Tabriz asked Molitor to take charge of the Alimentation Service was clear evidence of the absurdity of attacks against the Belgians taking place. Sharif al-Dowleh then showed Molitor a telegram sent by Heynssens authorizing him to become the Controller of the Alimentation Service. Even all the above arguments would not have convinced him, Molitor wrote later, but for the scandal of the embezzlement of funds by his compatriot M. Deflines, which mainly influenced his decision to accept the new task.[41] If he accepted the job, public opinion might forgive this misdeed by a Belgian. Moreover, and in my view the main, if not the only reason, he felt pressured by the fact that his appointment letter was signed by Sharif al-Dowleh, the chief of the prince's court, the leader of the Democrat party, and was countersigned by the prince himself. Also, given the misery of the people of Tabriz in the midst of war, he accepted in the interest of the public weal, thus having the opportunity to save thousands of lives. Finally, he felt that combining his function of Director of Customs with that of Controller of Alimentation Service was acceptable, since

41. V. Deflines had worked in Iran since 1900 and in November 1910 had been accused of embezzlement of the Treasury. Destrée 1976, pp. 304, 333. This noble argument, in my view, was but a cover justification for his acceptance of the job as Controller, one, which he knew, was difficult for Heynssens to denounce and disagree with.

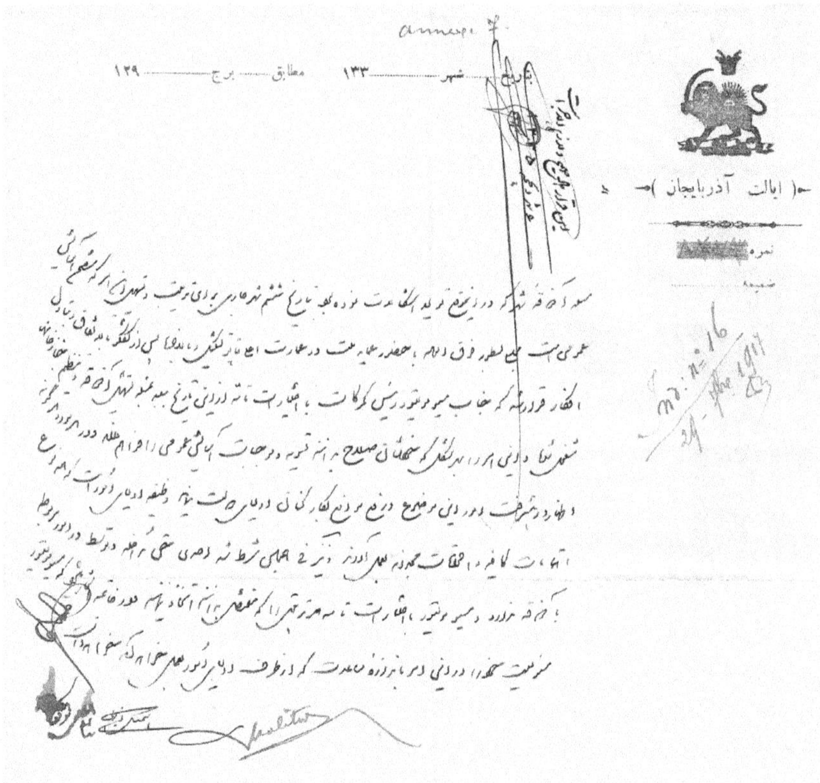

Fig. 3. Decision by the meeting at the Ala Qapu to appoint Molitor as director of the Alimentation Service, signed by Nowbari, Hariri and Mossadeq al-Molk, dated 6 Sonboleh 1335/29 September 1917.

Heynssens also had accepted the directorship of Treasury after the exodus of Belgian officials in May 1915, in addition to his function as Director-General of Customs.[42]

42. MA, Farde 36, 3610.pdf, Molitor to Heynssens (01/12/1917) Persian Notables (You are all robbers. We know we are all robbers, and that is why we ask you remain in your post." Tehran). MA, Mémoires, p. 325; Idem, Farde 38, 3801.pdf, Robinson Note; Molitor related the message he received during that meeting at the palace, where the Iranian attendants stated that if the Alimentation Service was left in the hands of Iranians then abuse would occur. Also, the people had lost faith in the Financial Administration "and by accepting you will send a calming message to people." MA, Farde 36, 3607.pdf, Extract private letter to Heynssens 06/12/1917.

The meeting at the palace decided the following: Molitor, the provincial director of Customs was charged with full powers to organize the bread supply system in a manner beneficial to the public weal and with the full support of the local authorities. Whenever appropriate he would submit reports to the authorities, who had to accept and implement them seriously. It was further decided that nobody might interfere or serve as intermediary concerning the Alimentation Service, which had full and sole authority.[43]

Heynssens still opposed that Molitor took on tasks other than Customs, "as he would only reap the ingratitude of the Persians." He finally gave in to the exhortations by the government, also, because Molitor remained director of the Customs Administration. Heynssens' worry was not exaggerated, for even Molitor realized that he faced an almost impossible task. He noted that "Persians always ask for the physician when the case is *in extremis*, and seeing that the case was hopeless, the Iranians in Azerbaijan appealed to Molitor, an honest man, who, at that time, was director of Customs."[44]

These were the arguments Molitor gave Heynssens four months later, but given the fact that he did not inform him months earlier about what he really was doing and where (from his home) suggests two things. First, he knew that Heynssens would forbid him to be director of the Alimentation Service, and second, which is related to the first one, is that Molitor probably liked the challenge of taking up an almost impossible task. It may have reminded him of his early years in Iran, when, totally ignorant about public health matters, he was told to lead the anti-plague campaign in southern Sistan in 1905. As he himself wrote, it had been a task that he was totally unprepared for. Fortunately, for everybody concerned, it was one that he performed quite well, which earned him the respect and accolades of all parties concerned.[45] This explains why Heynssens only learnt in November

43. The decision was signed by Esma`il Nowbari; Ali Hariri (a.k.a. Karbala'i `Ali Aqa), Movassaq al-Molk, see Fig. 3.

44. MA, Farde 38, 3802.pdf, Note-Resumé, p. 1; Idem, Farde 38, 3801.pdf, Alimentation, p. 1.

45. See Floor 2022 (forthcoming)

1917 through "a private letter received by one of our compatriots in Tehran, who informed me in confidence," that Molitor "had gradually become director responsible for taxes in kind of the province, of the municipal council charged with the public alimentation from your residence, which is not in line with your report of 15 August 1917." Heynssens wrote that Molitor should have remained a mere advisor to the Alimentation Service rather than accepting to be its director just because the authorities were too weak to tackle the hoarders and grain speculators.[46] I return to how Heynssens reacted to this news in what follows.

Even though Molitor had been given full powers and access to all support and means that he asked for, it also meant more work, more trouble and more headaches for him. Nevertheless, Molitor did not ask for an additional salary. However, he asked for a car from the government, because he still was director of Customs and this required much travel. He did so, because when he was still merely an advisor to the Alimentation Service he had incurred high expenses for hiring a vehicle. This may have been the reason for his claiming an indemnity in August, one not related to his work for the Customs Administration (see above). Molitor further demanded the creation of a Commission of six persons, elected by the notables and approved by the governor-general, to support the director's responsibility of the various steps to be taken.[47]

When the Alimentation Service had achieved its fullest form it consisted of the following services: i. a central commission; ii. a director; iii. grain warehouses, both government (*dowlati*) and private (*arbabi*); iv. bakeries; and v. research, collection and requisition of other food products (rice, almonds, vegetables, meat, etc. to supplement the bread shortage). The director of the Alimentation Service

46. MA, Farde 36, 3611.pdf, Heynssens to L. Molitor, 03/02/1918.

47. MA, Farde 36, 3610.pdf, Molitor to de Romero Dusnuet, Minister of Spain charged with Belgian interests in Persia, 24/12/1917 refers to his report to Heynssens and asks Dusnuet to bring it to the notice of M. de Raymond, the Belgian minister who was coming; MA, Farde 38, 3801. pdf., Alimentation, p. 2.

and the deputy directors of the various services were in constant contact with the special commissions (see below) to update data and suppress abuse, etc. Towards the end of his stay in Tabriz, Molitor argued for the establishment of a complaints and investigation service. Experience had shown that there were many disputes and incidents requiring investigation, which made it is indispensable to have such a special service headed by an honest agent directly under the director.[48]

The director of the Alimentation Service was guided by a Central Commission called the *Komisiyun-e Ta'min-e Adhuqeh* (food security commission), which had full powers conferred on it by the authorities.[49] It had six members appointed by the governor-general and it was an official government organization. Each morning the Central Commission worked in the office of the director of the Alimentation Service. The Central Commission's tasks were above all:

I. to look for ways to ensure the supply of grain (in particular by pressing for the collection of taxes in kind);
II. to ensure the funds for additional cost to the normal cost of collection;
III. to mobilize sources of finance by organizing public collections, imposing extraordinary fees on big landlords in case of absence of grain;
IV. to research all means to bring food products of grain and rice, wherever they are, to the city;
V. to decide on the distribution of grain to the bakers and of bread to the consumers taking into account how much grain there was still in stock locally and the quantities calculated to be recovered until the next harvest;
VI. to fix the price of grain sold to the bakers and the price of bread; control and supervision of the organization linked to the Alimentation Service, notably the grain transport service;
VII. to authorize and ratify all other committees etc, formed in the interest of public food supply;

---

48. MA, Farde 36, 3617.pdf, Note concernant, pp. 2-3, 6.

49. Its members included: Esma`il Nowbari, Mirza `Aliqoli Ganjeh'i, Mo`tamad al-Tojjar, Nazem al-Dowleh, Mo`in al-Ra`aya and Lambert Molitor as its president. Kasravi 1350, pp. 694-95, 802.

VIII. to decide in matters of food supply concerning regions or places in the province, notably the in kind taxes that effect that regional supply and how much may be converted into cash by the tax payers.

The Central Commission established a number of special sub-commissions, one of which was charged with the collection of the deliveries of grain promised by the landlords. This sub-commission examined the claims of the interested parties and submitted the results of its work to the Central Commission. The mandate of the Commission was based on the full powers given to the Alimentation Service to take control over all taxes in kind of Azerbaijan province by all means to secure the food supply of Tabriz.[50]

Past experience in Azerbaijan had not been very satisfactory. As soon as the harvest was reaped the authorities should have sent agents (*ma'mur*s) everywhere to make an inventory of the grain harvest and seal the granaries in the villages. However, the Alimentation Service had begun too late with the sealing of the village granaries thus, giving landlords the time to disperse their grain among their peasants, or to sell it to third parties.[51] Thus, it was decided to agree to a proportional discount to the agents (*ma'mur*s) of the quantity of grain inventoried and transported to the city. This had the result that the Alimentation Service brought 19,000 *kharvar*s into the government granary in that year, when the maximum in good years had never exceeded 13,000 to 14,000 *kharvar*s, because fewer towns contributed. It should be mentioned here that these deliveries were not always voluntary by certain landlords, because they were imposed by the Central Commission in a special meeting that was attended by persons who knew the

---

50. MA, Farde 36, 3617.pdf, Note concernant, pp. 2-4.

51. What also happened was that the Russians sealed the granaries in Maragheh and its environs as well as in other places, so that they could reserve it for the use of their troops. The Democrats were in discussion with the revolutionary committees of Russian soldiers to convince them to return the grain. Kasravi 1350, pp. 690, 698, 699 (2,000 *kharvar*s of wheat was bought from Maku and when the Russians left Tabriz they also left almost 2,000 *kharvar*s in Sharaf-Khaneh at Tabriz), 709.

properties of the notables of Azerbaijan. Those landlords, who were unable to supply grain from their property, had to pay the assessed value of their contribution at a unit price fixed by the Central Commission. This aspect of the Commission's work was based on its other mandate, viz. to requisition all private grain at a price of 40 *tumans*/ *kharvar* for wheat. Moreover, the Central Commission bought grain at any price where it could in other places, where the local or political situation did not allow confiscation. Although Molitor was authorized to confiscate grain anywhere in Azerbaijan, he was unable to do so in places where tribal chiefs were too powerful and diplomacy had to be used when buying grain.[52]

Another special sub-commissions collected funds subscribed by the merchants and notables of Tabriz in accordance with a list drawn up by the sub-commission itself as a function of the estimated wealth for each person taxed. The collection of these dues was not without difficulty in practice, but they were collected and as much as possible the above-mentioned list was adhered to.[53]

A third special sub-commissions collected funds to help refugees and operate soup kitchens for truly poor persons. This sub-commissions had full powers to organize this aid and was managed by a trusted agent, who was assisted by a *nazer* or supervisor. This Commission also had to take care of poor people, who were not Tabrizis. With the help of the police, the sub-commissions found the poor, who walked around the streets as well as identified those that were from villages in the province. In case of the latter, the Commission immediately forced

52. MA, Farde 38, 3801.pdf., Alimenation, p.1; Idem, Farde 36, 3617.pdf, Note concernant, p. 5; Kasravi 1350, pp. 689 (there were many *mojtaheds* and *Imam Jom`eh*'s among the landlords, who were hoarding grain), 695 (in a special meeting the Commission led by a furious Nowbari forced the *mojtahed* and others to give up their grain). Also, places like Maragheh, Sarab, Deh Khvarqan (Adhar Shahr) and other places flatly refused to give up their grain and kept it for themselves. Kasravi 1350, p. 699.

53. MA, Farde 36, 3617.pdf, Note concernant, p. 3. This was the so-called *A`aneh* Commission, which, in addition to the existing *Dar al-Mo`jezeh*, established the *Dar al-Masakin*. Kasravi 1350, pp. 699-700.

their landlords to take care of them. The other poor were gathered in shelters where they were looked after.[54]

Despite the full powers granted to him, there still were many difficulties and obstacles to overcome. When Molitor asked for money to finance the purchase of grain the central government in Tehran refused to permit the Financial Agent in Tabriz to make funds available needed for the food supply of Tabriz. In reaction, the Democrats in Tabriz, the most powerful political group in the city, sent armed men to collect tens of thousands of *tuman*s despite the protests by the central government and the Financial Agent, who said that they had no authority, but gave in under pressure. Molitor accepted the funds, under condition that he should only be held responsible for how well he spent them, but not for the method of their collection. This episode showed that the Tabriz government neither cared for nor accepted the authority of the central government at that time. Molitor requested that he should be considered only an administrator. However, the Democrats in Tabriz wanted him to be successful, because they and they alone, not the Iranian government, would get the credit for the successful handling of the bread crisis.[55]

There also was powerful interference by the Russians, who were beyond the control of the Iranian government. The presence of Russian troops was Molitor's greatest obstacle. The Russians were requisitioning grain for themselves in areas that were under their armed occupation. The Gendarmerie was unreliable. Moreover, the Russian occupation was an excuse for every self-interested landlord to flout

---

54. MA, Note concernant, p. 4.

55. MA, Farde 38, 3801.pdf., Alimentation, p. 2; Idem, Mémoires, pp. 331 (the chief of the Democrats Esma`il Nowbari, as president of the Democrat Committee, was the real power in Azerbaijan; the governor-general seemed to be his very devoted assistant. He allowed all illicit affairs pass that he was unable to stop. This gave rise an anarchic situation, where people without written authority took uncontrolled action. "Such as the moudjaheds, the instruments of the Democrats in iffy affairs, who inspired terror among everybody, and there are few people who dare to oppose them), 341, 363. For the Democrat's attitude toward the government in Tehran, see Kasravi 1350, pp. 696-97.

the government to pursue their own purpose and interest. At that time, although not officially, it may be said that Molitor was merely the collector of taxes in kind, nothing else. Although the administration of the Crown lands (*khaleseh*) was in the hands of Iranian officials he controlled government grain by requisitioning it.[56]

Apart from bad roads and their blockage due to wintry conditions, the major logistical problem was that the transport service in Azerbaijan was badly organized and people suffered because of it. The Alimentation Service had a bad experience with the brokerage system (*dallali*) to gather camels and other pack animals. The transport service was the most vital one of the Alimentation Service, because the city's supply of food depended on its good performance. Also, it had to be managed perfectly and operated as a machine to the smallest detail. Therefore, its chief and main agents had to be trustworthy persons. However, the agents of this service, according to Molitor, were "*mojahed*s, so-called revolutionary patriots, thieves and scoundrels, a mob one may not get rid of." Therefore, Molitor decided to establish a rational transport service over which he had perfect control to ensure good performance, which he considered himself as his main success.[57]

Bakeries Service

Because bread was scarce, it was absolutely necessary that the chief of the Bakeries Service was an honest person, because allowing the least abuse signaled less conscientious agents that they also might misuse their function as a source of income. The chief was assisted by a staff of record keepers, clerks, a bookkeeper, a cashier, orderlies (*farrash*es), Cossacks and police. Although the regulations developed by Mokhber al-Saltaneh and M. Ransquin in 1912-13 were sensible, they were formulated for a normal situation. However, they were not adequate in time of famine and thus, were accordingly adjusted. For

56. MA, Farde 38, 3801.pdf., Alimenation, p. 1.

57. MA, Farde 36, 3617.pdf, Note concernant, pp. 5-6. Molitor's submitted that his main victory was in transport, see MA, Farde 38, 3801.pdf, Alimentation, p. 2.

during times when abuse of power was very profitable, it was highly necessary to have strict rules concerning the inspection of bakeries and flour mills, the more so, because both bakeries and flour mills had a long history of taking advantage of consumers.[58]

Tasks of the Bakeries Service

Molitor placed the bakeries and flour mills as if under military regulation. He stressed that direct control of bakers was required to avoid a worsening of the quality and equitable distribution of bread at a low price to only those who were entitled to it. Therefore, in his opinion, this executive branch was the most important one of the various services. It consisted of inspectors of the bakeries, who were distributed over the city quarters and worked under chief inspectors. The division of city quarters adopted by the Alimentation Service was the one used by the police department, in view of the frequent need to call on police support. However, even if the Alimentation Service would know how much grain it had at its disposal over the next few months, it had no precise knowledge of the number of consumers in the city. This was essential, because one thing was certain: the normal quantity of grain was not available. Therefore, Molitor was forced to introduce a system of bread rationing. It had the additional benefit that it allowed to save grain for use in the more difficult periods ahead. This required knowing how many consumers there were in the city, which would allow the Alimentation Service to fix the number of bakeries needed to ensure the bread supply as well as to fix the quantity of grain to be given to each baker. Moreover, the Bakeries Service had to fix the price of bread in cooperation with the Central Commission. This meant in practice that the price of bread was totally controlled by the director, i.e. Molitor. The elements to fix the price of bread were: the sales price of grain to the bakers, the operating cost of the bakery (depending on output), and a reasonable profit for the bakers.

58. MA, Farde 36, 3617.pdf, Note concernant, pp. 8-9. In 1919, when Jamal asked for the regulations written by Molitor the Finance Administration was unable to find them. MA, Farde 37, 3705.pdf, Djemal/Tabriz to Molitor/Tehran, 22/01/1919.

It was estimated that 100 *batman* (300 kg) of flour gave 150 *batman* (150 kg) of *sangak* bread.[59]

The census of the population of Tabriz was facilitated by the fact that it had a Municipality and some administrative structure in the city quarters, although the census was done per area of each police Commissariat. As noted above this was done to have easy access to police support, when needed, but also because city quarter committees were formed per Commissariat at the initative of the Central Commission. Their main role was to inform the Central Commission and above all the deputy-director of the Bakeries Service of the bread needs of each quarter. Each sub-committee appointed five of its most notable members, who formed the *komiteh-ye motahhadeh*, which presided over the sub-committee's meetings and paid for the consumption of tea, pipes and cigarettes served.

The census was not executed by asking the inhabitants for the required information, but through special agents who were assisted by the police, the *kadkhoda*s (chiefs) and the *rish safid*s (elders) of the quarters. The census was adjusted through lists with information from the city quarter sub-committees. However, because it was impossible to have complete confidence in the sub-committees in identifying consumers, therefore, the *komiteh-ye motahhadeh* (united committee) appointed inspectors to verify the list of consumers per bakery, and the inspectors of the Bakeries Service did the same. The fact that the members of the city quarter sub-committees were mostly Democrats meant that there was no opposition to the census, but only strong cooperation. At that time, the Democrats had complete control over the city.

With the help of the sub-committees it was possible to launch a system of bread ration cards; each sub-committee drew up a list of consumers patronizing which bakeries. Based on the data collected the

59. *Sangak* bread is bread that is baked on a bed of hot stone pebbles, see Floor 2015, pp. 70-74 At that time *sangak* bread was sold at 14 *shahi*s per *man* of 1,000 *mesqal*s (one *mesqal* = 4.6 g). However, when the Alimentation Service found out that many of the rich also bought this bread the Commission decided to hold a census. Kasravi 1350, p. 693.

inhabitants of Tabriz were divided into four categories. i. landlords; ii. merchants; and iii. middle class consumers, who were able to buy bread at a price that was somewhat higher than the price fixed for category iv. the lower class consumers a.k.a. the poor, the vast majority of the city's population. Based on his experience in Tabriz, Molitor later recommended to immediately make several kinds of cards, with different colors for at least two bread prices and not to make the mistake made in Tabriz, where to become more popular with the people, the Alimentation Service Central Commission, composed of Democrat deputies, would have given bread free of charge to everybody, if he had let them do so.[60] According to Molitor, the local political committees were less interested in the food supply situation than in their political differences. He had to continuously press upon them the importance and severity of the food situation in Tabriz.[61]

The census allowed Molitor to issue bread ration cards to every middle class and poor family (categories iii and iv). The landowners and merchants were only allowed to have enough grain for auto-consumption. They were not allowed to buy bread from the controlled bakeries. The Alimentation Service also searched homes of wealthy inhabitants to check violations, such as having large stocks of grain and/or buying bread at government bakeries. In case of infraction they were liable for punishment. Because the Alimentation Service issued permits for grinding grain for auto-consumption to private persons as well as permits for transport of grain into the city, it knew who had grain stocks at home.[62]

Although developing, managing and using the system of ration cards was difficult, Molitor considered it essential. He argued that these difficulties should not be an excuse not to use the system, because it ensured control of equitable distribution of bread among consumers.

---

60. MA, Farde 36, 3617.pdf, Note concernant, pp. 4-5, 11-12; Kasravi 1350, pp. 694, 699. According to Adhari 1354, pp. 130-31, Sheikh Mohammad Khiyabani used the bread shortage to mobilize support for his Democratic cause, but Molitor never mentions him.
61. MA, Mémoires, p. 335.
62. MA, Farde 36, 3617.pdf, Note concernant, pp. 8-9.

The actual ration was fixed at 62.5 *mesqal*/p.p./day or one *charak* (287.5 grams), which the Alimentation Service considered to be the absolute minimum.[63] The ration cards were issued per family and listed the number of consumers (adults; children) in that family. It also specified the quantity for each presentation of the card. For three months, one space was crossed daily. All consumers had to get bread in their quarter based on the ration card given by the sub-committees. The only exception was for the police, the military and their families, who had special shops that also were under the Bakeries Service. The baker had to write down each card with its number in a register of daily sales, so that each day it was easy to inspect how much was sold per shop. As to the other food items sold by government shops consumers also had to present their ration card. *Dampokht* (steamed rice) was also distributed by card.

The Alimentation Service established two kinds of bakeries, which baked bread of the same quality, but sold it at different prices to consumers with different means, i.e. cheap and expensive bread, because the sale of these two in the same bakeries would result in abuse. It was necessary to oblige bakers to bake bread at night and to display the bread at one hour before sunrise so that inspectors could easily see it and were able to easily verify that the quantity of bread responded to the quantity of grain given to the bakery. This inspection plus the ration cards ensured an effective control. Increase or decrease of the grain quantities supplied to the bakeries was in accordance with their needs, which were based on discussions with the quarter sub-committees. The Alimentation Service punished bakers, who were found to be engaged in abuse, based on the inspectors' reports

---

63. MA, Farde 36, 3617.pdf, Note concernant, p. 11; Kasravi 1350, p. 699 writes that 120 bakeries in Tabriz received grain from the Alimentation Service and supplied bread to 180,000 people. Until the end of Adhar (22 December), each day a ration card was issued entitling each person to 125 *mesqal*s or one *siyeh*. After two months the ration was reduced 62.5 *mesqal*s (one *punzeh*). Sometimes, to compensate for this shortage, people were given three *shahi*s to buy rice or other foodstuffs, which were available, but were expensive. Middle class people could afford to buy those items, but the poor could not and they started to look sallow.

and after investigation. Likewise, there was inspection of the flour mills through a special service of inspectors. In case of infractions and abuse millers could be fined, imprisoned, or given the bastinado in case of abuse, based on reports by inspectors.[64]

Free sale of grain created the possibility of special bakeries that baked *khasseh* or high quality bread for wealthy consumers. This situation did not happen in Tabriz at that time. *Khasseh* meant bread made only from wheat without barley, although sometimes it might forcibly contain barley. Molitor recommended to only allowing *khasseh* bakeries to open, when the government granary was well-stocked, so that the government might earn money. Moreover, these bakeries needed watching, because they often operated thanks to the fraudulent sale of flour received from the government granary.[65]

Although the Alimentation Service had decided that 62.5 *mesqal*s p.p./day was the minimum in a country where bread was the poor people's staff, it doubted that this quantity was enough for an adult person. Therefore, it developed a program for the promotion of substitute foods. A special sub-commissions was tasked to find those other foods to be sold in special shops to those who had ration cards. This required an additional financial sacrifice by the government, because ration card holders were unable to pay the real price for these food stuffs. The substitute food items considered consisted mainly of almonds, raisins, dried and fresh fruit (when in season) and they saved the day, permitting people to survive with a small amount of bread.[66]

Even when Molitor was struggling to establish a viable and effective stored and feed the people of Tabriz, the extent of his involvement with the stored became known to his superior, the Director-General of Customs and Treasurer-General, Mr. Heynssens. In November 1917, Mr. Moreau,[67] Molitor's deputy at the Customs Administration,

---

64. MA, Farde 38, 3801.pdf., Alimentation, p. 2; Idem, Farde 36, 3617.pdf, Note concernant, pp. 8-9, 11-12.
65. MA, Farde 36, 3617.pdf, Note concernant, p. 12.
66. MA, Farde 36, 3617.pdf, Note concernant, p. 12; Idem, Mémoires, pp. 332, 336; Idem, Farde 38, 3801.pdf., Alimentation, p. 2.
67. G. Moreau served in Iran at least since 1913, see Destrée 1976, pp.

had spread the rumor that Molitor had totally ceded his function as provincial director of Customs to the Tabriz director to focus exclusively on the Alimentation Service, because of the special payment he received, while certain Customs employees were detached permanently, requiring replacement by others who were untrained.[68] Molitor denied that he received more salary because of his work for the Alimentation Service and expressed his surprise that Heynssens lend credibility to such and other rumors.[69] In December 1917 Molitor submitted a detailed explanation of his activities.[70] On 3 February 1918 Heynssens replied to Molitor's letter.

> I accept that these rumors are totally unfounded and, exceptionally, approve of measures taken by you, be it that you should have asked my approval beforehand. It is regrettable that you wanted an official follow-up that required a coded telegram. I am displeased that you gave your report, in which you take to task your 1st assistant, a Belgian official, to a native agent, however discrete he may be. You should know that this may have a negative impact concerning Belgian officials among natives, whom you should defend and support. I understand that this was due to resentment, unlike your normal measured attitude, about which you expressed regret.[71]

The reference to his first assistant is to Joseph Jamal, in whom Molitor had complete confidence and whom he left in complete charge of the Alimentation Service in the afternoon, when he took care of his responsibility as Director of Customs.[72] Of course, Heynssens

---

327, 342.

68. MA, Farde 36, 3611.pdf, Heynssens to L. Molitor, 03/02/1918.
69. MA, Farde 36, 3606.pdf, telegram Molitor to Heynssens, 25/11/1917.
70. MA, Farde 36, 3606.pdf, Extrait de ma lettre Molitor to Heynssens, 06/12/1917.
71. MA, Farde 36, 3611.pdf, Heynssens to L. Molitor, 03/02/1918.
72. MA, Mémoires, p. 364. Jamal had already been a trusted collaborator of Ransquin since 1912 and had an excellent knowledge and experience with the financial affairs of Azerbaijan.

was concerned about this arrangement, given the sometimes virulent criticism of the mere presence of Belgian officials in Iran by opponents of the government, as signaled above. The fact, that an Iranian, be it an Armenian, was able to replace a Belgian official would be powerful ammunition for those dissenting and opposing voices. Heynssens hoped "that soon the results will be such that the Persians will be appreciative of this disinterested effort, of which they themselves are incapable, as we know from sad experience. I hope that your involvement will not last beyond the next harvest, as increase in trade will require all your attention and without extraordinary help you would not be able to assume additional tasks."[73]

Heynssens clearly was upset with Molitor and intended to rap his knuckles. Without any care to the possible impact on the functioning of the Alimentation Service in Tabriz, on 2 March 1918, he ordered Molitor to resign from his posts in Azerbaijan and relocate to Enzeli. Due to the occupation of that town by the Jangalis, the Belgian Customs official with his family had fled to Russia.[74] However, Heynssens plans to 'exile' Molitor to Enzeli was not appreciated by the authorities in Tabriz. Mohtasham al-Saltaneh[75] immediately informed Heynssens that despite serious start-up problems Molitor had done an excellent job of actually making the Alimentation Service (*edareh-ye arzaq*) work perfectly. If Molitor would depart this would have serious consequences for the food situation in Tabriz reason why he refused to accept Molitor's resignation. "We hope you revisit your decision and again appoint him to this function."[76] Molitor did not want to go to Enzeli and was glad that the government supported him in this matter.

73. MA, Farde 36, 3611.pdf, Heynssens to L. Molitor, 03/02/1918; Idem, Farde 36, 3612.pdf, Heyssens to Molitor, telegram 28/02/1918.

74. MA, Farde 36, 3615.pdf, Mohtasham al-Saltaneh to Heynssens 4 Jomadi II 1316 (Persian and French); Idem, Farde 36, 3614.pdf, Telegram Heynssens 20/02/1918.

75. He was the chief executive (*pishkar*) of the *Vali `Ahd* in 1917. Mohtasham al-Saltaneh 1396, vol. 1, p. 325.

76. MA, Farde 36, 3615.pdf, Mohtasham al-Saltaneh to Heynssens 9 Jomadi II 16/March 1918.

Fortunately, for him and Tabriz, Heynssens temporarily capitulated and gave in to the government's request.

The fall-out of the Russian Revolution had consequences for the food supply of Tabriz in particular and Azerbaijan in general.

> Early in 1918 the Russian forces commanded by General Baratoff had degenerated into a rapidly disintegrating horde of disbanded and demoralised soldiers, who, plundering as they went, and finally selling their arms and accoutrements for food made their way homewards in irregular bands, many of which perished on the way. The west of Persia, except the province of Khuzistan, was by this time completely devastated and stricken by famine for the Russians had pulled down all the villages they passed to obtain firewood, and the Turks had driven off all the cattle that were left. To cope with the appalling and widespread distress an American mission of relief proceeded thither in the autumn of 1918 and aided by the British authorities at Baghdad and Basra is doing its best to alleviate the misery of these famine-stricken districts.[77]

In the Russian warehouses, situated at Sharaf-Khaneh, a village near Tabriz, not only food but also arms were stored. In early March 1918, this attracted all kinds of unsavory elements; the more so, because the local political situation had become chaotic and necessary steps to improve the food supply had not yet been taken. Moreover, the transport situation worsened, because of frequent attacks on the railway, which caused that the Russians abandoned its maintenance. Also, fuel for the train was in short supply, and after a while the rail service to Tiflis was discontinued. The *mojahed*s and Iranian troops who guarded the warehouses at Sharaf-Khaneh first served themselves, while they also terrorized the local population. Much of the equipment, including lorries, became defective. In the winter of 1917-18, Molitor was able to persuade the departing Bolsheviks

---

77. IOR/L/PS/20/C188, p. 50. In October 1917, at Maragheh and environs, the Russians took control over the local granaries. Adhari 1354, pp. 130-31.

to transport by train grain destined for the Russian army instead to Tabriz, which was very important as many roads were blocked due to snow.[78] In February 1918, Molitor found 17,000 *pud* or 278 ton (one *pud* = 16.38 kg) of salted meat that the Russian army had left in their slaughter-house (near the train station at Sharaf-Khaneh) when it returned to Russia. This meat would have allowed him to add it to the *dampokht* or to other popular soups. However, the Moslem inhabitants of Tabriz refused to eat meat that was not *halal*, so that only the Armenians of Tabriz accepted to eat it.[79] Among the abandoned meat there were barrels filled with cow tongues, which Molitor believed to have been set aside for Russian officers, which he distributed among a number of Europeans in the city. After having unsalted the tongues they turned them into excellent smoked tongues. When Molitor left Tabriz in June 1918 there were still many barrels of meat left, but he did not know what happened with it.[80]

On 14 March 1918, the government warehouse, which fed 100,000 people, only had grain for another six days of consumption. This was because for several weeks no camels had come to Tabriz, while roads were blocked by snow and made things worse. The growing anarchy in the province was not helpful either, the more so, because the usual grain supply centers for Tabriz that still had a surplus did not want to send it to the city. Fortunately, the railway chief, Mr. Mamatzeff was willing to transport about 1,500 *kharvar*s of grain that the Russian army had stored at Sharaf-Khaneh. The railway only had three locomotives and a few wagons with which it also had to evacuate Russian troops. Nevertheless, Mr. Mamatzeff exerted himself to ensure that the grain, which was being pilfered and sold left and right, reached

78. MA, Mémoires, p. 333; Laureys 1996, pp. 62-63.

79. MA, Mémoires, p. 336. According to Kasravi 1350, p. 709, the meat was conserved in small tins and came from Russia, however, this must have concerned part of the meat, because Molitor mentions that the meat was kept in barrels.

80. MA, Mémoires, pp. 332-33 (Molitor intended to send the meat to Sauj Bulagh, Sarab and the environs of Tabriz, where people were ravaged by famine), 366.

the city. Nevertheless, Molitor felt obliged to reduce the daily ration to one *punzdeh* or 63 *mesqal*s. [81]

There also was a large quantity of barley stored at Sharaf-Khaneh, which was used to supply rye bread, but this amount only served a few weeks of bread rations. Molitor feared that he might not be able to feed the poor. Therefore, he hoped that spring would soon arrive with the growth of plants and herbs that might be used as a food substitute, the more so because the expected rice from Gilan did not arrive at the expected time.[82] Because there was no sufficient supply of bread, potatoes were also bought so as to contend the poor somewhat.[83] As of 16 April 1918, the daily ration was reduced to 30 *mesqal*s of bread with 30 *mesqal*s of almonds and dried raisins. Many people were dying in the streets of hunger, mainly villagers who had fled to the city hoping to find food, and whose number only increased. However, even in Tabriz the poor suffered from hunger. Therefore, many people who before had refused to eat the Russian meat, now, driven by hunger, changed their minds. The Americans wanted to help them, but were inhibited from doing so by the limited number of missionaries and the hostile attitude of the Democrats, who made virulent attacks against them in their newspaper *Tajjadod*.[84] When the American Relief wanted to organize *dampokht* kitchens in the lower part of the city (in the upper city Iranians had already established such kitchens) the local Democrats were very much upset and opposed to this plan. When Molitor consulted the chief Democrat about the Rev.

---

81. MA, Mémoires, pp. 332, 335.

82. MA, Mémoires, pp. 336, 366. Meanwhile, the *mojahed*s and other vandals (*de gens sans foi ni loi*) continued to pillage the warehouses at Sharaf-Khaneh stealing anything of value, while terrorizing the local population. One of Molitor's staff, Mirza Janiyantz together with two companions was killed as well as many others, but the local people did not dare identify the killers out of fear. MA, Mémoires, pp. 333, 337 (the *mojahed*s spoiled an immense quantity of applesauce contained in large barrels of 50 *pud*s, by throwing gasoline over it).

83. Bahrami 1344, vol. 1, p. 549. For the limited use of potatoes in Iran, see Floor 2003, p. 353.

84. MA, Mémoires, p. 339; Laureys 1996, p. 63.

Jessup's proposal to organize these soup kitchens Nowbari flew into a rage and said the Americans were arming Christians against Moslems in Urmiyeh and he held the Americans responsible for all massacres of Moslems that had occurred in Urmiyeh. Despite the bread shortage there were still people in certain city quarters, who wanted to make trouble, because they refused to eat the *dampokht* and the meat.[85]

The low bread ration and the need to partially switch to substitute food, of course, had an impact on the population's mood. Therefore, it was necessary to watch over the people's morale. This was done by the city quarter sub-committees through their continuous contacts with inhabitants. The committees were instructed not to hide the seriousness of the situation from the people, under the pretext of not wishing to cause panic. Through print, the people were informed of measures taken, those to be taken to redress bad situations, and above all to warn them against the more serious inconveniences in the future. E.g., Molitor asked the inhabitants of Tabriz to save bread and sow millet, maize, beans etc. seed in spring, i.e. those vegetables that ripen before the grain harvest and might constitute an extra help to ease the public food supply. He also encouraged the cultivation of vegetables in stead of flowers in the city's gardens. The written Notices also invited the inhabitants to report (even anonymously) persons who had secret grain depots and those who had sufficient grain, but nevertheless bought cheap bread from the government bakeries. Because even during the famine there were persons that had more grain stored than they needed, which surplus had to be extracted and bought for the central granary, and even confiscated it in case of recalcitrant persons. Molitor stressed that one should always try to buy grain and at a good price, reason why ample funds were needed. He further noted that it was unnecessary to state that nothing was perfect, given the mentality of Iranians, "who cannot help but

---

85. MA, Mémoires, pp. 339-40, 366; Idem, Farde 38, 3801.pdf, Alimentation, pp. 2, 4; Kasravi 1350, pp. 695, 710-42. Because of the growing anti-Christian mood the Democrats through their force of terror, the *mojaheds*, expelled all Armenians from the Finance Department of Azerbaijan. However, they did not interfere with Molitor's Armenian staff in the Alimentation Service and the Customs Department. MA, Mémoires, p. 331.

favor their family and friends, and above all taking into account that the mojaheds (the revolutionary fighters) may impose themselves, but the director has to try and keep these abuses to a minimum."[86] Fortunately by 20 April 1918, the price of grain began to fall slowly, because the hoarders realized that it would be more profitable to sell their grain before the new harvest, as it had been raining abundantly since early April. However, the fall in price stalled and remained high at 20 *qran*s per *man* of 1,000 *mesqal*s. The good news was that there was an abundance of bread at Maragheh.[87]

How difficult the start-up problems were, referred to by Mohtasham al-Saltaneh, is clear from the Rev. Jessup's letter in October 1917, when he writes that conditions in Tabriz were going from bad to worse and he wondered how people would get through the winter. The price of bread had almost quadrupled compared to the summer. Also, there had been as yet no rains, which was bad for the prospect of sowings. Fortunately, the rains came in January 1918, which had a downward pressure on grain prices. Speculators who had driven up the price of wheat from 20 to 140 *tuman*s per *kharvar* for wheat and from 12 to 100 *tuman*s for barley saw prices drop to 80 for wheat and 60 *tuman*s for barley in January 1918. By that time, the Alimentation Service had become fully operational, which had a positive impact on the food situation in Tabriz and environs. Although there was still considerable suffering, the US Consul Paddock opined that the situation in Tabriz could not be described as one of famine.[88]

Despite all difficulties and suffering the result of the work of Alimentation Service was a positive one. It was clear that if nothing had been done 5-6 months later there would have been a catastrophe. Molitor submitted that if he would have been director of the Alimentation Service before August 1917, he might have been able to save almost the quantity necessary for two months bread for the poor of Tabriz. His work from September 1917-June 1918 was a record of

---

86. MA, Farde 36, 3617.pdf, Note concernant, pp. 6-7.

87. MA, Mémoires, pp. 339 (the hoarded stocks in Azerbaijan were small, contrary to those in Tehran), 340.

88. Majd 2003, pp. 30-32; see also Kasravi 1350, p. 695.

reorganization with most satisfactory results in a general situation of indescribable disorganization. One cannot imagine, Molitor submitted, what he had to do to ensure the food supply of the people by only leaving the peasants enough for subsistence and seed grain. At that time, the means available were at the most precarious minimum. Molitor was able to enter into government granaries more grain than ever before in normal years. He also had been able to create a bread and a substitute food rationing system in a town, where no population statistics or records existed. He realized that new systems were difficult to put into operation, which explained why the Alimentation Service was only fully operational by January 1918. Nevertheless, in Tabriz there were few deaths in the streets unlike in Tehran at that time. True, poor people were eating very little bread and a lot of almonds, raisins, dried fruit, vegetables, *dampokht* and fresh fruit, but it was adequate. Nevertheless, the worst incidents that one expected for the winter of 1917-18 did not happen and spring 1918 came without any disorder. By April or May 1918 the situation in Tabriz was considered to be saved.[89] In June 1918, Molitor had to leave due to the Turkish invasion of Tabriz,[90] which totally demoralized the Alimentation Service.

Before Molitor left Tabriz he wrote a Note for the use of the government in Tehran in which he explained what he had done in Tabriz. He had written the Note not only to inform the Ministers in Tehran, but also to argue the case for the establishment of a national government policy to manage the bread supply to the big cities.[91] In his Note, Molitor explained why and how the government could and should play a positive role in that regard. He submitted that in normal times, when grain was abundant, the government Granary only distributed part of its grain, the rest of their grain requirements bakers bought in the market, as needed. The taxes in kind and grain from Crown lands, stored in the Granary, gave the government control over the market,

89. MA, Farde 38, 3801.pdf., Alimentation, p. 2; Majd 2003, p. 32; MA, Farde 38, 3802.pdf, Note-Resumé, p. 3.

90. For details about the evacuation of the Belgians and other foreigners, see Laureys 1996, pp. 57-59; MA, Mémoires, pp. 342-51.

91. MA, Farde 36, 3617.pdf. Note.

because, the price of bread was fixed by combining the reduced price of government grain with the price of grain bought in the free market. The price of bread was lower as a function of how much cheap grain government was able to supply. Even when government shops were not filled public supply was assured. Therefore, the government always needed to have as much as possible grain in stock to control the market. In times of dearness and famine or even of insufficiency of government stocks one faces the following situation: 1. the bakers find little grain in the market, at a high price, then the government has to give them more grain and at prices lower than market price to allow a reasonable price of bread. 2. the bakers don't find grain at all in the market, or insufficient quantities at exorbitant prices, in which case the government has to ensure grain supply, which means an enormous financial sacrifice, above all when stocks are low. If government stores are not well-stocked in time of abundance then government is to blame and is responsible for too high price of bread by bakers. Therefore, there always needs to be a permanent Alimentation Service and a good functioning Finance Department.

In times of famine it was highly necessary to ensure the collection of grain to supply bakeries. The current crisis should be a lesson for the government and show clearly the waste by the Finance Department, because since a long time the supply of bread has not been assured in large cities by an absolutely stable and normal organization to collect the taxes in kind. Moreover, the in kind taxes had to guarantee the supply to the bakeries, certainly partly, while ensuring seed stock for new plantings.

Therefore, one has to decide in cities where the warehouses are emptied to make now serious and rigorous steps to get the following result: to have an important balance in the warehouse to face sudden shortages. To do so one has to continue to ration the bread consumers as of the next harvest, which appears to be abundant. It is unnecessary to point out the need to do so in Tehran in particular. The abuses and disorder existing in the transport service are the cause of the bad collection of taxes in kind. The government should not be afraid to establish regional warehouses that receive the grain before sending it off to the central granary, because of the expense. It would not receive grain directly any longer, but only in the regional ones. This would eliminate the problems that bedeviled the central warehouse at that time.

It was absolute necessary to establish an exact estimate of the grain needed to supply food to the city for one year. Also, to calculate exactly the quantity of grain (wheat and barley) that really might be collected without too much difficulty via taxes and the Domains. If these quantities were considered to be sufficient to supply the bakeries that served the lower and middle class of people (the others were able to take care of their own supply) the Central Commission had to demand from the main landlords living in the city to undertake a formal commitment beforehand to supply the necessary surplus, at a price to be determined beforehand, a price that ensured a reasonable profit to the landlords. Thereafter, once the taxed quantity per land lord was formally decided, one might decree the sale of grain to be free. The strict application of steps that preceded this stage was only indispensable when the year had not been a good one. In times of abundance, it sufficed to sell the bakeries half or two-third of their grain needs from the government granary, or the quantity that would be considered to be sufficient for them to bake bread; the remainder of their needs the bakers would buy in the market.[92]

II

After Molitor's departure, due to the Ottoman occupation of Tabriz in June that lasted until 23 August 1918, the bread situation did not improve and the people of Tabriz suffered much due to the presence of Turkish troops. When the Turkish troops left Tabriz, after having looted the city, the American Relief committee came back and brought

92. Molitor's Note end here. At the end he had added a list of 34 model documents, records, notes to the public, landlords, and bakers.

relief to 25,000-50,000 people.[93] During the Ottoman occupation, the local committees asked Joseph Jamal, Molitor's deputy, to organize an Alimentation Service, but given the precarious and dangerous situation for Christians he preferred to excuse himself.[94] This was understandable given Turkish treatment of Christians. Jamal wrote to Molitor: "The massacre of Christians [by the Turks] was planned and we escaped by a miracle. What was decisive was the success on the battlefield by the Allies in the Balkans and above all in Europe. As a result, the Turks became polite to the Christians!" When, after the Turkish withdrawal, the Iranian authorities returned to Tabriz the city was a great mess. Also, politically, because the leaders of the Democrats: Mirza Esma`il Nowbari, Aqa Sheikh Mohammad Khiyabani and Hajji Mohammad Ali Badamchi had been arrested by the Turks and imprisoned at Urmiyeh. After the Turks left Tabriz they were released, but they were rearrested by the Turks before their arrival at Tabriz and were exiled to Qars. Later they were released again and arrived in Tabriz at the beginning of November 1918. Since then, they "did not engage in activities, and, in my view, they await the arrival of the British to see what position they should take."[95]

Probably in or after a meeting concerning the food situation held on 14 Ramazan/24 June 1918, which was presided by Mohtasham al-Saltaneh, Jamal was asked to take charge of the Alimentation Service. For reasons discussed above he declined the honor. However, in early July 1918, he wrote a programmatic outline of measures that needed to be taken to ensure that the bread price might be held at 4 *qrans/man*. However, there was no government in Tabriz at that time to whom he might submit his proposal.[96] In this proposal, drawing

---

93. Post 1920, p. 71. Jamal wrote to Molitor that during the summer the poor in Tabriz still ate more almonds and dried raisins than bread. MA, Mémoires, p. 367.

94. MA, Farde 37, 3702.pdf, Djemal Note 15/12/1918.

95. MA, Farde 37, 3702, Jamal to Molitor, Tauris 15/12/1918.

96. MA, Farde 37, 3702.pdf, Djemal Note 15/12/1918; Idem, Farde 37, 3701.pdf, Note by Jamal, 06/07/1918; 15 Saratan1297; 26 Ramazan1336.

on his experience as Molitor's deputy at the Alimentation Service he described the food situation of Tabriz as follows:

Given the famine: 1. there is no grain reserve left in the province, while during normal years, as of the new harvest, the province always had several thousands of *kharvar*s from the preceding year; 2. due to lack of grain peasants have no seed to plant; 3. due to anarchy and insecurity in parts of the province the harvest is very small; 4. movement of troops in the province are an obstacle to the free movement of grain to the city; and 5. the exorbitant price of grain last year stimulated greed among landlords and led to artificial shortages.

Jamal submitted that a well-organized Alimentation Service was urgently needed to overcome these problems otherwise bread in city would become very expensive. This required the following measures:

1. For the year Yunt'il don't permit any transport in the province except for regions very far from Tabriz. In a meeting with government on 14 Ramazan presided by Mohtasham al-Saltaneh the total transportable quantity was estimated to be 29,000 *kharvar*s, which suffices if point 9 of this note is implemented.
2. Propose landlords to transport themselves this year's taxes in kind to the city's granary, transport that will be paid by the Alimentation Service. Once commitment is given and landlords neglect to do so then the Alimentation Service and the Finance Department have the right to transport it themselves, after the fixed delay has passed, by its officials (*ma'mur*) whose expense the landlord has to pay.
3. Stronger steps need to be taken regarding major payers whose recalcitrance and bad behavior is habitual and notorious if they constrain implementation. To show their selfish behavior to the famished people we need to do the following: taking into account the total quantity of taxes in kind they have to pay, both for the current and previous years, both for taxes and under the title of mosaedeh [advance], etc.[97] based on

97. "A good landlord gave seed to his tenants each year. If he supplied them with 10 kharvar (1,000 lbs) for sowing the peasants had to return at harvest these 10 kharvar plus 5 kharvar for the use of the loan. In addition,

the daily supply of grain to bakers into the *ambar*, given the distance of their property to Tabriz. Based on these elements impose on the big landlords concerned (each in turn) the obligation to ensure the supply of grain to the city's bakers during a certain number of days (a function of their fee); the proximity will be in relation to the distance between the properties and the city. The public will be informed beforehand through affiches of these measures during the period that the *ambar* will not supply grain to the bakers, but that the people have to address themselves to such and such landlord when they are unable to buy their daily bread during that time.

4. Charge the Finance officials with the task of transporting the taxes of those tax payers, who are unable to transport it; to that end these officials will be given extra subaltern staff as required by the Finance Department. The Cossacks and gendarmes could supply this additional staff.
5. Create a special transport service for in kind taxes that takes care of transport of those who have committed to transport it, but lack the will to so, and to do the necessary. It has to be attached to the Finance Department in connection with the granary.
6. It is indispensable to organize a serious service for grain transport consisting of honest members. Also, rules are needed to requisition camels.
7. Strict sentences need to be applied to those of the Finance staff who are dishonest and negligent. They need to be informed about this beforehand.
8. It is necessary to have landlords transform their in kind taxes that are in arrears and of last year's *mosa`edeh* at a price of 100 *tumans*/*kharvar* of *ghalleh*. These

---

they had to give two-tenth's of the crop - one tenth going to the landlord the other to the government. Thus, a peasant must set aside 10 batman, deduct from that 1 batman for the government/divan and the other for the landlord. This system is called musa`edeh looks advantageous, because both landlord and peasant contribute 10 kharvar, or a total of 20 kharvar for sowing. This would yield at least 200 kharvar of grain. From this two-tenths or 40 kharvar is deducted, plus 10 kharvar borrowed from the landlord in addition to 5 kharvar, so that there remains 145 kharvar for the peasant." DCR 423 (1888), p. 4.

funds will serve to partially cover the loss suffered by government and if need be may be used for the purchase of additional grain when needed for the city.

9. The system of the sale of bread on the basis of ration cards also needs to be maintained this year and given the quantity of transportable grain as per art. 1 it is required to fix a bread ration of 1/16 *batman*/day/p. p. Nevertheless, one should contract with the bakers so that as of next 19 Asad/13 August 1919 they increase an equal quantity of grain through purchase elsewhere, so that we may give 1/8 batman/p. p. and the price of grain from the granary will be changed in accordance with the day's price of additional grain that the bakers buy in the market, so that they may provide people with bread at the official price (see art. 10).
10. To avoid major losses for the government a reasonable bread price should be fixed. I think that 4 *qran*s per *batman* is not exaggerated. In case on 15 Asad/9 August 1919, the grain price in the market has not sufficiently fallen to allow the government to provide bread without major losses at the above price, one may organize the people into three groups, of which the third one may receive bread at the above price. Those of 1st and 2nd group will get bread at variable rates depending on the market price combined what that which is supplied to the granary.
11. It goes without saying that the authorities have to see to it that security is established on the roads in the province so that transport can take place without difficulty.

Given the Turkish occupation, the state of disorder after the Turkish withdrawal, the restoration of a semblance of order and of Iranian authority in the city and province it took some time to address the bread situation again. Then the pandemic struck and it was a harsh winter with many deaths.[98] Nominally there was an Alimentation Service in Tabriz by the end of 1918. It was under Hajj Nazem al-Dowleh, the ex-chief of the Municipality. However, the Alimentation Service did not do a proper job, because the bakers bought their grain in the

98. Kasravi 1350, p. 701.

bazaar at the day's price, which yielded them enormous profits. The Chief of the granary, Mr. Vahan, was the same as in 1917. He told Joseph Jamal that the Ark contained more than 6,000 *kharvar*s of grain and did not supply more than 10 *kharvar*s/day to special shops that supplied bread to government officials and the military at 6 *qran*s and 40 *dinars* per *batman*. The cases of death due to hunger were numerous; the streets were full of beggars. Without exaggeration, Jamal submitted, one-third of the population was reduced to begging and there was misery everywhere. True, bread was now aplenty in the bazaar, but every day there were many deaths due to hunger in the city. This abundance of bread was explained by its price, 8 *qrans*/*batman* and because the landlords and speculators (*mohtakar*s) had achieved their objective by being able to sell their grain at 100-120 *tumans*/*kharvar*, when this price should be at most 30 *tumans*.[99] Jamal wrote to Molitor in December 1918:

> The people of Tehran gain with you as head of the Alimentation Service, we in Tabriz lose. There is much talk here how easy people have it in Tehran thanks to you as to bread and the Tabrizis are jealous. After you, more or less, had been able to feed the people with the available existing quantities of grain, which nevertheless were totally insufficient, due to the shortage caused by the drought, it is obvious that you will not allow people to suffer in a year of abundance.[100]

On 26 February 1919, the *Vali `Ahd* ordered *Majid al-Saltaneh* to appoint Mirza Agha Bilouri and Hajj Nazem al-Adalaeg (sic: Nazem al-Dowleh) as joint-chiefs of the Alimentation Service. In total the Alimentation Service Commission consisted of eight persons.[101]

---

99. MA, Farde 37, 3702.pdf, Djemal to Molitor, Tauris 15/12/1918.

100. MA, Farde 37, 3702.pdf, Djemal to Molitor, Tauris 15/12/1918

101. MA, Farde 37, 3706.pdf, Djemal to Molitor, Tauris 27/01/1919. According to Molitor, the Crown prince, who had been totally sidelined and ignored by the Democrats, used Mirza Aqa Boluri (who had arrived in April 1918 from Istanbul), a fierce opponent of the Democrats, to destroy and divide them. The Democrats accused Boluri of being an Ottoman spy

Apparently, somebody had second thoughts about this appointment, because the next day Joseph Jamal was appointed as director of the Alimentation Service. As director he had signing authority together with the head of the Municipality. He had to submit weekly accounts and their justification to the Central Commission consisting of representatives of American Relief, government and the people, to wit: Mr. Jessup, Hajj Arfa` al-Molk, chief of the Municipality; Hajj `Adl ol-Molk; Nazem al-Dowleh; Hajj Mirza Agha Farshforush; Heshmat al-Saltaneh; Hajj Rahim Aqa; Nazal al-Mamalek, Amir Nosrat, Sayyed Abu'l-Fotuh, Mirza Ali Khan, Ali Vakili, and Jamal himself.

The governor-general accepted to finance public works for the poor on condition that the Alimentation Service would be attached to the Municipality. Agreement was reached with Dr. Alam al-Molk concerning the composition of the commission charged with the distribution of grain seed to the villages most in need. Its members were: Hajj Adl al-Molk (later Safa al-Molk), Heshmat al-Saltaneh, Nazem al-Dowleh, Hajj Mirza Agha Farshforush, Hajj Arfa` al-Molk, Hajj Zoka al-Dowleh, and Asadollah Khan, inspector. This commission proposed a distribution system based on the following parameters. Given that a good part of the Azerbaijani taxes in kind were irrecoverable this year, the commission deemed it opportune to give a quantity of seed on account of taxes that had to be equally distributed over all needy villages of the same district. This quantity might be for example ¼ or ⅓ of the taxes in kind. The task of distributing it could be given to landlord, who in return had to give a receipt with the commitment to: i. distribute the same quantity to his peasants, ii. assume the responsibility for sowing, iii. pay the rest of taxes without procrastination, and iv. not submit claims of insolvability to pay in the next round. Jamal asked Molitor to confirm that the amount of financial assistance agreed upon would constitute the definite remittance

---

and tool and on 14 May 1918, he escaped arrest by seeking refuge with the governor-general, after a group of his armed supporters (also called *mojaheds*) had been arrested by the chief of police, a Democrat supporter. However, Molitor opined that the two sides would make up and he was proven right. MA, Mémoires, p. 342.

or merely a simple recoverable advance. As the sowing season was very much advanced Jamal proposed to give Commission certain powers to act quickly.

Because there was not enough grain to satisfy food demand Mazandaran rice was consumed as the main substitute. The rice was either sent to Tabriz by sea via Astara, or by land via Tehran, but this last option was very expensive. Therefore, Jamal asked Molitor to precisely indicate the eventual manner of use of the rice to be sent.[102] Was it for resale or to be distributed to the poor at a low price? Was it the balance of last year's Alimentation Service rice? By the end of February 1919, the price of rice in Tabriz was going down. *Sadri* rice cost 14 to 20 *qran*s and *gerdeh* rice 8-11/*batman* of 1,000 *mesqal*s. As usual there were payment problems. Therefore, Jamal asked Molitor to have the Ministry of Finance inform the *pishkar* in Tabriz to pay the necessary funds without difficulty to the aid commission. At that time, grain was sold at 30 *tuman*s/*kharvar* to the Tabriz bakers. Jamal requested that the cash grants be sent via the Imperial Bank of Persia, an amount of 50,000 *tuman*s, to sustain the current state of necessary work. Measures taken to help poor consisted in: i. gratis help for the sick and the disabled; and ii. creation of appropriate work for different categories of the poor such as weaving of carpets and fabrics, construction, repairs, street making, cleaning of streets, establishment of hospitals, hospices, artisinal and elementary schools. The Iran-American Relief Foundation (*Hey'at-e Kheyriyyeh-ye Iran va Amrika'i; Edareh-ye Markazi-ye A`asheh-ye Foqara dar Baladiyyeh*) accepted in principle to pay the daily wages of workers on condition that the government paid the administrative expenditures of control and materials. These expenses, according to Jamal, represented only 25% of the wages of the workers. Nevertheless, the result was very much appreciated by the people and government. However, the main difficulty was the payment of taxes allocated for these expenses. Since the end of January 1919, every Friday, American Relief distributed

---

102. In February 1919, food prices were high and famine reigned in Tabriz. Rice was being sent from Tehran and Mazandaran to Tabriz. Majd 2003, p. 34.

about 4 *qrans*/p.p./week as charity, or about 8,000 *tumans* per week, to the needy, but never to beggars. Jamal was afraid that if the administration of the public works was not started shortly that this would demoralize people. Moreover, 2,700 beggars were looked after in two hospices paid for by municipal taxes on transport of packages inside the country, which yielded about 7,500 *tumans* per month. However, the streets were still filled by thousands of beggars, because the above sums were insufficient and the Americans formally had decided not to pay for support of beggars. If the government would not send financial support the 2,700 beggars would be thrown into the streets and, therefore, Jamal begged Molitor to ask the government to send cash in sufficient amount immediately.[103]

By the end of February 1919, the government granary held 6,300 *kharvars* in storage. As of 25 February 1919, bread was sold at the bazaar price of 6.40 *qrans*/*batman*. Government grain (*ghalleh-ye dowlati*) was sold at 65 *tumans*/*kharvar*. At that time, the government granary daily supplied 50 *kharvars* to the bakers. Jamal intended to have the government issue a formal decree to discontinue the sale of grain or save the remaining grain, so as to sell it three months later at a lower price, which would have the effect to much reduce the price of all grain categories for the next fiscal year (i.e. the year starting 21 March 1919).[104]

Molitor quickly responded to the needs of Tabriz,[105] for he approved an allocation of 300,000 *tumans*, of which 25,000 *tumans* were transferred directly from Tehran and these were being recovered through daily payments of 1,500 *tumans* by the Finance administration through the sale of 50 *kharvars* of the granary grain (*ghalleh-ye ambar*)/day. Because Tabriz was able to count on this line of credit the Alimentation Service had undertaken to feed an average of 5,000 poor persons, of

---

103. By the end of March 1919, American Relief was "helping to feed about 25,000 people daily in Tabriz, who are also victim of typhus epidemic." Majd 2003, p. 35.

104. MA, Farde 37, 3798.pdf, Telegram Djemal to Molitor, 27/02/1919.

105. Although now based in Tehran, officially he still was Director of Customs of Azerbaijan.

whom about 1,000 were begging in the streets, and were supported daily through work. The public works activities launched consisted of:

1. Road work, paving of streets with cut stones,[106] based on a contract, but in accordance with the instructions by an engineer;
2. Construction of two levies that were indispensable to protect the city against flooding and that provided work to about 2,500 workers/day during three months.
3. Cleaning the *Shahgölü* [now *El Gölü*] pass with about 4,000 workers;
4. Permanent cleaning of the streets provided daily work to 600 persons;
5. Establishment of two temporary carpet factories that provided paid employment to about 1,200 children and women without means of subsistence. All these activities were paid regularly by the American Relief Foundation. Apart from direct aid, this amounted daily to about 400,000 *tuman*s in this province up to the end of May 1919, but it was diminishing.
6. Maintenance of hospices, where about 1,500 poor, who were unable to work, were taken care of;
7. Establishment of hospitals for the poor;[107]
8. A plan to establish a school for 150 orphans[108] picked up in the streets with an annual budget of 18,000 *tuman*s for teaching and upkeep;

---

106. "During the war, the local committee had followed the general policy of giving aid in return for labor. More streets were repaired, more permanent improvements were made for the general benefit in Tabriz than in any other place as a by-product of the distribution of relief." Barton 1930, p. 101.

107. These 'hospitals' must have been, if established, very temporary. In June 1918, the American missionary hospital was looted and occupied by the Turkish occupation force. When the Turks left Tabriz in October they only left an empty building. The hospital was open for business (be it only with 10 beds) in November 1919. At that time, the only other hospital in Tabriz was the *Ahmadiyyeh* hospital. Floor 2021, p. 428.

108. With financing of the American Relief Foundation a small orphanage was maintained in Tabriz. Barton 1930, p. 101.

9. Special services for the distribution of free rice to about 34,000 poor as well as the sale of rice at lower price to other needy persons; and
10. Dispatch of cash and rice to needy people in Ardabil, Sarab, Heris, Maragheh, Solduz, etc. to support American aid activities etc.

Given the budget it was planned that all these activities would be completed by the end of next Asad 1298/22 August 1919. The total cost would amount to 290,000 *tuman*s, of which 124,000 were paid by the American Relief Foundation, which money was remitted on 24 May 1919. The monthly expenditures were verified and certified by a group of competent Europeans and Iranians.[109]

Arfa` al-Molk and Joseph Jamal expressed their regret that the Finance Administration, although selling daily more than 50 *kharvar*s of grain and despite objection by the commission, had reduced its daily payments from 1,500 to 1,250 *tuman*s as of 19 Hamal/10 April 1919, and then to 1,000 *tuman*s from 25 Thowr/17 May 1919 onwards. Furthermore, although the Finance Administration had paid the commission from 25 Hut to 21 Jowza/17 March to 21 June, the amount paid was only 102, 500 *tuman*s instead of 132,000 *tuman*s. As a result, the Alimentation Service Commission had no cash on hand, because it had paid Toumaniantz for the transport cost of 1,500 *kharvar*s of rice. Moreover, Tumaniantz still claimed 15,000 *tuman*s to settle the payment of transport of that same rice plus an advance of 25,000 *tuman*s to undertake the transport of 1,500 *kharvar*s plus payment of 60,000 *tuman*s per *havaleh* by the center,[110] probably

109. "Having received your orders to examine the accounts of the Aid Administration of Tabriz led by Mr. Jamal, we had access to all documents and found them in good order. Also, we were given the minutes of the Comm.'s meetings. Implementation was scrupulously in accordance with Comm.'s decisions." MA, Farde 37, 3703.pdf, Charles Stevens, Nourollah Djavid, Modjir ed Dowleh to the Governor-General, 21 Jozveh 1298/25 May 1919.

110. I am not absolute sure about the translation of this part of the sentence, which in French is: "*plus soixante mille tomans havaleh centre.*"

representing the price and two-third's of transport cost of 2,000 *kharvar*s of rice. Apart from these transport cost, the Alimentation Service urgently needed 20,000 *tuman*s to pay the contractors, who shortly would complete the road works. Fortunately, the price of grain had dropped and *gerdeh* rice in the bazaar cost 7 *qrans*/*man* of 1,000 *mesqal*s in May 1919, but it was difficult to sell and then only in small quantities. Nevertheless this reduction placed the Aid Commission (presumably, the Alimentation Service Commission) in a critical situation, because the Commission had to pay about 170,000 *tuman*s, while the sale of 2,000 *kharvar*s would yield about 80,000 *tuman*s, thus showing a deficit of 90,000 *tuman*s. The remaining credit amounted to 210,000 *tuman*s, which was sufficient to complete the works. The Alimentation Service Commission only asked Molitor to: i. order the Finance Administration to reimburse the Commission for the payment arrears of 1,500 *tumans*/day or 29,500 *tuman*s until 21 Jowza/12 June, because without it the relief works would be stopped, which would be very regrettable, because the American Relief Foundation had given the Commission one-fourth of the budget to pay the workers. ii. cancel, if possible, the transport of 1,500 *kharvar*s of the remaining rice to avoid a loss of about 30,000 *tumans*; iii. order the commission of Urmiyeh to immediately reimburse the Alimentation Service Commission 18,000 *tuman*s, the price of 200 *kharvar* of rice and 50 *kharvar* of millet that it had lent and sent to Urmiyeh; and iv. not to demand from the Commission the price and cost of transport until Astara of 2/3 of 2,000 *kharvar*s mentioned in the second letter, but to deduct the amount from the credit of 300,000 *tuman*s allocated to the province of Azerbaijan as humanitarian aid, in case the same transport of 3,000 *kharvar*s of rice to Tabriz would take place.[111]

Jamal feared that as soon as the crisis was over and the work of the Alimentation Service completed he would be criticized, if not accused of malfeasance by persons whom he had prevented from benefiting from the crisis situation. Therefore, in March 1919, he had insisted that the accounts of all seven services under the Alimentation

---

111. MA, Farde 37, 3704.pdf, Arfa al-Molk, head of the Municipality and Djemal, chief of the Aid Admin./Tauris to Lambert Molitor, Tehran. 22 Djozva 1298 = 24 May 1919.

Fig. 4. Letterhead of the American Food Relief Foundation in Tabriz in 1919.

Service would be audited, despite objections and assurances that this was not necessary. He mentioned a few examples of cases where he had intervened to prevent fraud. In view of the difficulties of having Tumaniantz transport rice for 16-17 *qran*s instead of 22 or a savings of 15,000 *tuman*s on the first 30,000 *pud*s already transported, members of the Alimentation Service Commission and the authorities wanted to benefit from these money savings. Jamal also took away the management of the hospice for the poor from dishonest people and thus, reduced its daily cost from 400 to 200 and then to 150 *qran*s, while the number of poor was even greater than in 1917-18. Thanks to Molitor's intervention with the government its little support tided over the Alimentation Service until the end of Asad, when it discontinued its activities. Jamal informed Molitor that of the credit of 300,000 *tuman*s some 170,000 *tuman*s would suffice, if it arrived in time. Unfortunately, the Finance Administration did not or was unable to assist the Alimentation Service.[112] Despite the good work done by the Alimentation Service and the American Relief Foundation, the famine in Azerbaijan lasted till the end of 1919, despite the good harvest,

112. MA, Farde 37, 3709.pdf, Djemal to Molitor, Tauris 09/07/1919. In an earlier letter, Jamal had complained of the lack of cooperation from the staff of the Finance Department of Azerbaijan. MA, Farde 37, 3705.pdf, Djemal/Tabriz to Molitor/Tehran, 22/01/1919.

which suggests that the bread situation was not yet totally under the control of the Alimentation Service.[113]

Although I have found no information about the food situation of Tabriz between 1919 and 1923, the Alimentation Service continued to function after 1919. This is clear from a document dated 7 August 1922 in which a certain Esma`il Khan is appointed as horse rider of the requisitioning branch of the Central Municipal Food Security Administration of Azerbaijan. The translation of this document is as follows:

14 Saratan 1301 = 11 Dhi Qa`deh 1340 or 6 July 1922

Because it was necessary for the Municipal Food Security Service to have sufficient and honest horse riders for the operations of its [animal] requisitioning branch, therefore, by this order, as of the first of the month of Saratan of It'il [Dog year] we have written that you have been appointed and designated [chief] horse rider of the requisitioning branch. You need to acquaint yourself with this position and carry out relevant missions and administrative tasks. Your wages and clothes [are paid] according to expenses that will [be] submitted to the Office. You must serve with total integrity. If you commit [even] a minor violation and abuse, you will not receive [your] wages and will be severely punished. Date ...[114]

113. Majd 2003, p. 44.

114. MA, Farde 42, 4214.pdf

CHAPTER THREE

THE SITUATION IN TEHRAN 1918-1922

As noted in chapter one, during the preceding winter of 1917-18, Tehran had been ravaged by a serious shortage of grain and above all by activities of grain speculators. The spring rains that started to fall on 26 April 1918 gave hope for a good harvest.[1] In fact, according to Abdollah Mostowfi the food crisis was over and everyone could resume his or her old life. However, even with sufficient rain, the problem for peasants was that they had fewer animals left for plowing, due to mortality of ploughing oxen from rinderpest. Moreover, the remaining animals were weak and for which peasants had insufficient or only bad substitute fodder, while the government still insisted on payment of taxes in cash.[2] Moreover, in May 1918 there still was drought all over Iran.[3] As a result, in early May 1918, there was a bread demonstration

1. Eyn al-Saltaneh 1376, vol. 7, p. 5200.
2. Eyn al-Saltaneh 1376, vol. 7, pp. 5163-65, 5190, 5228-30; IOR/L/MIL/17/15/23, p. 112.
3. Eyn al-Saltaneh 1376, vol. 7, p. 5138.

in Tehran incited by the Democrats. Some houses were plundered and the bazaar's police chief's belly was slit. This led to the order to evict all the poor from the city, including some 3,000 beggars. Also some Democrats were evicted, while tribesmen were armed and the police was put on alert. The price of wheat was 130 *tumans*, barley 100 *tumans*, millet 67 *tumans*, beans (*lubiya*) 100 *tumans*.[4] In short, the prospect of a good harvest in 1918 did not look promising. The short-lived government of Samsam al-Saltaneh (1 May-8 August 1918) had been unable to develop an effective policy and/or a mechanism to address the bread question. Given the political risk of failing to do so, the government of Vosuq al-Dowleh, which came into office on 8 August 1918, wanted to avoid a repeat of the bread crisis at all cost. The man who chosen to achieve that objective was Lambert Molitor.

With most other Europeans of Allied nations, Molitor had left Azerbaijan in June 1918 before its occupation by Ottoman troops following the collapse of Russian troops after the October Revolution. After arrival in Tehran, Molitor counted on being occupied with Customs affairs. However, when he arrived in Qazvin on 24 June there was a telegram from Heynssens waiting for him, which informed him that he was appointed Director of the Customs Administration of Gilan and would be based in Enzeli, where he did not want to go. Although General Dunsterville, who was in Qazvin at that time, forbade Molitor to go to Enzeli, because of the insecurity prevailing there, Heynssens nevertheless insisted he had to go there. After further talks with the British military and his colleagues Molitor refused to go and was allowed to proceed to Tehran. Arrived at Tehran, Heynssens told him to go to Mashhad and assume the post of provincial director of Customs of Khorasan. Molitor again refused pointing out that only the Minister of Finance could change his contracted posting. Heynssens again had to give in, admitting to the Belgian Minister that he had only acted in this insistent manner at the urging of his deputy. At the end of July 1918, Moshar al-Molk, Minister of Finance and Mohassel al-Mamalek, Minister for Posts met with Molitor. Molitor's reputation and success in dealing with the bread question in Tabriz had preceded

4. Eyn al-Saltaneh 1376, vol. 7, p. 5211.

him and they wanted him as director of the Alimentation Service. With his Tabriz experience and his knowledge of Iran Molitor was believed to be the most likely person to succeed in this very difficult affair. The Ministers told Molitor that "if you can bring us to *Nowruz* or one month after we consider that you have rendered us a great service." Heynssens believed that the favor Molitor enjoyed would harm him, and therefore, energetically, unscrupulously, and disloyally opposed Molitor's appointment to the Alimentation Service. However, he had to give in to the demand of the government. On 8 August 1918, before Molitor could assume his new function he contracted a severe case of cholera and during one week it was uncertain whether he would live or die. After one month of cholera and convalescence, Molitor took charge of the Alimentation Service in September 1918. [5]

Heynssens was not the only one who was unhappy with Molitor's appointment, so were the opponents of the new government. After Vosuq al-Dowleh had formed his government (8 August 1918 – 3 July 1920), Abdollah Mostowfi was asked by Moshar al-Molk, one of its Ministers, if there was a problem with the bread supply of Tehran for that year. He replied that the harvest was good, and therefore, there was no need for an Alimentation Service.[6] He advised to make the transport and trade in grain free - prices were already going down - and to only inspect the bakeries to prevent that they might take advantage of consumers. However, the Vosuq al-Dowleh Cabinet did not listen

---

5. MA, Mémoires, pp. 352-58, 367, note (*Nowruz* remark); Idem, Farde 38, 3801.pdf, Alimentation, p. 4; Idem, Farde 38, 3802.pdf, Note-Resumé, p. 3.

6. Mostowfi 1324, vol. 3, p. 29 ("when you formed your new Cabinet, there was no longer a sign of famine"). In May 1918 there were still people dying in the streets of Tehran. Laureys 1996, p. 61; also Sadr 1364, p. 229 writes that the situation in 1918 the bread situation like in 1917 was bad due to lack of rain. According to Eyn al-Saltaneh, in September 1918, in the Alamut region bread was sold at 8 *hazar* per *man*, wheat at 40 *tuman*s, and rice 3.5 to 4 *tuman*s, although this was at harvest time and output was low. A few days later the price of wheat had risen to 45-50 and barley to 30 *tuman*s. Eyn al-Saltaneh 1376, vol. 7, pp. 5344, 5346.

to him, because, as Mostowfi alleged, it wanted to supply grain to the British. Later Mostowfi would fiercely attack Molitor and his endeavors. Vosuq al-Dowleh established the Alimentation Service (*edareh-ye arzaq*) that took control over the transport and collection of grain, to ensure that the state granary was adequately stocked for the regulated sale to bakeries and consumers.[7]

Tehran had just experienced a terrible famine, and its specter haunted its habitants, who besieged the government and the royal palace. In July 1918 the food situation in Tehran was very bad and led to riots. Therefore, appointing someone who had with success tackled the bread issue under very difficult circumstances made sense. Caldwell of the American Relief Foundation hoped that the government would give Molitor adequate powers and support to regulate the bread price and force owners to sell it at a reasonable price. He opined that if prices "don't further rise about their current high level and next year prices of staple foods will be reduced that would be an attainable objective. If he is unable to control prices famine conditions will once again exist like in 1917."[8]

During June-July 1918, Mirza Ahmad Khan Adhari was in charge of the Alimentation Service of Tehran. He was an intelligent, energetic official, but, as reported by the *Ra`d* newspaper, according to public opinion only a European was able to perform this task with success, because no Iranian official was able to resist taking advantage of his post, because of political and personal intrigues, which caused that during the last years no Iranian official had been able to do his job

---

7. Mostowfi 1324, vol. 3, p. 33. The government was very much aware of the highly political nature and risk of the bread supply question. Eyn al-Saltaneh 1376, vol. 7, p. 5372. How politically and financially sensitive and difficult the bread question was is evident from a discussion by a committee that took place on 28 August 1918, where each of the participants had a different view of and solution for the problem, some even self-serving ones. For a summary, see Eyn al-Saltaneh 1376, vol. 7, pp. 5820-21. For a more positive view of this commission, see Mostowfi 1324, vol. 3, p. 39, note 1.
8. Majd 2003, pp. 38-39; Kasravi 1350, p. 802; Eyn al-Saltaneh 1376, vol. 7, p. 5818.

neutrally and without fear.[9] According to Molitor, Adhari was efficient, but dishonest and mixed up in politics. Therefore, the American Relief Foundation had insisted that Molitor be appointed and after some parleying and with some British prodding the Iran government agreed. Mr. Adhari had taken intelligent steps; his rules were good in principle, but inapplicable in Iran, according to Molitor. He had taken the necessary measures to bring government grain of Tehran province to the capital (both from *maliyat* and *khaleseh*). Gendarmes controlled the roads to Qom, Semnan (Mashhad road) and Qazvin to prevent the export of grain from province, but he had not yet created the necessary organization to ensure success.[10]

How was the bread situation in Tehran at that time? At the beginning of August 1918 the Granary had only three days of supply of grain, while the daily consumption of the city exceeded 250 *kharvars*.[11] In 1918, Molitor estimated the total annual requirements of Tehran at approximately 112,000 *kharvars* (72,800,000 lbs) of wheat, and 70,000 *kharvars* (42,500,000 1bs) of barley. "In a normal year these can supply about 90,000 *kharvars* of wheat, the remaining 22,000 *kharvars* being obtained from Saveh, Iraq (Sultanabad), Kazvin, and in lean years from as far afield as Damghan, Hamadan and Malayir,

---

9. MA, Farde 41, 4110.pdf, *Ra`d* no. 147 (07/01/1338 – 2 October 1919).

10. MA, Farde 38, 3801.pdf., Alimentation, p. 4. According to Joseph Jamal, when the Rev. Jessup arrived in Tabriz he told him that Molitor had been forced to accept the job of Director of the Alimentation Service in Tehran, because the government had threatened in case he refused to cancel his contract. MA, Farde 37, 3705.pdf, Djemal/Tabriz to Molitor/Tehran, 22/01/1919. According to Mostowfi 1324, vol. 3, p. 35, restrictions imposed on the transport of flour for private use by Ahmad Adhari led to disruption of the grain market, which, if left alone, would have allowed bread distribution to work normally. As a result, the price of wheat shot up from 5 *tumans* (in Asad/July-August) to 40 *tumans*. Majd 2003, p. 98 also posits that food control is harmful, without an explanation why that is the case.

11. MA, Farde 41, 4102.pdf, Yaddasht, see Appendix II, p. 229. Mostowfi 1324, vol. 3, p. 34 argued that Vosuq al-Dowleh's interference in the market led to this situation and the call for the establishment of an Alimentation Service.

and the whole 70,000 *kharvars* of barley. In addition they have a small surplus of barley for export to Qum."[12] According to Marling, the British Minister in Tehran, the situation in and around the city was as follows:

> 1. Grain question. Prices are still abnormally high and Government has to secure considerable quantities in order to regulate prices in the capital during winter. Main difficulty is transport owing to mortality amongst animals last winter and spring. Our own purchases of wheat at Sultanabad necessitated by the arrival of Syrian [sic; Syriac speaking Christians from Urmiyeh and Salmas] refugees at Hamadan also tends to increase their difficulties, as Sultanabad supplies Teheran to a certain extent.
>
> 2. Arrears of salary. This is a serious question. Government employees are several months in arrears and their impoverishment is particularly severe owing to late famine. These two questions are matter of money only (? Mal-administration of) last 15 months, disorder in Fars, occupation of Azerbaijan by Turkish troops etc., all contributed to prevent money reaching Treasury except from Southern Customs and telegraph revenues from which together with tomans 250,000 which His Majesty's Government have authorized as an advance will not do much more than cover current expenses.[13]

Marling's description gives a rather desperate description of the food situation in Tehran, which differs from the optimistic picture that Abdollah Mostowfi drew. As is clear from what follows, Mostowfi's narrative, written with political bias, is not borne out by reality. When

---

12. IOR/L/MIL/17/15/23, p. 113. The quality of grain was not very good in some areas such as the Alamut. Eyn al-Saltaneh 1376, vol. 7, p. 5409 (with prices of various foodstuffs).

13. IOR/L/PS/10/550/2, tel. Marling to FO, 22/08/1918 (no. 731). According to Eyn al-Saltaneh 1376, vol. 7, p. 5352, in August 1918 there was a shortage of grain and bread in Tehran. Bread cost 3 *hazar* per *man* and the bakeries were doing brisk business. Allegedly, the reason for the shortage of grain supply was the lack of pack animals. People were also hoarding and bread rings were being formed. Eyn al-Saltaneh 1376, vol. 7, pp. 5381-82.

Molitor effectively started at the Alimentation Service on 10 September 1918, he found that the government Granary was empty, the Crown lands (*khaleseh*) service was in shambles and that of Taxation (*maliyat*) was totally disorganized and staffed with incompetent officials.[14] Molitor was quite aware of the peril of the task that he had accepted. He wrote to his wife's family on 30 November 1918: "It is an important and exhausting task. If I succeed I will be the hero! If I fail ...?[15]

Molitor, having just arrived in Tehran, did not know what jungle of political intrigue and conflict of interests there were to make his task most difficult. Before taking control Molitor demanded great authority and that the government created a permanent Alimentation Service, with a contract of five years for himself, and a line of credit, under government control, from the Imperial Bank of Persia. The government did not accept these terms; it decided to transfer Molitor provisionally from the Customs Administration to quickly re-establish a normal situation in the food supply of Tehran. He was given full charge of the Crown lands and Taxes in kind of Tehran province. Molitor made it clear that he only wanted to concern himself with food supply of Tehran province and that he only could take over the direction of the Crown lands of Tehran. For as long as an organization on European principles was not possible Molitor refused to take responsibility for the abuses of the various services of which he was invited to take charge. The Crown lands outside Tehran province were not very important for the Tehran food supply. In all provinces the administration of Crown lands was part of the Finance Administration. Due to private interests and intrigue, Molitor's request to take charge of and reorganize the Crown lands department was refused. The government, at first also did not place the department of Taxes under Molitor, which was a

14. MA, Mémoires, p. 358. Eyn al-Saltaneh 1376, vol. 7, pp. 5393-94 reports that before that time the government had issued instructions that changed all the time. First, the bakeries had to bake bread by mid-night so that in the morning bread was ready. Two days later, that only half had to be baked at night and the rest by noon; three days later bakers were instructed that as before they had to bake throughout the day.

15. MA, Mémoires, p. 369.

serious error, because the taxes supplied much of the grain to Tehran. Later the government was obliged to recognize the need for this step and finally Molitor was given control over Customs, Finance and the government grain of Semnan, Qom, Arak, Malayer, Hamadan and Qazvin. This was needed because the harvest of Tehran province was insufficient to satisfy the needs of the city of Tehran. The long delay in granting this authority made Molitor's task much more difficult, a delay due to the huge profits made by the agents responsible for collecting government grain. Molitor started work on 10 September 1918.[16] On 18 Sonboleh 1336/11 September 1918 Molitor's contract was finalized by the Ministry of Finance as follows:

> 1. Molitor will be Director of the Domains (*khaleseh*);
>
> 2. The Granary (*Ambar*) of Tehran will be under Molitor's direction; he will also be charged with the transport and collection of taxes and purchase of grain;
>
> 3. Molitor is director of the Alimentation Service and manages the service of bakeries;
>
> 4. Separately the Minister of Finance will indicate Molitor's powers and duties in the above services;
>
> 5. Molitor's salary remains the same: 26,000 franc as per his contract payable by Customs. For as long as he is in charge of the services mentioned in i., ii., and iii he will receive an indemnity of 120 *tumans*/month; 40 *tumans* fodder, and 40 *tumans* house rent, or a total of 200 *tumans*/month to be paid monthly by Treasury. Signed Moshir al-Molk. [N.B I did neither receive the *jireh* [ration] nor the rent thereafter][17]

---

16. MA, Farde 38, 3801.pdf, Alimentation, p. 4. According to Eyn al-Saltaneh 1376, vol. 7, p. 5822, Molitor started work on 2 September 1918.

17. MA, Farde 41, 4106.pdf, 18 Sonboleh 1336/11 September 1918 by the Minister of Finance, no. 18415; Idem, Farde 40, 4001.pdf, Projet de 'Cheraietnameh," [Sept. 1918] plus attached documents. Molitor's indemnity of 100 *tumans* was approved. MA, Farde 41, 4106.pdf, Cabinet to Molitor, 19/03/1919 (cheque 241302). On 02/05/1919, Molitor received a note from Hajji Heydar Khan, director

وزارت مالیه

ادارهٔ ارزاق عمومی

Administration

de l'Alimentation publique

Fig. 5. Letterhead of the Alimentation Service in Tehran in 1919.

---

of camels, No. 39127 6 Sor [sic; Thowr], Farde 41, 4106.pdf, stating that: As Molitor is Controller General of the Alimentation Service, the Crown lands are exempted from Customs service and as serving the Alimentation Service he has not received his share of the fines distributed to Customs officials, therefore, the Cabinet decided that as gratification he receives 7,500 francs or 1,500 *tuman*s, equivalent to 3 months' salary. Treasurer-General Khalil Fahm al-Molk.

Molitor's remit was published in a decree by the Council, ten days after his appointment. Measures of implementation taken for the above were printed in Persian and made public. The decree issued on 21/09/1918 spelled out the main Alimentation Service regulations:

> 6. The government appropriates all wheat produced in the province of Tehran for the use of the capital, except the amount needed for planting and the annual supply of the farmers and the landowners;
>
> 7. Transportation of wheat from Tehran and its environs is strictly prohibited;
>
> 8. Buying and selling of wheat for commercial purposes is not allowed;
>
> 9. Only the government can buy wheat; and
>
> 10. Those who obstruct the carrying out of the measures in regard to the food control and disobey the food regulations will be punished in accordance with separate articles approved by the Cabinet.[18]

This decree gave Molitor the authority to search for grain in all villages in the province of Tehran and to legally confiscate surplus grain (above what was needed for auto-consumption and seed). A special service of requisition was created to take possession of such surplus grains in the villages and in private granaries.[19] The Alimentation Service also bought large quantities of grain in Arak (a great center of production), Qazvin and in Damghan. It also brought in tax payments in grain from Arak and Qazvin. All grain coming into the province of Tehran was for the use of Tehran. It had to enter via the city gate and then taken to the Granary, be it government grain or grain bought by the government, or grain brought by private persons for their own use or for sale to the government in its Granary. This

18. Majd 2003, pp. 99-100; Kasravi 1350, p. 802.

19. MA, Fardc 38, 3801.pdf, Alimcntation, p. 4.

applied only to grain. As yet, no peas and vegetables were collected in the Granary, although this would be the case later.[20]

Those Tehranis who had bought wheat and barley before the issuance of the decree were allowed to bring it into the city before 14 October 1918; after that date they had to sell it to the government. However, households were allowed to bring grain for auto-consumption, after having obtained permission from the Alimentation Service. Those importing grain from outside Tehran province were allowed to do so, but had to submit a Bill-of-Lading (*barnameh*) signed by the Finance agent of the place where the grain had been bought. Also, the owners needed to get a pass or *javaz* beforehand. Grain hoarded for speculation was confiscated. Grain holders had two months to inform the Alimentation Service how much grain they had and where it was held. After that period it would be confiscated.[21]

All food stuffs (i.e. wheat, barley, rice, and vegetables) were allowed into Tehran, but nothing could leave without Molitor's permission. He refused to give permission for export for purposes of trade, but facilitated the import of food stuffs. Premiums were given, as of the first week of June 1919. Landlords who delivered their wheat to the government Granary within one month before the end of Saratan (after 40 days) were paid 30 *tumans*/*kharvar*, five *tumans* more than the official price, obtaining for three months. The official grain prices were not lowered for the harvest. It was expected that through the natural market process the price would fall below the 25 *tumans* figure.

Requisition of grain was a special office cooperating with the Tax revenue (*Maliyat*) service. It employed young well-paid men who were accompanied by Cossacks or Gendarmes. In each provincial district (*boluk*), an Agent of Taxes or *Amin al-Maliyat* was the man who, with his staff, collected grain of the Crown lands and *Maliyat* and took charge of forwarding it to Tehran. Molitor made a list of grain that had to be requisitioned and gave it to the *Amin al-Maliyat* and his sub-agents, who then took the grain, paid what was told them

20. MA, Farde 38, 3801.pdf, Alimentation, p. 4.
21. Majd 2003, pp. 99-100.

to pay and ensured transport to the Granary. Initially, all requisitions were a most inaccurate and inadequate operation, due to the lack of organization and precise information. Later it was decided that all grain had to be taken. When Molitor began implementing these measures all those who before that time had sold their wheat at 150 *tumans* per *kharvar* or more (Ahmad Shah himself sold his grain to the kitchen of Lady Marling, the wife of the British Minister, at an even higher price) began opposing him and his work. He frustrated their opposition "by applying the rules with the strongest severity and this in a country where in both spirit and letter it is almost impossible to apply laws." Landlords being unaccustomed to the firm application of administrative rules constantly complaining about their inability to do so, but backed by Vosuq al-Dowleh it was possible to force the issue in each case.[22]

Although having the monopoly of buying all grain in the province of Tehran the Alimentation Service had to buy it at a reasonable price fixed by the government and ensuring an adequate benefit for the owners. The latter was purely Molitor's decision. In the beginning Molitor's control extended only to wheat and barley. Later it was extended to the control of all transport of other food, consisting of rice, vegetables and dry food (like peas, etc, substitutes for bread), not including dried fruit, as well as the ban of export of the same from the city of Tehran. This extension of the monopoly was done to ensure that there was a reserve of bread substitutes, which was considered essential. The control established for transport of all bread substitutes prevented the rise in price of rice and other necessaries.[23]

Because there was no serious statistical service concerning agricultural production it was difficult to know how much grain was available. Realizing that perhaps there was not enough grain, it was

22. MA, Farde 38, 3801.pdf, Alimentation, p. 7.

23. MA, Farde 38, 3801.pdf, Alimentation, p. 5. "Wood also is scarce and coal and charcoal very expensive owing to cost of transport. Sheep, vegetables, fruit, etc., are fairly plentiful and available from the surrounding districts. Rice, as in the other plateau towns, is brought from Mazandaran." IOR/L/MIL/17/15/23, p. 113.

decided to create a large reserve of rice in Mazandaran as a provision against the possible eventuality of shortness of grain at the end of the season. The government bought 3,000 *kharvars* of rice and stored it in the Granary, which quantity could save the town from danger of famine. Moshir al-Molk himself bought this through Tumaniantz, but it was Molitor's plan. Moshir al-Molk first had opposed it, but then became Molitor's first assistant.

An effective military cordon was organized at the province's borders to control the application of Alimentation Service rules and to confiscate any serious quantity of grain leaving the province. There was a post at every 25 km on the border, composed of one gendarme, one Cossack and two private horsemen (*savars*) (the former were likely to develop into first class rascals under temptation, Molitor believed). The military cordon was efficacious, because all orders came only from the chief of the Alimentation Service. According to Molitor, "at the moment it is impossible in Persia, whoever it is, to delegate to others who have to obey different masters." The cordon was organized with the help of Mr. Hajian, an Armenian who had been a Ottoman army official many years ago. He had fled from the Ottoman Empire before the Armenian persecutions and acquired experience in requisitioning etc. in the time of Mornard (probably in 1912). He had the confidence of the Prime Minister, was active and intelligent. The Armenians were recruited among the refugees from Azerbaijan and being responsible to Hajian, were absolutely reliable. The military cordon around the province was the best element of support in the success of the Alimentation Service, because it formed a wall and moat for the Granary. It forced those landlords who had doubts about the cordon's efficacy to finally offer their grain later at prices less than the original figure of 40 *tumans*.[24]

---

24. MA, Farde 41, 4110.pdf, *Ra`d* no. 147 (07/01/1338 or 02 October 1919 - Hajin); Idem, Farde 38, 3801.pdf, Alimentation, p. 7. "Hajian.— Commands "Brigade d'Alimentation" about 500 strong, composed largely of Armenians. Is himself an Armenian and professes devotion to the British cause." IOR/L/MIL/17/15/11/3, p. 117.

The Alimentation Service also created a transport service, which established confidence among transporters, who had suffered much by the dishonesty of the officials. Molitor requisitioned all means of transport in the province. During the famine at least one-third of the means of transport had died and the greatest difficulty in supplying Tehran was due to the shortage of animals. Therefore, only a strict and military organization of the transport service and under centralized control could guarantee success. Furthermore, the government took complete control of the bakeries and flour mills of Tehran. All were placed under military supervision; the directors having punitive powers. Molitor also had full powers to draw up regulations for those bakeries, which only received grain via the Alimentation Service. The above measures were executed with the help of a few old, reliable and competent officials of the Ministry of Finance as well as by the government.[25] Already in September 1918 Molitor took punitive actions against a hoarder and transgressor, Karbala'i Hasan, one of Tehran's chief bakers, who, instead of using grain that he had received from the government to bake bread had stored it. He was arrested and given 100 lashes. At that time, large quantities of grain entered into Tehran, which the Alimentation Service sent to the Granary. It then informed the owner, who received a part for auto-consumption; the rest was kept by the Alimentation Service, which paid the owner a price of 45-50 *tumans* per *kharvar*.[26]

By the end of September 1918, Molitor tried the fill the Granary by requisitioning half of the grain brought into Tehran at the prevailing market price. Grain was also bought in from the provinces and those that did not sell to the government forfeited 10% of their grain each month. At the same time, Alimentation Service supplied grain to the bakers and fixed the price of bread at 3 *qrans* per *man* of 3 kgs. The price of bread in 'normal' times was 1.1 *qran*. It was expected that the price of bread could be held at this level. By January 1919, although the situation in Tehran had much improved, *sangak* bread was still

25. MA, Farde 41, 4102.pdf, Yaddasht, see Appendix II, p. 234; Idem, Farde 38, 3801.pdf., Alimentation, p. 6.

26. Majd 2002, p. 39.

sold at 3 *qrans*.[27] As a result of Molitor's insistence the Alimentation Service not only had control over the grain output of the Crown lands, but also over its output of beans (*hobubat*) such as peas (*nokhud*), vetch or chickling pea (*mash*), and other products, which were collected by fiscal agents (*omana-ye maliyeh*) and transferred to the Granary where it was stored in special warehouses. The sale of grain from landowners was paid for in cash through the intermediary of a grocer (*`allaf*), for each landowner sold his grain to the grocer of his choice. If there was a disagreement between the Granary and a grocer about the grain sold then Arbab Heydar `Ali, a leading grocer and de-facto the leader of this group, acted as arbiter. The latter was each day until noon in the Granary to deal with such matters.[28] There was both staff to control incoming and outgoing grain in the Granary. When grain left the permits (*patehha*) of bakers and grocers were checked, because the bakers each day took delivery of 300 *kharvars* of cleaned grain for the city's bread consumption and 30 *kharvars* that were bought by the oil-bread bakers (*khoshkeh-paziha*).[29]

But to get at this positive situation Molitor had to overcome many problems that threatened to undo the Alimentation Service's objectives, such as the general disorganization, imperfect functioning and demoralization that reigned in the Finance Department when Molitor took control. When the Minister of Finance transferred that job to Molitor, he said: "To my regret, I don't know two trustworthy officials that he would recommend to him." Given this state of affairs Molitor had no choice but to adopt the strictest measures, although it was very difficult. Molitor compared his task to that of "being the driver of a very delicate car driving over one of Persian roads full with obstacles. He had to carefully overcome each obstacle, while driving the car forward with energy and firmness. Each detail or the organization and execution of the Alimentation Service required his attention. However,

27. Majd 2003, pp. 42-43.

28. Qodsi 1342, vol. 2, p. 33.

29. Qodsi 1342, vol. 1, p. 511.

this inspires confidence and the strict implementation of the decisions and plans with the support of the Prime Minister."[30]

The political enemies of Vosuq al-Dowleh immediately launched their attacks on the Alimentation Service, because it prevented them from making the enormous profits they had made in the previous year, when so many had died of hunger.[31] The opening salvo was against the use of the Armenian soldiers guarding the roads, who effectively blocked the diversion of grain. On the one hand, Molitor considered these immediate attacks and intrigue as a sure sign of success; on the other hand, it impeded the effectiveness of the Alimentation Service. Most of the opposition and intrigues came from greedy landlords, who so far had enjoyed large profits from grain sales. Ahmad Shah was one of those landlords. The Shah asked a high price for wheat and each time when the buyer agreed he upped the price until finally saying that he would not sell, "preferring to wait until later when the price would certainly be higher."[32] In the beginning this intrigue threatened Molitor's position. Mullahs, chiefs of certain parties, and who not, all made complaints. A group of them even pitched tents at the Sheikh `Abdol-Hoseyn Mosque under the guise of *rowzeh-khvani* to protest that a Christian was put in charge of the bread question, which was 'contrary to religious law" (*bar khelaf-e shar`*). Also, like Abdollah Mostowfi, many said that Molitor would only collect grain to sell it to the British. Vosuq al-Dowleh, who had used similar tactics against the previous government, took action against the crowd that had gathered around the mullahs and sent police and gendarmes to scatter them. Some of their leaders he arrested and sent them outside Tehran.[33] Vosuq al-Dowleh acted with such firmness, because his political power was absolutely bound to the Alimentation Service's performance. The intriguers soon realized the hopelessness of their plots

---

30. MA, Farde 41, 4110, pdf, *Ra`d* no. 147 (07 Moharram 1338 or 02 October 1919).

31. For a short overview of the kind and nature of these attacks, see Eyn al-Saltaneh 1376, vol. 7, p. 5822.

32. Majd 2003, p. 127.

33. Kasravi 1350, p. 802.

in face of hostile public opinion, which could not forget the crimes of the previous winter. Such an organization involving perseverance to the end with clear plans formulated to specific ends, nonplussed and discouraged the enemies of food control. The plans, at first, scoffed at and said to be impracticable, for such a place as Tehran were later, step by step, implemented.[34]

Molitor did not react to the intrigues other than to write a few notes to Vosuq al-Dowleh, copies of which he transmitted to Sir Percy Cox, asking that such and such intrigue should be squelched so that it might not interfere with his work. Sir Percy promptly spoke on each occasion to Vosuq al-Dowleh, who arranged everything shortly after. The government was convinced that its fate depended on the food situation. Therefore, Molitor was certain of Vosuq al-Dowleh's support, who consistently did so.[35]

On 23 October 1918, Molitor wrote to Vosuq al-Dowleh asking him to take a stand against the continuing intrigue targeting the Alimentation Service, because doing nothing would result in disorder.

> We give enough grain to the bakers to satisfy public need. Nobody ignores this. But the people and in particular the women are incited to buy more bread that their daily ration. The decision by the Council of Ministers of Sombaleh [September] stipulates serious punishment against the women, who via intrigues complot against the safety of public food supply. I cannot act against the leaders of the complot, which is beyond my remit. But the government's duty is spelled out in the decree. If corrective steps are not immediately taken against the inciters, who are well-known, the impunity will only encourage them. I urge the government to act against these criminals. It has now considerable military and police force at its disposal led by integer men, who are willing to do the necessary. Now it the time to act and show the enemies

34. MA, Farde 38, 3801.pdf, Alimentation, p. 8.
35. MA, Farde 38, 3801.pdf, Alimentation, p. 8.

> of order and the people that the government is ready to do everything to prevent the events of last year to happen again.[36]

Vosuq al-Dowleh's political opponents and grain speculators were not the only ones causing problems for Molitor, so was the Cabinet itself. In December 1918, Molitor called Vosuq al-Dowleh's attention to the fact that the government, although it had placed him in charge of the Crown lands, as he had to depend on them for 30,000 *kharvars*, had made a great mistake in refusing to put him also in charge of Taxation (*maliyat*), from which he expected 18,000 *kharvars*. This was because the fiscal agents (*omana-ye maliyeh*) were under Molitor's control for the requisition as well as for collection of grain from the Crown lands, but for fiscal grain in kind they were under the command of the director of Taxation. Clearly, it was not an ideal situation for these agents, who had to serve two masters. Therefore, Molitor asked that they be placed entirely under his orders as director of Taxation. Molitor did not exclude the possibility that the former director of Taxation might want the Alimentation Service to fail. Molitor's request caused some dismay to his boss, Heynssens, who told Raymond, the Belgian Minister: "Molitor will break his neck. It is impossible work" Shortly thereafter, Heynssens again talked to Raymond and said: "The Tarpeian Rock is near the Capitol."[37] Molitor called the chiefs of parties to his office and drew their attention to the fact that his work was extra-political. Vosuq al-Dowleh did not like this. They solemnly promised full co-operation for the benefit of the people whom Molitor was trying to help. The leaders of the various parties were asked to furnish inspectors for special occasions.[38]

36. MA, Farde 41, 4103.pdf, Molitor to Vosuq al-Dowleh, 23/10/1918. Bread was expensive in Tehran at that time; flour cost 14 *tuman*s. Eyn al-Saltaneh 1376, vol. 7, p. 5431.

37. The Tarpeian Rock was used as a place of execution during the Roman Republic by throwing the condemned from its sharp cliffs. Heynssens quotes a Latin aphorism, *Arx tarpeia Capitoli proxima* ('the Tarpeian Rock is near the Capitol'), a warning that one's fall from grace may come swiftly.

38. MA, Fardc 38, 3801.pdf, Alimcntation, p. 8.

When Molitor had accepted the job, the Minister of Finance had told him that there were not any officials in the Ministry that he could rely on. Moreover, there was little scope to replace the existing staff with new ones. According to Willemsens, the old staff instead of trying to help Molitor was doing a good job to do the opposite. The agent who had the responsibility to draw up the sales contracts for grain on purpose left out the well-known phrase of *oft* (droppage) and the overworked and badly organized accounting office only found out after the harm was done.[39]

Likewise, the financial agents and collectors who were accustomed to pay the cost of transport on the spot were discharged, because their main interest was how to enrich themselves to the loss of the tax payers, the treasury and the transporter. Therefore, the Granary organized its own transport service (with the monopoly of the means of transportation) and paid the transport cost in Tehran. There were no complaints, because the *charvadars* were paid regularly and without any withholding. Likewise, the intermediaries for the purchasing of grain were abolished, which presented a considerable saving for the Treasury. Also, the grain was carefully sieved, so that the taxpayer and the transporter both received the correct quantity. This was possible, because the Granary had a grain sifter (*bujar*), where grain after delivery was cleaned before it was supplied to the bakers. Every day, each baker sent one or two workers to the Granary to receive the cleaned grain and take it to the flour mill, which activity was proverbially known as 'double carriage' (*do sareh bar kardan*), because first the grain was carried to the mill and then by the millers to the bakeries.[40]

---

39. MA, Mémoires, p. 373. The term *oft* is an abbreviation of *oftadeh* or 'fallen.' There could indeed be quite a problem with the level of droppage, see, e.g., MA, Farde 42, 4201.pdf, Modir al-Molk, the Treasurer-General, 20/12/1920 and the preceding letters that are attached to it. Therefore, the term is also used to mean 'deduction in weight' or 'loss in weight' due to insect damage and the like.

40. Qodsi 1342, vol. 2, p. 33. As to the manner of collection of grain in the Alamut region, see Eyn al-Saltaneh 1376, vol. 7, pp. 5479-80.

As an example of how careful Molitor was in determining the parameters within which the Alimentation Service had to operate in an area in which it had little experience, in this case that of transport), the following calculation may serve, even though this calculation was made for the Alimentation Service in 1920.

Table 3.1 Transport tariff 22/07/1920.

Food Grain Transport Service with Mashhadi Ali Aqa Qafqazi [note: to use as a basis for control of transport cost of wheat]
Approximate basis

Income:
Transport tax from Aragh [Arak] to Tehran per *kharvar* of wheat = 165 *qrans*. One *fourgeon* contains 6 *kharvar*; there are 50 fourgons at the man's disposal. Duration of route between Arak and Tehran and v.v. is 15 days. Income per month is as follows:
6 *kharvar* x 165 *qrans* = 990 *qrans* x 50 fourgons = 49,500 *qrans* times two per month = gross income per month = 99,000 *qrans*

Expenses
Cost of one horse *kemend*[41] per day

12 *batman* of barley at 1.50	18,00 *qrans*
12 *batman* of straw at 0.40	4.80
02 *batman* of lucerne at 1.50	3.00
Wages of *surchi* [driver] and the groom 12.00	
Blacksmith	1.00
Others, incl. wages of *nayeb*s (assts.)	3.20
Total	42.00 *qran*s
Result: 50 fourgeons ar 43 *qran*s x 30 days	63,000 *qran*s
Net benefit per month	36,000 *qran*s

NOTE: in 50 horse teams [*kemends*] one has to allow for two sick ones and not working; the difference (3,960 *qrans*) due to the idleness of these horses is amply compensated by the fact that the entrepreneur adds to his *forgons* for his personal account, travelers and merchandise freight cost.

The capital of about 500,000 *qrans* that represents the price of the fourgon, horses, tack, etc. has been paid for previously by the government. The horses that die and that become useless are replaced.

41. *Kemend* or *kumund*, meaning 'halter, team of six horses.'

Source: MA, Farde 42, 4202.pdf.

M. Majesky was Molitor's only European assistant in the first weeks of his work, but apparently he was not available thereafter, at least he is not further mentioned in the available documents.[42] This may explain that, given the heavy workload and staff problems, Molitor asked for a European official "to assist me and to acquaint himself with my tasks so that he eventually replace me when I my contract ends and I may not return."[43] He proposed his compatriot Willemsens as candidate to which proposal the Minister of Finance had replied that he would do the necessary. When nothing happened Molitor contacted the British Legation and asked for its support to get the required assistant. However, Molitor's proposal was thwarted by an unnamed and unemployed Belgian official.[44] In February 1919, Molitor again urged the Minister of Finance to provide him with a European assistant. He argued that to make the organization for the food supply of Tehran more effective and permanent the merger of the provincial Directorate of Finance with that of the Granary had been decided by the Cabinet. Therefore, "his detachment is more than ever needed, given the multiplicity of new task that this reorganization entails."[45] Finally, after eight months Mr. Willemsens was appointed his assistant, during which time Molitor had basically been alone battling the grain speculators, the political opponents, the unreliable staff, and the slow to react Cabinet, while trying to make sure there was enough bread for sale in the city.[46]

The rains had been abundant in the winter of 1918-1919 and the 1919 harvest was good. However, despite the fact that seemingly there was enough grain it did not reach the poor, due to the undermining

42. MA, Farde 38, 3801.pdf, Alimentation, p. 5.
43. MA, Farde 41, 4105.pdf, Molitor to Minister of Finance, 02/02/1919.
44. MA, Mémoires, p. 372.
45. MA, Farde 41, 4105.pdf, Molitor to Minister of Finance, 02/02/1919.
46. MA, Mémoires, p. 372.

activities of the grain owners.[47] Although Vosuq al-Dowleh had taken steps against those intriguing against the Alimentation Service after Molitor's request in October 1919, these steps had neither been firm nor effective enough. There were still many landlords, who thwarted the Alimentation Service's activities, which had a negative physical and monetary impact on the food supply of Tehran. Therefore, Molitor wrote several times to Vosuq al-Dowleh asking him to take firm action, which he did not. On 24 January 1920 Molitor wrote him again, this time clearly putting the ball in the Prime Minister's court. He submitted a note on the food situation of Tehran to Vosuq al-Dowleh, while in his cover letter he stressed that this subject was too serious, above all in these times of the threat of revolutionary Bolshevism, to be neglected. Moreover, he would be remiss in his duty not to inform the Prime Minister what needed to be done.

In this note Molitor emphasized that Ahmad Shah was one of the major problems in supplying Tehran with grain, which explained Vosuq al-Dowleh's earlier reluctance to act. As indicated above, the Shah was one of the landlords, who wanted to benefit from the bad food situation.[48] The Shah's negative behavior towards the work of the Alimentation Service created additional and unnecessary obstacles to collect the available grain in the province. For example, in January 1920, the agents charged with grain requisition in the Sauj Bulagh district reported that because they neither made an inventory of grain nor collected any in villages belonging to the Shah, out of respect for his person, some landlords abused that situation and transported much of their grain to the Shah's villages, to avoid it being requisitioned. At that time, there was no less than 2,000 *kharvars* of grain in the villages concerned, including that which belonged to Ahmad Shah, which alone was estimated at 1,000 *kharvars*. In short, the Shah's villages formed a center for speculation and formal offense against the measures promulgated by the government to ensure the food supply to Tehran and environs. What was worse was that it was public knowledge

---

47. Sadr 1364, p. 229.

48. This self-serving interest in the price of grain earned him the nickname of Ahmad *`Allaf*, or Ahmad the grocer. Forbes-Leith 1927, p. 150; MA, Mémoires, p. 374.

that the Shah's grain in the village granaries was already spoiling and was filled with weevils. The dilemma for Molitor was that while the Alimentation Service did everything and at great expense to get grain from faraway places such as Arak, Damghan, Qazvin, and Shahrud, speculators kept thousands of *kharvars* of grain at a few *farsakhs* from Tehran and the Alimentation Service was unable to get hold of that grain because it was held in the Shah's villages. He needed that grain, because if he would be unable to collect it, Molitor expected a crisis to occur in the food supply of Tehran in about 40 days. He informed Vosuq al-Dowleh and his Cabinet that it was their responsibility to take the required action and to do it in time. He ended his note: "I have done my duty; in fact, I have done more than my duty, because this note was written after several unsuccessful demarches."[49] In his cover letter Molitor added in a PS the statement: "The day that we take grain from the villages from H.M. we will not have any problem with the other landlords." To bring home to the Prime Minister that the matter was too serious to be ignored he added even a PPS, in which he wrote: "One has to buy at all cost [grain of H.M., which was struck through in the draft letter], because it is very urgent and the delay caused by Sadeq Soltan at Araq [Arak] will cause us difficulties. H.M. should be informed immediately that it is essential that his grain be put at my disposal."[50] Finally, Vosuq al-Dowleh took firm steps and, as a result, the shah sold his grain to the Alimentation Service at a very moderate price, which example forced the others to do likewise.[51]

As noted above, the Alimentation Service had established a cordon around the province of Tehran. However, because the Alimentation Service estimated that the quantity of grain within the cordoned off area would be insufficient, the government bought grain outside Tehran province such as in Arak, Qazvin and Damghan. By the end of the harvest season 20,000 *kharvars* had been bought there. Transport from Araq cost 22.5 to 25 *tumans* per *kharvar* by camel. Although price of grain was reduced to 16 *tumans*, the average price was between 21 and

---

49. MA, Farde 41, 4104.pdf, Molitor to Minister of Finance, 24/01/1919.
50. MA, Farde 41, 4104.pdf, Molitor to HH, 24/01/1919.
51. Majd 2003, p. 43.

26 *tumans*, for wheat only. Thus, transport was the greatest expense, in fact, it was more expensive than the grain itself, but there was no choice. A special service for Arak and the other supply centers was organized to buy and transport grain to Tehran, which had to rely on a number of small tribes and a number of villages that traditionally dominated the transport sector.

> The chief camel transport owning district in the vicinity of Tehran is Saveh, where the Inanlu and Baghdadi Shahsavan tribes (see Chapter VIII) own many thousands of camels. The tribes of Varamin and Khar, who spend the summer in the "Yailaq" of Lar and Firuzkuh, also own a considerable number. After the harvest, and to a lesser extent in winter, camels find local employment in carrying grain from Varamin, Khar, Saveh, Sauj Bulagh, Shahriyar, etc., into Tehran. On entering Tehran camels go to caravansarais in the Pa-i-Ghapu quarter. Mules are owned by all the villages of the mountain valleys- East, North and North-West of Tehran and the carrying trade between Mazandaran and Tehran is one of their chief sources of livelihood. Of the Shimran villages close to Tehran the vicinity of Kand owns the greatest number, about 400, and Lavasan, beyond the Jajarud, about 300. Quite half the mule convoys coming to Tehran are natives of Larijan. Mules on entering Tehran go to caravansarais in the Ghesariyeh quarter.[52]

In April 1919, Francis White reported that the situation in Tehran had much improved. Bread was plentiful and cheap thanks to a good harvest and the food control by Molitor.[53] By July 1919 the famine was over with an excellent abundant harvest. The Alimentation Service removed all restrictions on the sale of barley and did not need grain from Arak any longer, so that other cities like Qom could be assisted. Bread cost 2.6 *qrans*, but the scarcity of pack-animals was still a problem.[54] The purchase of Mazandaran rice proved to have been mostly unnecessary. Fortunately, the pessimistic previsions by the

---

52. IOR/L/MIL/17/15/23, pp. 112-14.
53. Majd 2003, p. 35.
54. Majd 2003, p. 43.

government, shared by the public, did not manifest themselves and until the next harvest the Alimentation Service was able to supply sufficient grain to the consumers. Only a small quantity of this rice was used to make *dampokht*, which was organized by the American Relief Foundation during Ramazan. That organization was very helpful in the supply of grain as well during a few weeks that the Alimentation Service had difficult moments, when in the granary there was only a minimum of grain left. After the end of Ramazan (29/06/1919) the American Relief Foundation organized *dampokht* public kitchens. Molitor was much pleased with the American Relief Foundation *dampokht* initiative, not only because it was one that was different in quality from the *dampokht* organized by the Iranian authorities in 1917-18, but because it had achieved its intended objective. This was because the American Relief wanted to make Alimentation Service of Tehran realize that it was possible to save bread at the time when there was a temporary stop in grain transport, due to the problems suffered by the camel drivers. As a result, after the *dampokht* service had functioned barely two weeks, the Alimentation Service was able to discontinue several bakeries in the quarters where the American Relief kitchens were set up. Molitor wrote to the American Relief Foundation "that the Alimentation Service will appreciate if you pay for the cost of the *dampokht* at half the price of rice." [55] For the future, Molitor recommended storing only *sadri* but not *gerdeh* rice, which later was very difficult to sell. The role of the American Relief Foundation in the success achieved by the Alimentation Service was not inconsiderable. By May 1918, American citizens had given more than $2 million to Tabriz and Tehran for relief operations[56] with which "More than 300,000 people have been helped in Teheran alone."[57]

Because he had not been back to Belgium since 1913, Molitor needed and was owed furlough and thus, he left Tehran on 17 October 1919. However, before he left he did two things to pre-empt further

---

55. MA, Farde 41, 4108.pdf, Molitor to Mr. Robinson, Dir. American Relief, Tehran, 02/07/1919.

56. Majd 2003, p. 125

57. Barton 1930, p. 95.

وزارت مالیه
نظارت کل مالیات
وخالصجات و ارزاق عمومی ایالت طهران

Contrôle Général des Finances
Domaines et de l'Alimentation
de la Province de Téhéran,

Fig. 6. Letterhead of the Inspectorate-General of Taxes and Domains and the Public Food Supply of the Province of Tehran, 1919.

intrigue and criticism by the Cabinet's and his own opponents. In early August 1919, he informed Vosuq al-Dowleh that at his request, the Minister of Finance had formed a Commission of three persons to audit the financial accounts of the Alimentation Service (1337-38). The commission had to look at the invoices to verify whether expenses were justified and appropriate in light of the *shariyat-nameh* or his remit. Molitor wrote that, "Apart from my remit there is also the decree of 29 Sombaleh [21 September 1918], and the Commission also should take that into account."[58] He felt confident about the verification, because during the year 1918-19, the Alimentation Service had been able "to gather 80,000 *kharvars* of grain in the Granary that began to yield an income of 45,000 *tumans* per year. The Crown lands of Varamin supplied the Granary with 14,000 *kharvars*, whereas formerly

58. MA, Farde 41, 4109.pdf, Molitor to Prime Minister, 05/08/1919 draft.

it produced only one-third of that quantity, as shown by the records of the Granary."[59]

When it became known that Molitor would depart, one newspaper accused him of going to Europe to hide the many millions that he had embezzled during his time at the Alimentation Service. In Iran, this was quite a credible accusation, for that is what everybody expected what an Iranian official in his place would have done. To set the record straight and keep control of the story Molitor, at the request and approved by the Cabinet, wrote an article for the newspaper *Ra`d* of 7 Moharram 1338/ 2 October 1919 in which he carefully outlined what he had done as head of the Alimentation Service between September 1918 and September 1919 and what the results were.[60] In this article Molitor did not claim that the success of Alimentation Service was due to him. He wrote:

> Only by having worked in the Alimentation Service during last year one may realize how difficult and delicate the work of the chief and officials of the Alimentation Service was and how many nights they had not been able to sleep, because failing to do the job would make the city's population suffer. It shows that Persians are capable of doing great things, when they want to and when they are guided by the public interest. A final element that contributed to the success was that despite the various intrigues people soon understood that it concerned a work for the public weal, that disorder and disorganization would result in numerous deaths, and that is why the Alimentation Service finally obtained the cooperation of all in the interest of the public weal. [...]
>
> Lastly, the chief Alimentation Service deplores absence of a civil registry that would allow one to know the number of "consumers of bread" of each family. This allows to issue of ration cards as was done elsewhere. Of course, waste could not be avoided, and savings in one month represents

59. MA, Farde 41, 4102.pdf, Yaddasht, see Appendix II, p. 228.
60. MA, Farde 41, 4110.pdf, *Ra`d* no. 147 (7 Moharram 1338 or 02 October 1919).

> consumption of days. In this way one arrives at managing bread over many months. In the future all major cities in Iran are able to protect themselves against famine by adopting proper rules and organization. One of these rules should be the execution of a census. The accounts of the Alimentation Service for 1 Asad Yunt'il 1337 to 1 Asad Quy'il 1338 will be published soon. Meanwhile, we give a table here of entries and departures from the Ambar that gives a clear picture.

It was no surprise that Vosuq al-Dowleh was very pleased with the result of the Alimentation Service in general and of Molitor in particular. On 8 April 1919 he wrote to Molitor:

> Thanks to your continuous and astute efforts the Alimentation Service has been able to spare the government the concern of a repetition of last year's misery. The Cabinet joins me to inform you of its total satisfaction and to confirm once again that its confidence [in you] had been well placed."[61]

Due to the vigorous efforts and stringent measures of control by the Alimentation Service the period 1918-19 was tided over without a shortage.[62] When Molitor left, the government Granary was well-stocked with a quantity of grain having a value of 900,000 *tumans*. Moreover, it exceeded the quantity of grain that had been stored there until then. The Granary Service was even obliged to rent neighboring storage space to be able to stock the grain that continued to be brought into Tehran. According to Molitor's assistant, Willemsen:

> At the moment, the organization of the Alimentation Service operates like a clock-work that keeps the hours. This service ensures the arrival of flour and the baking of daily bread for both poor and rich. Disorder has made place for a model of order and the Treasury amply benefits from this.[63]

---

61. MA, Mémoires, p. 373; Idem, Farde 41, 4106.pdf, Vosuq al-Dowleh to Molitor, 08/04/1919 (in French).

62. IOR/L/MIL/17/15/23, p. 113.

63. MA, Mémoires, p. 373.

Abdollah Mostowfi was one of the strongest critics of Vosuq al-Dowleh and Molitor, who had led the Alimentation Service in Tehran during the great famine of 1917-18 (see chapter one). Although he himself believed that he had done an excellent job in feeding the inhabitants of Tehran, others pointed out that the situation in Tehran had been disastrous, with many, according to some 20,000 dead in the streets.[64] According to the Americans (both of the Legation and to Mr. Judson of the American Relief Foundation), "The year before [1917], famine situation was 'shameful.'"[65] Therefore, it was no surprise that the Americans had pressed Vosuq al-Dowleh to appoint Molitor, with whom they had successfully collaborated to combat hunger in Tabriz. Abdollah Mostowfi was a political enemy of Vosuq al-Dowleh and had no good word either for any of the Belgian officials, whom he wanted to replace all with Iranians.[66] He accused Vosuq al-Dowleh of having appointed Molitor by a hand-picked committee; moreover, there was no need for an Alimentation Service or a Food Controller. He supported this argument by pointing out that the grain price had dropped from 40 *tumans* in August 1918 to 25 *tumans* per *kharvar* at the end of December 1918. At that same time, Molitor sold this grain at a price of 39 *tumans* to the bakers, which forced bakers to charge 3 *qrans* per *man* of 3 kg of bread. Thus, consumers had to pay 3 *abbasis* more for their bread than it cost the government. As a result, the Alimentation Service made a profit of 9 *tumans* per *kharvar* or a total profit of 300,000 *tumans* by March 1919. However, this revenue

64. Mostashar al-Dowleh Sadeq 1367, pp. 106, 109, 114, 123-24, 145, 148, 164, 176, 179, 180, 182-84, 186-87, 190-94, 197-201, 203, 205, 211, 213-14, 221, 224-25, 228-30.

65. MA, Farde 38, 3801.pdf., Alimentation, p. 7.

66. Mostowfi 1324, vol. 3, pp. 36-37. Not everyone agreed with this point of view. Other towns and regions (Semnan, Qom) asked Molitor to organize their Alimentation Service, "because they distrust their Finance Agents and governors. He advises them to organize an administrative board under the charge of their officials. The invariable reply is: 'we don't trust these officials. They are the worst robbers of all.'" MA, Farde 38, 3801.pdf., Alimentation, p. 3.

was not shown anywhere in the reports, while, moreover, Molitor had asked for 3.5 million *tumans* in cash to operate the Alimentation Service between August 1918 and March 1919. This amount of 3.8 million *tumans* would have served to supply the entire city's population with free bread for an entire year. Therefore, Mostowfi lambasted both Vosuq al-Dowleh and Molitor ("this serious government servant"), for refusing to allow proper accounting of their books. "No, they did not even prepare a fake account, but just hid behind power!"[67]

In the absence of more data it is difficult to assess whether Mostowfi's criticism is borne out by reality and to what extent. A fact is that Mostowfi is plain wrong concerning the financial audit, while he assumes, if the grain market had been left free, that cheap and abundant bread of good quality would have been available to the consumers. It is true that in a normal year that is what might have happened, but other sources disagree with Mostowfi and submit that 1918-19 was not a normal year. Also, even in a normal year landowners might create an artificial shortage to make money.[68] The fact that prices came down again in the fourth quarter of 1918 is not proof that Mostowfi is right, as he contends. After all, one may argue that it was only due to the work of the Alimentation Service that grain hoarding was kept within bounds, that supplies were delivered to the central government Granary and thus, prices did not rise but trended downward. Moreover, as was indicated above, the hoarders had already made a killing in the market, until the Alimentation Service was able to put a stop to that practice. Of course, it is possible that the supply of bread could have been managed in cheaper way, but parts of these costs were the cost of learning, as the Alimentation Service and its staff had to learn how to operate most effectively, while at the same time establishing new structures and rules. Whatever the truth of this matter, in October 1919 foodstuffs were cheap; wheat cost 15 *tumans*, while other products,

67. Mostowfi 1324, vol. 3, p. 36.

68. In fact, Eyn al-Saltaneh 1376, vol. 7, pp. 5382 reports that in August 1918 bread rings were formed in Tehran.

due to the end of World War I and the resultant revival in trade, also were much cheaper than they had been before.[69]

Molitor had clear ideas what government food policy should be and what policy instruments it should have to execute such a policy. In June 1919, in an interview with Mr. Robinson of the American Relief Foundation he set out his ideas based on his experience in both Tabriz and Tehran. First and foremost, he submitted, now was the time that the government had to take this matter seriously and to be forced to look after it. He added a warning that not only the entire system of government was threatened if nothing was done, but also the social position of the upper class, because growing Bolshevism would take advantage of a neglected bread situation. Secondly, there had to be a central organization of food security with exchange of data between provinces to determine the relative needs and arrange for the exchange of grains (e.g., Tehran must, in normal years, give to Qom and so must Arak). However, it was an obstacle that Tehran had no accurate census.[70] This central organization should be under an assistant of the Treasurer-General, who would be the director of Alimentation Service and only concentrate on that task. The employment of honest technical agents was a must. Moreover, in every province there should be a general director of Finances, Crown lands and Alimentation, since all three were subsidiary to each other. At that time, there was only one director of the Alimentation Service, whose jurisdiction was restricted to Tehran province. The first task for the Alimentation Service should be to preserve the grain production of Tehran province for the city of Tehran. Later surplus might be sent to Qom, Semnan. Also from Damghan (Sauj Bulagh west in Tehran province, sends wheat to Qazvin in normal years to make up for deficit by the latter sending wheat to Rasht, which returns rice). Moreover, in each province there had to

---

69. Eyn al-Saltaneh 1376, vol. 7, p. 5607.

70. "A census taken by the police in 1919 gave 250,000 as the population, which is supposed to be a decrease of 100,000 from the population of 1917-18 due to the famine, influenza and typhus. The birth rate is computed at 780 per month and the death rate at 580. Within the enceinte there are 23,428 houses." IOR/L/MIL/17/15/23, p. 112.

be a director of Finance and Crown lands, one man combining both functions. As in Tehran, Crown lands were very important, because they ensured that the greatest part of the grain (the government's share in output) is sent to the state Granary. Crown lands in Tehran province in a normal year supplied 40,000 *kharvars*, whereas taxes in kind only supplied 10-12,000 *kharvars* of wheat and barley. Therefore, there had to be a separate organization of Crown lands under the direction of the Alimentation Service director.

In Tehran province, Molitor argued that two Europeans were essential in addition to the director – one for provincial Domains and one for *Maliyat*. In other provinces one European and a European assistant would suffice. Such appointments wouldn't require extra funds as the Finance Agent must be under instruction to take these responsibilities. In other words, Alimentation required the reorganization of Finances, including the control of Domains. (Naser al-Din Shah always held part of the Crown lands of Tehran to control the grain from the villages and thus control the price of grain). The cost of petty administration and other unforeseen cost in the budget had to be met by special taxes on transport, bakers, etc. Molitor waxed philosophical when he concluded: "Persians live on hope. They are more concerned with honest effort than with results; in waiting, they can suffer much; this is a tremendous aid to the administrator."[71]

The fact that there are no reports that mention problems with the food supply of Tehran during 1919-20 indicates that it likely was a normal year. Nevertheless, Molitor made sure that the quality of his work and that of his staff was evaluated to which end he had asked three independent persons to verify the financial and other accounts of the Alimentation Service. The audit report of 6 November 1920 concluded that everything was in proper order.[72]

When Molitor left Tehran in October 1920 his deputy Willemsens had been left in charge. Later Kamal al-Vezareh was appointed chief

71. MA, Farde 38, 3801.pdf., Alimentation, p. 11.

72. MA, Farde 42, 4203.pdf, Office note re the three persons verifying the accounts of the Alimentation Service, 14 Aqrab 1299/06/11/1920.

of the Alimentation Service, who resigned when Molitor returned and was appointed as his successor.[73] Whether it was due to this change of the guard and/or to other causes, but it would seem that at the end of the spring of 1921 the bread situation in Tehran was not good. On 11 May 1921, Eyn al-Saltaneh noted that bread was in short supply and very bad in Tehran. Given the fixed price of flour baking bread was unprofitable. Therefore, most bakery shops were closed, while its owner and/or baker had gone into hiding. The bakeries that were still open needed protection from Cossacks and Gendarmes. He blamed that situation on a lack of interest on part of the two short-lived Cabinets that had succeeded Vosuq al-Dowleh's government.[74].

On his return to Tehran, on 13 July 1921, Molitor learnt that on 10 July 1921, the Minister of Finance had appointed him Administrator-General of Customs to succeed Heynssens, who had already left Tehran. This was the pinnacle of Molitor's career and gave him, of course, much satisfaction. Molitor was less pleased that he again was put in charge of the Alimentation Service. He had to submit a proposal to the Minister of Finance how he intended to operate the Alimentation Service.[75] Molitor's instructions arrived the next day. These were as follows:

> In accordance with order no. 10342, I herewith inform you of your attributions:

---

73. MA, Farde 52, 5202.pdf, Mo`tamad al-Saltaneh gerant/*kafil* Min. of Finance to Molitor, 18 Saratan 1300/July 1921, no. 10342 ; Idem, Farde 52, 5201.pdf, Mo`tamad al-Saltaneh gerant/*kafil* Min. of Finance to Molitor, no. 10386, July 1921/ 19 Saratan 1339 (French and Persian version).

74. Eyn al-Saltaneh 1376, vol. 8, pp. 5959, 6078 (on 17 June 1921 still a shortage). Hasan Pirniya (3 July-27 October 1920) and Fathollah Khan Akbar (27 October 1920-22 February 1922).

75. MA, Farde 52, 5202.pdf, Mo`tamad al-Saltaneh Administrator Mininstry of Finance to Molitor, 10/07/1921 - 18 Saratan 1300. The short-lived coup d'etat Cabinet led by Ziya al-Din Tabataba'i (24 February-4 June 1921) was succeeded by a series of other short-lived Cabinets, the first one led by Qavam al-Saltaneh (4 June 1921-21 January 1922).

1. Because you are also still Director of Customs you are allowed to have two other Belgian officials as assistants;
2. As Director-General of the Alimentation Service of Tehran you have to determine: (a) the system for farming out the Crown lands; (b) the manner of collection taxes in kind from the municipalities; and you are: (c) responsible for the collection of taxes in kind and to see to it that they are all collected and stored in the Granary; authorized to pay administrative and management expenses within approved limits; and have (d) to ensure food supply and to see to it that all taxes of Crown lands, *Maliyat* and of municipalities are collected and grain bought to ensure the food supply;
3. As Director-General of the Alimentation Service you will study the subject and organization of the Alimentation Service for the whole country and submit proposals to the government via the Minister of Finance;
4. Instructions will be given to officials in the provinces to give all food supply related information to the Director-General of the Alimentation Service of Tehran.
5. Instructions will be given to the Finance officials not to take any step concerning the conversion of government grain in the regions of Qazvin, Khamseh, Arak, Hamadan, Malayer, Semnan and Damghan, without the approval of the Director-General of the Alimentation Service of Tehran;
6. The Minister of Finance will give the necessary funds to Director-General of the Alimentation Service of Tehran for the purchase of grain, who will report on this in writing and inform him of the amount of credit needed;
7. The Minister of Finance will make an adequate force (Cossacks; gendarmes) available to the Alimentation Service to do its job;
8. Based on the report by the Director-General of the Alimentation Service of Tehran the government will impose severe punishments on people who take covert or overt action against the Alimentation Service;
9. The Director-General of the Alimentation Service of Tehran has full authority to change and transfer officials; he has

the same authority concerning the staff of Crown lands and *Maliyat* of Tehran up to the grade of *chef de section*. As to the *chef de section* and higher, he may provisionally revoke them and take steps without the approval of the Minister of Finance. In having these powers he has to take into account the existing rules concerning promotion etc. The Minster of Finance will never impose a particular official.

10. The Director-General of the Alimentation Service of Tehran has the right to all information that has to be given to him immediately; he must submit his accounts to the Minister of Finance when asked;

11. In urgent cases Mr. Molitor may contact the Prime Minister directly concerning the Alimentation Service, but has to give his questions to Minister of Finance in writing immediately;

12. The Director-General of the Alimentation Service of Tehran has to submit a detailed annual report; also quarterly reports to the Minister of Finance as well as a monthly recapitulation of income and expenses to the Minister of Finance;

13. The Director-General of the Alimentation Service of Tehran has to publish his list of the recapitulation of his accounts, annexing necessary information at the end of each quarter for public confidence;

14. The Director-General of the Alimentation Service of Tehran has to be thrifty in all his expenses, and has to have an eye for the balance between income and expenses in pursuing his objective;

15. Mr. Molitor may collect arrears as soon as possible.

16. Gérant of the Minister of Finance Mo`tamad al-Saltaneh.[76]

Molitor was pleased that many of his ideas about the desired organization and functioning of a national Alimentation Service had been adopted by the government. However, to be both Administrator-General of Customs for the entire country and also be in charge of the Alimentation Service he considered to be a too heavy a workload and, therefore, he immediately wrote to the Minister on 29 August 1921:

---

76. MA, Farde 52, 5201.pdf, Mo`tamed al-Saltaneh to Molitor, no. 10386, 11/07/1921 - 19 Saratan 1339 (French and Persian version).

Fig. 7. Letterhead of the Tehran Municipality, 1919.

This is to inform you that I can no longer continue as Director of the Provincial Directorate of Taxes, Domains [Crown lands], *Ambar* [Granary] and Bakeries. The work

> load of the two services (Customs and Alimentation Service) is too much. It is undesirable that one of the two services would be neglected because of the other. The Alimentation Service demands all attention and needs it and, therefore, immediate action needs to be taken.[77]

Of course, this did not mean that Molitor was let off the hook, for discussions were initiated how to resolve Molitor's position. The government felt that it had eased Molitor's burden as chief of the Alimentation Service by its appointment of two Belgian officials, Willemsens and Hunin to the Alimenation Service, who also were given an increase in salary.[78] When the government did not react to Molitor's letter, he informed the Minister on 1 November 1921 that his compatriot and assistant Hunin was sufficiently knowledgeable to take over alone the management of the Alimentation Service of the Crown lands and Taxes of Tehran province. He requested the Minister to transfer to Hunin the powers that had been given him by letter 10386 of 19 Saratan 1339/11 July 1921, whereby he was appointed Chief of the Alimentation Service, Customs and Taxes.[79] The Minister met Molitor's demand half-way, for on 3 November 1921, Qavam al-Saltaneh informed Molitor that in reply his letter of 1 November Mr. Hunin's appointment as his deputy of the Alimentation Service had been approved.[80] However, the government still did not release

77. MA, Farde 52, 5205.pdf, Molitor to Prime Minister, Confi, no. 23821, 29/08/1921.

78. MA, Farde 52, 5206.pdf, Molitor to gérant of Minister of Finance, no. 24821, Confi, 24/08/1921; Idem, Farde 52, 5203.pdf, Mo`tamed al-Saltaneh to Molitor 09/08/1921, concerning Hunin and Willemssens and their salary increase. (On 10/08/1921 Hunin had fled from Enzeli and was attached to Molitor) The Minister, referring to his letter 15 Asad 1300/07 August 1921, approved the appointment of Hunin and Willemssens (with information concerning their contract and tasks), see MA, Farde 52, 5203.pdf.

79. MA, Farde 52, 5207.pdf, Molitor to Qavam al-Saltaneh, no. 11122, 01/11/1921.

80. MA, Farde 52, 5208.pdf, Qavam al-Saltaneh to Molitor 03/11/1921.

Molitor from his function as director of the Alimentation Service, because it needed his experience to resolve a looming bread crisis.

By August 1921 there was a shortage of grain due to a bad harvest after a severe winter due to phylloxera (insect pest) that ravaged the crops in particular the villages (including Varamin and Zarand) around Tehran. As a result, by January 1922, a quantity of only 14,400 *kharvars* of wheat and 6,880 *kharvars* of barley had entered the Granary. To keep control over the situation the government maintained the monopoly on the trade in grain, fixed the price of wheat in the Granary at 20 *tumans* per *kharvar*, while the price of sale of grain to the bakers was fixed at 19 *tumans*. When Fatan al-Molk, the director of the Granary until January 1922, assumed the service at the Granary a quantity of 60,000 *kharvars* still had to be supplied to Tehran for the remaining seven months until the next harvest and 9/10 of that quantity had to come from Arak and Khorasan. Therefore, Fatan al-Molk signed two contracts; the first one for the delivery of 20,000 *kharvars* of wheat from Arak and one for 20,000 *kharvars* of wheat from Khorasan. Fatan al-Molk's successor in addition bought additional 5,000 *kharvars* of wheat.

Given the above conditions, for planning purposes, the Alimentation Service immediately determined that the quantity of wheat needed until the following harvest, i.e. *Asad It'il* [Dog year = July-August 1922] was 10,000 *kharvars* per month or 120,000 per year. The Service based this figure on the records of the Granary for the period of Asad/August until 15 Jadi/January. From the trend of grain entries the Service concluded that during 5.5 months a quantity of 52,700 *kharvars* had been consumed, thus, assuming the same consumption trend, the annual consumption was estimated to be 115,000 *kharvars*. (see the two Tables below). Therefore, for the remaining six months of the year, i.e. from 15 Jadi 1300/16 January 1922 to end Saratan It'il 1301/23 August 1922, a quantity of 65,000 *kharvars* of wheat was needed, minus 8,000 already in stock; thus, 57,000 *kharvars* had to be purchased and transported to the Granary. In January 1922, the government decided to raise the price of wheat to the bakers at 23 *tumans* per *kharvar*, i.e. 4 *tumans* more than the previous price, so that the government would not suffer a financial loss.

Table 3.2: Estimate of annual grain consumption in Tehran in 1921-22

No. of order	Description	Quantity of wheat in *kharvar*	Observations
1	Quantity available at Asad	2,000	
2	Grain (tax in kind) of Tehran *khaleseh* villages[81]	20,000	
3	Purchase in Tehran province	40,000	
4	Grain (taxes) in Arak	4,500	
5	" " in Malayer	1,000	
6	" " Damghan, Shahrud, Sabzevar, Nishapur	3,000	5,000 *kharvars* of which 2,000 are consumed by the bakers of Semnan, Damghan and Shahrud
7	Purchase at Arak	20,000	
8	" on way to Khorasan	25,000	
9	Grain (taxes) of Khamseh *3,000 *kharvars*)	-	
10	Grain(taxes) of Qazvin (2,000 *kharvars*)	-	
	Total in *kharvars*	115,500	

Source: MA, Farde 41, 4102.pdf, Yaddasht, see Appendix II, p. 232.

Table 3.3: Entry into the Granary from 1 Asad until 15 Jadi (22/07/1921-

81. It was suggested to impose direct government control over the Crown lands (*khaleseh*), above all those of Tehran and avoid farming of the Crown lands.

05/01/1922)

No. of order	Description	Quantity of wheat in *batman*	Quantity of barley in *batman*
1	Quantity available at 1 Asad	200,042	281,784
2	Entered from Tehran *khaleseh*	1,440,020.25	688,031.75
3	" " (taxes)	430,453.50	439,875.10
4	" from purchasing chiefs	3,707,097	634,360.25
5	" taxes Arak	282,067.25	20,557.75
6	" Khorasan	30,790.75	19,380
7	" from Qazvin	4,553.75	3,531.75
8	" purchased in Arak	35,299.50	-
9	" in Khorasan	-	-
	Total entered	6,080,324	2,037,521
	Entered into the Ambar until 15 Jadi/5 January	6,080,324	2,037,521
	Left the *ambar* until 15 Jadi	5,268,924	1,221,529
	Available in the *ambar*	812,400	815,992

Source: MA, Farde 41, 4102.pdf, Yaddasht, see Appendix II, p. 232.

Barley also had supply problems, but it would seem that these were less stringent than in the case of wheat. According to the statistics of the transport tax office (*navaqel*), the trade of barley, which was a government monopoly since the 1st of Asad/22 July 1921, the consumption by the military amounted to 1,500 *kharvars* and that of the city to 3,000 *kharvars* per month. Thus, for the eight months until the harvest, i.e. since the 1st of Oqrab/22 November until the end of Joza It'il/21 June 1922, there was an estimated demand of 36,000 *kharvars* of fodder. The Alimentation Service intended to satisfy demand mainly through purchase.

Available at the Granary at 1 Oqrab/22 November	9,000 *kharvar*s
Purchased in Tehran province	12,000
Idem in [other] provinces	15,000
Total	36,000 *kharvar*s

To receive the purchased grain two agents left for Arak and Khorasan, where they met with stiff opposition. Agents from Arak, Qazvin and Khamseh reported that due to lack of grain in these two towns it was impossible to transport the 5,000 *kharvars* of taxes in grain of these towns to Tehran. To improve the logistics of food supply, it was proposed that the roads of Varamin, Qom, Aragh and the bridge of Rudkhaneh should be repaired as soon as possible. Furthermore, the purchase of 10 big lorries was proposed to be used exclusively for the transport of grain by the government.

As to the food supply of Tehran it was decided that there was no choice but to make savings given the rise in price of grain in Arak, which increased daily due to transport of grain for sale to Hamadan and Qazvin. It rose from 9 *tuman*s to 16 *tuman*s, which gave rise to the fear that it would be impossible to send the grain surplus to Tehran. This was the result of incitement and misinformation by wealthy landlords. Things became so tense that the government was forced to send agents to Arak, who requisitioned the warehouses of the landlords and speculators and put pressure on them to sell their grain, so that they were unable to continue with their intrigues. Finally, the influential big local landlords agreed on a price at Soltanabad of 13 *tuman*s, 11 *tuman*s, 9 *qrans* and 10 *tuman*s. A cordon was created to prevent grain leaving the area.[82]

To shore up the Alimentation Service's work in the Arak region, a bakery was established at Soltanabad and Qom, which sold bread at a reasonable price to prevent that landlords and speculators might benefit from the uncertain grain supply situation. The opening of a

82. MA, Farde 41, 4102.pdf, Yaddasht, see Appendix II, p. 233–34 (the anonymous author also noted that the government needed to pass a law banning the practice of grain hoarding and speculation).

bakery at Qom aimed to prevent the transport of grain from Arak, ostensibly on behalf of the Qom bakeries, and then from there to transport it for sale to Qazvin, Kashan, and other places. For the same reason and to facilitate grain transport from Khorasan to Tehran, the Alimentation Service opened bakeries at Semnan, Damghan, and Shahrud. To ensure the viability of these bakeries 2,000 *kharvars* of taxes in kind of these regions that were allocated for Tehran were reserved for these bakeries. However, the revolution in Khorasan led by Mohammad Taqi Pesiyan in April 1921 caused a delay of several months. The Alimentation Service agents were forced to stay at Damghan waiting for the end of the revolution, which happened on 15 Rabi I. [16 November 1921]. The bakeries of Qazvin were placed under the control of the local military governor and the taxes in kind of Qazvin and partly those of Zanjan that had to be sent to Tehran each year were made available to the military governor.[83]

This was not the only problem the Alimentation Service had to face. The bakers had formed a union (*ettehadiyeh*) and demanded that the Alimentation Service acknowledged them as such.[84] The Direction of the Alimentation Service refused this as it was out of its area of competence and remit. The bakers went on strike (*e`tesab*), sat in *bast* at Shah Abdol-Azim, closed their shops and met several times with the authorities so that they did not have to pay the usual taxes (*`avarez*). Supported by the government, the Alimentation Service put an end to the intrigues and complaints of the bakers by making it clear to them that they should not allow themselves to be used by political intrigants. Also, given the shortage of bread in Tehran they would not be allowed to do so and they were made aware that they were absolutely to follow government instructions. If they did not the government would take over their shops, which actually happened in the case of 15 bakeries, which as of then were managed and owned by the

83. MA, Farde 41, 4102.pdf, Yaddasht, see Appendix II, p. 234.

84. At the end of 1921, the exact number of bakeries in Tehran was 129 (92 *sangak* and 37 *lavash*). MA, Farde 41, 4107.pdf, Eshagh undated informal note. Since the text of the note refers to the month of `Oqrab/ December 1921, it must have been written in early 1922.

government.[85] Another problem was that caravanseraidars, coachmen (*doroshkehchiyan*), and pack-animal owners complained about the barley (fodder) situation. They, to buy and transport barley, gathered each day in the Meydan. Thus was the situation of the Alimentation Service at the beginning of Asad of the current Year of the Cock (*Takhaqu'il* – July-August 1921).[86]

There continued to be criticism about the efficacy of the Alimentation Service. However, the various attacks were mostly for political and/or for financial reasons, not necessarily because these were driven by legitimate objective reasons. The price and availability of bread could make or break cabinets and at any given moment political opponents and landowners, who saw the opportunity for political and/or illict gains reduced, would launch attacks.

> On 14 December 1921 it was alleged that only 13,000 *kharvar*s are present in the *Ambar* (Granary) plus 4,000 *kharvar*s bought from Khorasan, which might not arrive, because of blocked road and/or lack of pack animals. There was also doubt about sale of grain at Qom and Araq [Arak] because of the incompetence of the officials in charge of buying. The bakery opened by Alimentation Service in Araq [Arak] only had created problems for the inhabitants, while the population of Semnan and other places feared famine would occur having only three months of grain. For this lack of grain they blame the new organization by Molitor who has sent incompetent agents to their area, who allegedly had hardly been able to buy grain. This situation was also due to the Alimentation Service transport service, which did not exist before and was solely created for the benefit of some known persons. The officials in charge of the transport of Alimentation Service at Semnan hinder transport rather than facilitating it. See what the Alimentation [*adhuqeh*] has done with the credit of 50,000 *tuman*s it obtained. It has

85. MA, Farde 41, 4102.pdf, Yaddasht, see Appendix II, p. 234–35. In fact, the anonymous author advocated that the government place all bakeries under control and bakers throughout the country.

86. MA, Farde 41, 4102.pdf, Yaddasht, see Appendix II, p. 234; Idem, Farde 41, 4101.pdf, Translation 14/12/1921.

> hardly been able to transport 200 to 300 *kharvar*s, a quantity that suffices hardly for two days. At Arak exists a commission assisted by Hajji Mohammad Hoseyn with 100 *tuman*s salary (approved by the Minister), by Mahan Khan and Nasrollah Khan with 80 *tuman*s (without authorization). One has no idea what this commission does. Now there are three chiefs for Araq [Arak]: Molitor, Hunin and another official who receive too high salaries without having any concern of their responsibility. The journal asks the Minister Finance to order an investigation whether the population is being helped.[87]

Intrigue also affected the internal functioning of the Alimentation Service, which given the volatile political situation and weak cabinets, and changing alliances, was but to be expected. In early January 1922, an incident happened at the Granary that intended to disrupt the proper functioning of the transport service, because the agent targeted was an expert and competent agent in transport affairs; it was thanks to him that thousands of camels were sent to transport grain to ensure that the bakeries of Tehran were working well. This was a rather sensitive issue (see above), because transport was still the major bottleneck for Tehran's food security. Therefore, towards the end of 1921 the Alimentation Service had created its own transport service at Arak and another at Shahrud.[88]

The incident happened, because when in early January 1922 Fatan al-Molk left as chief of the Granary to become Financial Agent in Kerman[89] the food supply entered a difficult situation. He was quite aware of the tense situation among the Granary staff, because he told them: "Man, az inja farar mikonam ta bahal kar asan bud. Ba`d az in … cheh hekayat!!!" (I flee from here; until now work was easy, but after this ... who can tell!!!) Fatan al-Molk and Molitor agreed to recommend Badi`ollah Khan Mesbah as his successor, who was

87. MA, Farde 42, 4208.pdf, *Setareh-ye Iran* 20 Qaws 1300 or 12/12/1921.

88. MA, Farde 41, 4102.pdf, Yaddasht, see Appendix II, p. 234.

89. MA, Farde 52, 5211.pdf, Molitor to Prime Minister, no. 16122, 22/07/1922.

very knowledgeable about transport matters and thus, his appointment allowed things to move ahead. This was necessary, because the least delay in their work would have a negative impact. In a few weeks he had been able to send an enormous number of camels to the supply centers and his presence at the *Ambar* was a guarantee for the success of the food supply.[90] Then an incident was caused by a certain A`zam al-Vezareh, (*une espèce de fou-furieux, épileptique*) who had contacted Badi`ollah Khan under the pretext of having valuable information. During their meeting A`zam al-Vezareh attacked and wounded Badi-`ollah Khan.[91] The attack happened at the time that Badi`ollah Khan

---

90. Hajj Shams al-Din Jalali Fatan al-Molk, the chief of the government granary had replaced Mirza `Abbas Khan with A`zam al-Vezareh Qodsi. According to the latter, at that time Modir al-Molk was director of the Alimentation Service and Eshaq Khan Baha'i had great influence with him. Mirza Eshaq Khan Baha'i was the father-in-law of Mirza Abbas Khan, who had been chief of the control over in- and outgoing grain of the government granary (*ra'is-e sho`beh-ye kontrol-e edareh-ye anbar-e ghalleh-e dowlati*) until March 1921. Qodsi 1342, vol. 1, pp. 511-14 (photo on p. 512); Idem vol. 2, p. 32. Mirza Mahmud Khan Jam Modir al-Molk was born 1885 in Tabriz. "Has had a long career in the Customs and other Government Departments, and was for more than ten years Persian secretary to the French Legation in Tehran. Director of the Granary and thereafter asst. Director of the Alimentation Department, Tehran, 1915-20, where he did good work. Minister for Foreign Affairs in Seyid Zia-ed-Din's short-lived Cabinet, 1921." Thereafter he was governor of Kerman, several times minister in various cabinets and was Prime Minister from Adhar 1314 until Aban 1318. IOR/L/PS/12/3451, p. 19; Burrell and Jarman 1997, (vol. 1931-24), p. 261; Najmi 1370, vol. 1, pp. 333-41 (with bio and more details).
91. For A`zam al-Vezareh's version of these events, see Qodsi 1342, vol. 2, p. 32, who alleges that Badi`ollah Khan cursed the prophet Mohammad. He also refers to a (religious inspired?) intrigue in the Granary, but against him, see Qodsi 1342, vol. 1, pp. 511-12. The post of head of the Granary was not without danger. In 1916, Mirza Esma`il Khan Banki, who held that function, was killed by the *komiteh-ye mojazat* (punishment committee), which, according to Mostowfi 1324, vol. 3, p. 25, was founded by Vosuq al-Dowleh. Mirza Esma`il's crime was that he was an Anglophile and therefore, also being head of the Granary, he was accused of being co-responsible for the famine that, of course, had been engineered by the British. `Emad al-Kottab 1284, pp.

had been chosen as chief of the Granary, because of his experience, honesty, and his special knowledge about the grain transport of 5,500 *kharvars* from Khorasan and Arak for the next 6-7 months. What happened then was baffling to Molitor, for instead of punishing the attacker the innocent Badi`ollah Khan was forced to leave the city. According to Molitor, the attack was not a religious matter, as was being bruited about, but an intrigue, probably mounted by people who didn't like that the Alimentation Service worked well despite their pessimistic predictions. Molitor further noted that A`zam al-Vezareh (whom he banned from entering the Granary) had earlier attacked Zahir al-Molk, governor of Mazandaran under similar circumstances.[92] In a letter to Reza Khan, the Minister of War, he wrote that this incident and the dismissal of Badi`ollah Khan had a negative impact on food supply "for your soldiers and the city's inhabitants." To the Prime Minister he wrote that A`zam al-Vezareh could not remain in the administration; "he is dangerous."[93] Moreover, Molitor drew the Prime Minister's attention to the fact that Badi`ollah Khan's dismissal and that his attacker, A`zam al-Vezareh was not punished, had a negative effect on the staff of the Granary. He added,

> I have no confidence in a regular conduct of business that is per force undermined after intimidation of the staff. Under these conditions I am forced to ask Your Highness to immediately replace me and Mr. Hunin, because we cannot continue to work under such conditions that offer foreign officials no assurance. Given that security is directly linked to public food supply and that the Alimentation Service ensures this, I realize that I will earn the reproach of the Minister of War if I don't inform him that these salaries are in danger in the future. I have asked him,

---

20-21, 216-17.

92. Qodsi 1342, vol. 1, p. 501.

93. The politically well-connected A`zam al-Vezarah was transferred to the Ministry of Finance in the office of reductions and reparations of the department of the revenue assessment of the Crown lands (*edareh-ye tashkhis-e `ayedat-e khalesejat sho`beh-ye takhfif va ta`mirat*). Qodsi 1342, vol. 2, p. 35.

> as I had already done for the service of bakeries, to place an officer at the *ambar*, while giving all services the protection by the authority, which now is the most feared and respected.
> As Badi`ollah Khan is ill I propose to you as chief of the *Ambar* one of the following three persons:
> Mirza `Ali Naqi Khan, currently chief bookkeeper
> Mirza Sayyed `Ali Khan, my assistant
> Mirza Sayyed `Isa Khan, inspector; all three are Moslem.
> We need somebody who knows the business. Meanwhile, Badi`ollah Khan continues to busy himself with grain transport.
> I add that if I don't have full support from the government in the difficult work of the Alimentation Service there might be serious consequences.[94]

Badi`ollah Khan's shabby treatment reinforced Molitor's wish to resign from his post as director of the Alimentation Service. On 29 March 1922, he informed Prime Minister Hasan Pirniya that contrary to some rumors he had indeed resigned as director of the Alimentation Service for health reasons, "which, after having given so many years of my life to it, I do with great regret." Molitor added that he would transfer the responsibility of the Alimentation Service to the officials the Prime Minister would appoint. Furthermore, he submitted that he would prepare a signed report concerning the situation of the Alimentation Service as well as of its loans from the Imperial Bank of Persia. To that end Molitor brought to the Prime Minister's attention that the general accounts of the Alimentation Service were included in

---

94. MA, Farde 52, 5211.pdf, Molitor to President du Conseil, no, 16122, 15/01/1922; Idem, Farde 52, 5210.pdf, Molitor to Minister of Finance, 05/01/1922; Idem, Farde 52, 5210.pdf, Molitor to Minister of War, 15/01/1922 (As you are responsible for the general security of the city and the country I considered it necessary to inform you and to take steps to ensure the proper performance of the Alimentation Service). The fact that Molitor explicitly mentioned that the proposed candidates were Moslem makes it likely that the conflict in the Granary may have had religious overtones, because Mirza Eshaq Khan and his son-in-law Mirza Abbas Khan were Baha'is and there was bad blood between them and A`zam al-Vezareh, who was a Moslem. Qodsi 1342, vol. 1, pp. 511-12; vol. 2, p. 32.

the monthly accounts of the Provincial Direction of Taxes, Domains, *Ambar* and Bakeries, which were kept and drawn up by Mirza `Ali Naqi Khan, who was in charge of the book-keeping section. Molitor also advised that he considered Mirza Eshaq Khan Haqiqi, inspector-general of the services, a very industrious man, who, moreover, was most knowledgeable of the general state of affairs of the service. He commented that Mirza Eshaq Khan Haqiqi might be the energetic chief that the Prime Minister wanted for the Alimentation Service.[95]

Since the government had not reacted to Molitor's request for his dismissal, on 1 April 1922, he informed Hasan Pirniya, the Prime Minister that he was unable to stay in function any longer. In 1921, he had already offered his resignation from the Alimentation Service to Pirniya's predecessor, Qavam al-Saltaneh, a function that required much energy and full commitment from its chief, which, given his medical situation, Molitor was unable to offer. Moreover, the food supply situation of Tehran as well as the transportation of grain from the regions far away from the city entered into a difficult phase. Also, the attack on Badi`ollah Khan and the non-punishment, nay the rewarding, of his attacker had a negative impact on the Alimentation Service. Once again, Molitor stressed that this affair had serious consequences. "I believe that the intrigants behind this deed knew whom to target so as to have the desired result in the future. If the Minister of War did not have the spirit and initiative to place an officer at the management team of the Alimentation Service it would have been a blow to its revival." However, there still might be an interruption or a halt in grain transport, which would have fatal consequences

95. MA, Farde 52, 5215.pdf, Molitor to Min. of Finance, no. 29322, 24/03/1922. On 25 March 1922, the newspaper *Iran* had an article it which it noted that the high cost of foodstuffs made life very uncomfortable and that the government, instead of making life easier for people, imposed high taxes. Eyn al-Saltaneh 1376, vol. 8, p. 6715.

for the food supply. Therefore, Molitor advised the Prime Minister to immediately order a 24/7 action plan for the requisition of pack animals at Tehran and in the regions of Arak and Khorasan.[96] Molitor received an immediate reaction. The next day Moshir al-Dowleh acknowledged receipt of his letter and expressed his regret that "we loose your services at Alimentation Service due to health reasons and therefore, I have accepted your resignation from Alimentation Service. I hope that measures taken as well as you having informed Minister of War and his measures will help the transport of grain."[97]

---

96. MA, Farde 52, 5215.pdf, Molitor to Min. of Finance, no. 29322, 24/03/1922; Idem, Frade 52, 5216.pdf, Molitor to Min. of Finance, no. 1422, 01/04/1922.
97. MA, Farde 52, 5217.pdf, Moshir al-Dowleh to Molitor, no. 358, 02/04/1922. Molitor himself wrote that he served until 21 March 1922. MA, Delcourt and Molitor n.d., p. 40.

Fig. 8. Types of bread from top left, clockwise: taftun, sangak, lavash, barbary.

CHAPTER FOUR

THE SITUATION IN TABRIZ IN 1923

Information concerning the bread question of the city of Tabriz and recommendations to fundamentally change it.[1]

PART ONE

THE BREAD QUESTION OF TABRIZ

People who are informed about the situation and developments of affairs in Azerbaijan know well that in the city of Tabriz the bread question was of special importance and that from the political and

1. For the Persian text by Jamal, see MA, Farde 36, 3605. For easy comparison I have inserted the original page numbers of the Persian text in bold between square brackets in the translation, which indicates the end of the original Persian text on that page.

economic point of view it is tightly linked with the government's interests. From the political point of view naturally the bread question and its disruption has been the first cause and factor for tension among the lower classes, the gathering of a mob of the common people, and the outbreak of sudden rioting. It is mostly seen that general turmoil initially began under the guise of the disruption of the bread [supply] and thereafter, through incitement by trouble-seekers, the course of its events was caused to go out of control, which led to many historical tragic events. In 1300 hijri/November 1882-83 the plundering of the house of the late Nezam al-Olama and the expulsion of Hasan `Ali Khan Amir-e Nezam from Tabriz etc.[2] were very tragic events and I refer to it, because it is one historical chain of events whose headstone has been chiseled in the name of the disruption of the bread [supply], and because every outbreak of turmoil has resulted in significant damage to the government. [**2**]

Also, from the economic point of view, careful study of the accounts of the Treasury shows that in normal years, every year the government suffered a loss from 50,000 to 100,000 *tuman*s due to a rise in price, cheapness of grain, and shortage of the bread in Tabriz and in years of hunger and drought this loss even rose to more than one half a million.

Therefore, it is surprising that during this long time, with all these material and significant losses that the government suffered, the authorities having to endure a loss in securing the food supply of the city of Tabriz every year, that until now the government has not given thought to put the foundation of this activity on a sound basis and fundament by adopting a proper method and remaining immune to outside attacks, as, until now, in the shadow of continuous disorder and disorganization, this situation easily has been corrupted and taken advantage of by some bad elements.

Therefore, for the preservation of the material and real benefits of the alarmed government I considered it necessary to submit the

---

2. On this event, which took place in August 1898 or Rabi` I and II 1316 (not 1300), see Floor 2015, p. 125.

results of my own comprehension and experience by submitting this Note to the attention of the authorities and to propose my own views as to its fundamental and permanent reform. [**3**]

PART TWO

The cause of the importance of bread to Tabriz

One may think that the cause of the importance of the bread question of the city of Tabriz is one of the simple and plain problems that is only due to external factors. However, on the contrary, some natural problems and obstacles in the province of Azerbaijan exist that were totally interfering with this matter and its importance is greater than in other parts of Iran and deserve more attention by the authorities. These problems are twofold:

1. Natural causes peculiar to Azerbaijan.
2. External causes due to mismanagement.

First, Natural causes:

1. The geographical location. This region of Iran consists completely of highlands, rising valleys and large rivers such as the Aras and the Qizil Uzun that are situated in the north and east and in their course don't irrigate any of Azerbaijan's regions and without any benefit wind through the valleys and flow into the Caspian Sea. Likewise, most of the small rivers have been beset by the same natural obstacles and have been unable until now to be of benefit. Therefore, 70% of all wheat and barley cultivation is limited to villages and to highlands and the basis for good and bad crops [**4**] is linked to precipitation.

2. Dryness of the area. The calamity of a dry year due to natural drought threatens the crop of the region of Azerbaijan every year.

3. The variation in water, weather, and rainfall. In case of rainfall most places in the summer and winter quarters differ greatly from

each other. In the whole of Azerbaijan it has a single result, viz. at times that rainfall in Garmrud, Arunaq and Anzab is very beneficial it has an opposite effect in the villages of Sahandabad, so that naturally each year part of the crop suffers damage.

4. The difficulty of roads and highways. Because the roads and highways are natural pathways and traverse valleys and floods and are subject to natural destruction the use of carts etc. is impractical and the means of transportation are limited to pack animals, even on small paths that connect the villages with the highways as most of them pass through valleys and pastures. The roads of most villages on the slopes are closed for three to four months so that the pack animals also cannot pass. Only in the north-western part of Azerbaijan the Russians during war to enable the execution of military operations have constructed and operated a railway of a length of 19 *farsakh* from Jolfa to Tabriz and over a length of seven *farsakh* from Sharaf-Khaneh to Sufiyan, which line in Sufiyan also connects with the Jolfa line. **[5]** These aforementioned establishments now belong to the government of Iran and, with great ease, transport of grain takes place via this line and via boats on Lake Urmiyeh to Marand, Arunaq, Anzab, and parts of Maragheh, Hashtrud and Qurichay. However, for the transport of grain to the station and the lake ports pack animals are needed.

5. Lack of means of transportation. Except for the railway that was mentioned above the means of transportation in this province are limited to camels, horses, mules and donkeys. For the transport of grain horses and mules are not used; the major part of grain is carried by donkeys and a part also by camels, because of the difficulty of the road. The use of bikes, carts and other means of transportation is not possible.

6. Insecurity of the roads and attacks by bandits and tribes. Although this subject is not one of the natural obstacles, however, since for many years it is a permanent and lasting occurrence in Azerbaijan and thus, may be mentioned among the natural obstacles. Each year, it begins in the middle of spring and continues until the end of fall in most of the grain-cropped areas and causes much standstill to cultivation and transport of foodstuffs from one area to another. In

fact, effective activities by the Ministry of War in establishing security in the area of Azerbaijan are making progress and it is hoped that this obstacle also will eliminated. [**6**]

Secondly. External causes

External causes to the importance of the bread question are twofold: First, the absence of the allocation of fixed and adequate funds by the government for the transport of grain due to the constant tightness of the treasury each year results in extraordinary difficulties and obstacles in the transport of grain and is the main problem for the muleteers. Therefore, the best opportunity to transport grain is lost and results in a major standstill in collecting and delivering grain to the central Granary. But as was mentioned in the beginning, the major reason is the internal disorganization of the management of bread supply due to the absence of a permanent agency and a solid foundation for food security. This is because the bread question is left to different commissions and managed by temporary agencies. It is evident that such agencies that have no official status and legal responsibility and have not foreseen future dangerous situations always seek the future success of their own agency, and this will result in nothing but the destruction of the central role of the office's activities, the destruction of the responsibility of the person in charge, and of the accumulation of sources of incomes for the staff of the food security office, so that finally the only output is the arising of a situation of chaos that totally disrupts the management of the bread supply.

Although by virtue of article 2 (sub 3) and article 70 (sub 11) of the Municipality Law in case of absence of drought control as well as fixing and regulating the price of bread is one of the tasks of the municipal office, up to now a legal Municipality has not been established and because of the great importance [7] of disruption of the bread supply of Tabriz most of the time, in case of necessity, the authorities have managed the bread question separately and independent from the Municipality. In both cases a fixed system and basic plans have not been adopted. For the same reason, trusted and reliable people have not opposed this and those who have accepted this job, because they knew it was temporary and were in a state of shock and anxiety, did not have the opportunity and desire to acquire the necessary experience to bring about fundamental reform. Because, whether their activities were good or bad, they did not have to fear castigation and punishment they, without any shred of moral trouble and with total lack of concern, abused [their position] and secured their own future. It is clear that in case of the food [supply] to a city such as Tabriz, whose daily consumption reaches about 200 *kharvar*s of bread and in case of misappropriation of only one *shahi* per *man* the daily amount will exceed more than 100 *tuman*s each year, from 50 to 60,000 head of camels transport this, for the delivery of each load the cameleers are ready to give a present of five *hazar* to one *tuman*, nay, even more. If the responsible agent wants to take advantage of this he may collect substantial sums and in such a case the members of the Alimentation Service (*edareh-ye adhuqeh*), who are upset and anxious in their assignment will all the more engage in bad behavior. It is evident that the value of every illicitly misappropriated *qran* will be tenfold in case of the disruption of the bread question. [**8**]

In years of plenty, which is the time of natural bounty and of abundant harvest, food matters will take a course following natural rules. Nobody thinks about the future or foresees days of hunger, on the contrary, government officials for their own interest and to obtain a good reputation show a strange urge to bring down the price of bread and gradually go to extremes in this matter so that government grain has become the main means to lower the price of bread for the authorities and it is sold to the bakers at a low price. Even the cost of transport that has been paid to bring it to the city is not received and the government is forced to suffer a loss. The peasant class likewise due to the sale of grain doesn't earn enough to cover their cost and loses interest in cultivation and only tills that which their own family needs and engage in other activities. In that case the following year with little help from nature the price of wheat and barley again goes up and the previous problem happens again. From this point of view experience has always confirmed and established that excessive cheapness is the news bearer of future dearness. In fact, when problems and obstacles such as a failed crop, insecurity in the country, closure of roads by snow, lack of means to pay for the transport of grain, and the extraordinary need of the government to supply the army on the move or the occurrence of other unrelated obstacles, immediately the city's bread supply is disrupted and, given the presence of incompetent officials, this problem will worsen so that the inhabitants of the city all will become afraid, and, as a result, the causes of anxiety of the authorities [**9**] increase and daily turmoil and havoc threaten the city. At that time government officials begin thinking about corrections and are forced to look for various solutions with extraordinary proposals and tough measures concerning the transport of grain etc. and try with the dispatch of officials and pressure on peasants and tax payers concerned, requisition of pack animals, etc. etc. to remove the impediment. Meanwhile, to help reflection and borrowing money for the cost of transport of grain and in particular for sharing in the responsibility for the food supply they form a commission of the wealthy of the city composed of a number of the elite, notables, and merchants etc.; most of its members, from several points of view, were not reformists, nay, they are harmful to the welfare of the general public. On the one hand, the formation of the commission, the worry of the authorities and the extraordinary activities increase the distress of the public, and the price of bread rises. On the other hand, after the peasants, the group of cameleers and some penniless small landowners concerned have been put under pressure by the officials in every respect the country's situation becomes a mess and the opportunities for profiteering by the officials come available. The owners of grain and powerful landowners also benefit from these circumstances and with jests they deceitfully try to extend its durance. The price of grain rises daily, bread becomes scarce and then again the government's loss becomes inevitable. At the orders of the authorities, to please the people, government grain is given at low prices to the bakers to be mixed with purchased grain from the bazaar and perforce the difference in market price and the reduced weight coincide with the bread price and it is quite clear, if the price of bread is lower than the daily market price everybody, without exception, bought bread from the bazaar and sold their own existing wheat and flour [**10**] at their desired price. Preventing this in a big city such as Tabriz and keeping people away from bazaari bread is impossible. Moreover, in any case, mostly in a year of drought and plenty government grain is revenue from the Crown lands. The non-existence of a permanent and statuary office is the reason that the abovementioned abuses are found as a revolving cycle. It is for many years that this situation has lasted and together with the cause of loss for the government's treasury and a major cause of the threat of the general security of the country.

PART THREE

INFORMATION AND DATA ETC. CONCERNING URBAN FOOD SUPPLY

1. The number of inhabitants of the city of Tabriz. Now the number is 175,000 and the number of houses is an estimated 35,000, of which 165,000 are Moslems and 10,000 are Armenians, Europeans, Russians, etc.

2. The commissariats and the quarters of the city. They are as follows: [**11**]

3. City's consumption of foodstuffs

Est. no. of people	*Kukeh-pazi-ye rowghani**	*Lavash pazi*	*Sangak pazi*	Description of the quarters	No. of Commissariats and names of the quarters	No. of the column
25,000	1	-	11	Kucheh-ye Sarbaz-khaneh, Darband-e Dowreh; Kucheh-ye Hajji Sheikh; Kucheh-ye Ark; Darb-e Nowbar; Kucheh-ye Laleh Bek; Maqsudiyeh; Kucheh-ye `Azab daftarha; Kucheh-ye Hajji Jabbar Na`eb; Kordughliha; Charandab Nowbar; Kucheh-ye Bagh-e `Eyn al-Dowleh; Rasteh-ye Aqa Mir Fattah Marhum; Rasteh-ye Bagh-e Shomal; Kucheh-ye Sadr; Kucheh-ye Qullar, Kucheh-ye Mirza Nasrollah; Darb-e Baghmisheh;	1. Nowbar	1.
16,000	-	-	-8	Rasteh-ye Khiyaban; Kucheh-ye Hajji Ehtesham; Dalan-e Mirza Reza; Dimashqiyeh; Kucheh-ye Sadbashi; Bagh-e Saheb-e Divan; Kalantar Kucheh; Qurt Meydani; Kucheh-ye Hajji Seyf; Meydan-e Chupur; Ghayath; Armani Donan; Rasteh-ye Maralan; Sheytan Kucheh; Baramleq; Golkhaneh; Masjed-e Karim Khan; Kucheh-ye Qarehbaghiha	2. Khiyaban	2
15,000	1	1	7	Kucheh-ye Mojtahed; Kucheh-ye Haramkhaneh; Rasteh-ye Sheshgalan; Kucheh-ye Qa'emmaqam; Kucheh-ye Yakhchal; Dash Darband Sheshgalan; Kucheh-ye Moshir-e Nezam; Silab-e Qushkhaneh; Pol-e Sanki; Vaplankuh; Baghmisheh	3. Sheshgalan	3
38,000	1	-	15	**Sorkhab**	4. Shotorban-e Sorkhab	4
				Kucheh-ye Molla-Bashi; Darvazeh; Sorkhab; Takiyeh-ye Heydari; Rasteh-ye Sayyed Hamzeh; Kucheh-ye Qushdashi; Kucheh-ye Bagh- Amir; Silab-e Molla Zeynal; Kucheh-ye Bagh-e Soffeh; Masjed- Hasan Darzi; Aqa Janabad; Bazarcheh-ye Hajji Ali Akbar		
				Shotorban		

*. Except in Tabriz and Urmiyeh, the common name of this bread in the rest of Iran is *barbari*.

Est. no. of people	*Kukeh-pazi-ye rowghani**	*Lavash pazi*	*Sangak pazi*	Description of the quarters	No. of Commissariats and names of the quarters	No. of the column
				Kucheh-ye Hammam-e Geru; Hajji Aqa Baba; Shekalleli Masjed; Dash Darband-e Shotorban; Sayyed Ebrahim; Meydan-e Kahforushan; Kohneh-ye Emamzadeh; Kucheh-ye Naser al-Hokama; Rasteh-ye Akunum; Mehar Mahin; Maghazeh-ha-ye Sangi; Kucheh-ye A`rab; Kucheh-ye Hammam-e Mostashar; Kucheh-ye Barun Avak; Rasteh-ye Leylabad; Mariz-khaneh-ye Amrika'iha; Shahr-e Now; Golzar Kucheh; Charandab-e Armanistan; Masjed-e Khuni; Dowreh-ye Ark-e Jahanshahi; Ziqler; Ustad Shagerd		
14,000	-	-	53	Rasteh-ye Kucheh; Darb-e Eslambul; Kucheh-ye Hajji `Azim Khan; Yakeh Dokkanlar; Kucheh-ye Qarrehchiha; Chost duzan; `Amu; Zeyn al-Din; Jamshidabad; Aji Kenar; Lakeh Dizaj; Kucheh-ye Taj Ahmadi;	6. Amir Khiz	6
26,000	-	-	12	Kucheh-ye Angaj; Darvazeh-ye Gajal; Qarreh-ye Aghaj; Akhunkhuyeh; Hokmabad; Rasteh-ye Vagzal; Kazeran; Du Qal`eh; Kucheh-ye Bagh; Shahabad; Vazirabad	7. Darvazaeh	7
Counted as part of the quarters	10	2	15	…	8. Bazaar	8
175,000	18	12	86	Total		

First. On average about one *man* of grain satisfies the daily need of bread of ten people [**14**] and based on this calculation provisions of 175,000 people comes to not more than 175 *kharvar*s daily. As to fodder for animals also about 10 *kharvar*s of barley is brought in, which in total comes to the daily needs of the city to not more than 185 *kharvar*s, 5,550 per month, and 66,000 *kharvar*s per year.

Secondly. From the daily abovementioned amount 125 *kharvar*s per day is for the baking of the *sangak* bakeries, which is considered official bread. 25 *kharvar*s are for the baking of the *lavash* bakeries etc. and 25 *kharvar*s for the baking of those who bake at home (*khaneh-khvor*) and 10 *kharvar*s for animal fodder.

Thirdly. From the above consumption the manner of the use of wheat and barley is as follows:

The baking of *sangak* bakeries, *lavash* bakeries, and *kukeh* bakeries uses three-quarters wheat and one-quarter barley and those baking at home only use wheat. Therefore, of the amount of 185 *kharvars* about 135 *kharvar*s is wheat and 50 *kharvar*s is barley.

4. The number of working bakeries. At this time:

Sangak bakeries	86 shops
Lavash bakeries	12
Kukeh bakeries	18

(description as mentioned in section 2) [**15**]

5. The number of mills.

First. Water mills that are all working:

1. Qanat-e Kalantar-e Bozorg-e Barenj	16 mills
2. Qanat-e Shah Chelebi	10
3. Qanat-e Shahzadeh	9
4. Qanat-e Mirza Hashem Baghmisheh	15
5. Qanat-e Kalantar-e Kuchek	10
6. Qanat Emam-Jom`eh	12
7. Qanat-e Hasan Pasha	7

8. Qanat-e Tajer-bashi - sar-e Khiyaban	7
9. Qanat-e Shamsabad	16
10. Qanat-e Qurchi-bashi – Maralan	16
11. Qanat-e Shahzadeh	5
12. Qanat-e Aqa	8
13. Qanat-e Laleh Dizaj, in all	26
Total	149 mills

Secondly. There are three [fuel] fired mills of which none are working. [**16**]

6. Estimated total and cost of managing a *sangak* bakery and the proportional price of the kinds of bread (*jensbanan*):

First. To ensure that the revenue of a bakery covers its cost its daily batch has to be at least 25 portions (*parcheh*). One portion consists of 5 *man* and 3 *charak* of flour so that 25 portions equals 142.5 *man* of new weight plus 1,000 *mesqal*s of flour.

Secondly. In fact, the baking of one *man* of bread requires 750 dinars; the use per portion is 4.30 *qran*s and consumption of one *kharvar* is 75 *qran*s. But, in exchange of this each *man* of flour yields 5 *man* of bread.

Thirdly. In accordance with the above method the relationship of the price of the kinds of bread in a bakery that daily bakes 25 portions (*parcheh-pokht*) is as follows:

Price per	One *man* of bread	Price of one *man*	New weight of grain	Price of one *man*	bread	Price of one *man* of grain	New weight
Qran	*Sadam*	*Qran*	*Sadam*	*Qran*	*Sadam*	*Qran*	*Sadam*
3	20	3	60	1	60	1	50
3	60	4	20	2	-	2	-
4	-	4	80	2	40	2	50
-	-	-	-	2	80	3	10

[**17**]

7. Estimation of the collection of the requirement of 66,000 *kharvar*s of grain.

The city's annual [needs]. The above amount must be collected from the places hereunder and from areas from which it may be carried because of the distance and the saving of transport costs:

1. Government taxes in kind (grain)
2. Rent from Crown lands
3. Grain from landowners
4. Grain from peasants and farmers after deduction of their needs on account of auto-consumption and seed.

Government grain in the province of Azerbaijan after deduction of the taxes of the Crown lands conform the actual tax records is almost more than 55,000 *kharvar*s, but that which was collected in It'il 1301 was as was expected, which may be considered a normal and natural year. It was about 26,000 *kharvar*s of which 17,700 *kharvar*s were able to be transported to the city and 83,000 *kharvar*s were in remote regions and its transport was not to the government's advantage and from the amount carried to the city 3,000 *kharvar*s were transported by the tax payers (*bar kardeh*) and the remainder by the government (*gheyr bar kardeh*) and detailed statement is as follows: [**18**]

Amount		Places from where grain could not be transported to Tabriz	No. of column	Amount		Places from where grain could be transported to Tabriz	No. of column
Kharvar	*man*			*Kharvar*	*Man*		
2,200	-	Khoy	11	1,400	-	Immediate surrounding Tabriz	1
200	-	Sarab	12	3,100	-	Bolukat-e Tholtheh	2
500	-	Garmrud	13	600	-	Arunaq and Anzab	3
1,900	-	Sa'en Qa-l'eh	14	600	-	Alan Baraghush and districts	4
2,500	-	Maragheh	15	1,200	-	Sarab	5
1,000	-	Ardabil	16	1,000	-	Garmrud	6
-	-	-	-	1,300	-	Qarajeh-dagh	7
-	-	-	-	2,800	-	Maragheh	8
-	-	-	-	2,400	-	Marand	9
-	-	-	-	3,400	-	Hashtrud; Qurichay	10
8,300	-	Total of grain unable to transport to city		17,700	-	Total able to transport to city	
17,700	-	Total able to transport to city					
26,000	-	Total estimated amount collected in It'il					

[19]

The rent of the Crown lands in the year It'il was equal to 7,000 and odd *kharvars* (almost half of that can be transported to the city) as follows:

Summary	Amount		Number of village	Place	No. of column
	Kharvar	*Man*			
Total transportable Total not transportable	439	50	11	Arunaq; Anzab	1
17,000 *kharvars* 26,000 *kharvars* taxes	60	-	2	Mavaze` Khan [Arasbaran][3]	2
3,300 7,285 Crown lands	300	-	4	Rudqat [Marand][4]	3
21,000 33, 285 Total	256	75	1	Deh Khvarqan[5]	4
	319	-	13	Sarab	5
	623	50	9	Bolukat-e Tholtheh	6
	145	-	1	Misanj	7
	6	-	5	Salmas	8
	392	-	5	Marand va Gargar	9
	781	65	17	Khoy – Qotur	10
	2,769	-	49	Maragheh	11
	326	96		Qarajehdagh	12
	31	-		Shahr [Tabriz]	13
	835	-		Alan Baraghush	14
	7,285	36	36		

[20]

The total of the two entries of the above [grain] revenues was more than 33,000 odd *kharvars* and of this quantity recently 21,000 *kharvars* were transported to the city. Based on proper research and information the total of government grain that actually can be transported at one *farsakh* of the city – on all four sides – is almost equal to 750 *kharvars*. This means, it is estimated that the government may collect 750 *kharvars* from the villages located at one *farsakh* from the city and from [villages at] a distance of 5 *farsakh* 3,750 *kharvars* and from a distance of 10 *farsakh* from the city 7,500 *kharvars* and from villages at 20 *farsakh* 15,000 *kharvars* of government grain. Concerning the grain of landowners and peasants, after deduction

3. For a description, see Adamec 1976, vol. 1, p. 444.
4. For a description, see Adamec 1976, vol. 1, p. 547.
5. For a description, see Adamec 1976, vol. 1, p. 153

of their personal needs for food supply and seed, the government may also collect an estimated amount equal to three times the above quantity. In this case, government grain, in addition to the transportable revenue of the Crown lands and the surplus of the landowners and village peasants located up to 16 *farsakh* from the city in normal years, suffices for the food supply of the city of Tabriz, which is estimated to be 66,000 *kharvar*s.

8. The capacity of the government Granary of the city of Tabriz. Actually the Granary consists of the warehouses located in the government Ark, whose capacity is only 8,000 *kharvar*s. At the time of collection of the grain most of the above quantity is needed and after the warehouses of the Ark have been filled additional warehouses and caravanserais have to be rented, which from the point of view of conservation is highly unsuitable. [**21**]

9. The situation of the roads in Azerbaijan .

1. The railway.

a. From Jolfa to Tabriz almost 19 *farsakh.*

b. From Sufiyan[6] to Sharafkhaneh[7] almost 7 *farsakh.*

2. Boats. On Lake Urmiyeh now four boats are operating and commute between the following ports:

a. Bandar-e Sharaf-Khaneh, which is the main center of navigation.

b. Bandar-e Golman-Khaneh

c. Bandar-e Heydarabad.

d. Bandar-e Danalu.[8]

e. Bandar-e Chubanlu

f. Two small ports that have been established on the royal island.

---

6. See Adamec 1976, vol. 1, p. 618.
7. See Adamec 1976, vol. 1, p. 600.
8. See Adamec 1976, vol. 1, p. 140.

All of these ports are connected by normal roads over which droshkes and carts run.

3. Metalled roads. On all sides of Tabriz	20 *farsakh.*
a. Road from Jolfa to Tabriz	20 *farsakh*
b. Road from Maragheh to Tabriz	19 *farsakh*
c. Road from Chubankareh[9] to Danalu	12 *farsakh* [**22**]

The above roads are in need of major repairs.

4. Normal roads over which droshkies and carts travel: From Tabriz to Miyanj 24 *farsakh.*

10. Means of transportation in Azerbaijan. These are camels, horses, mules, donkeys, bicycles, four-wheelers, carts, and fourgeons. In some areas of Qarajeh Dagh cows are also used for transportation. However, the main means of transportation are donkeys and camels. Normally, one *kharvar* of grain of new weight is transported by 7 to 8 head of donkeys or three camels.

Observations concerning fundamental reforms of the food supply of the city of Tabriz

PART FOUR

The first and most important duty of the authorities is this that by careful consideration of the above-mentioned arrangements and information a stable and correct method concerning the bread question of the city has to be adopted:

---

9. See Adamec 1976, vol. 1, p. 131.

> [i] For the permanent security and regularization of food supply of 175,000 inhabitants of the city of Tabriz;
>
> [ii] For the deterrence of political damage and the prevention of uprising and riots;
>
> [iii] For the prevention of the annual occurrence of important losses to the government;
>
> [iv] Against drought, and finally,
>
> [v] For the closing of the road to illicit income, giving peace of mind to the people of the city, the peasants in the surrounding areas and the transporters as well as establishing a just market price for grain in a permanent manner as an encouragement of peasants and farmers [**23**]. Natural problems such as drought, market price, loss of means of transport, impassable and insecure roads etc. have to be resolved and improved with practical methods and proper organization so that the well-being of all people is achieved and the country's affairs may develop towards the best conditions. In my view, the accomplishment and realization of this important subject will only be successful when employing one of two of the following methods:

First. The government should have the monopoly of the purchase and sale of grain, i.e. nobody, except for the government, has the right to trade in grain. The total implementation of this rule will fundamentally resolve and settle the bread question and all imaginable obstacles will disappear and it will be possible that within the course of one year people's bread supply will be secure with a just price that takes into account the benefit and welfare of the inhabitants of the city as well as of the peasants and farmers. In doing so, after deduction of cost and necessary use by the monopoly, without being a burden to people, it will enable the government to make an annual profit from this trading monopoly. Moreover, as the price of grain with the application of this system is fixed, the people of the city will have complete peace of mind, because of the abundance of bread and having a just fixed price. Also, each year and at any time, the peasant and farming class will be able to sell the surplus of their own crop without any apprehension and all of it at the same just price and with utter contentment and tranquility may engage in cultivation and tillage. However, in case [**24**] of the implementation of this system that which should be of significance is this that the Alimentation Service (*edareh-ye arzaq*) in the beginning will have a need for ample funds that the government has to give as a loan. After the said Service has been in operation, it has to pay it back in installments from the surplus of its revenues. Until the time that the above loan has been paid back to the government it is necessary that from the buying and selling of grain the Alimentation Service assigns two *tuman*s of the profit of each *kharvar* to the benefit for its own treasury (*sanduq*), so that the revenues of the difference of the sale of 66,000 *kharvar*s of grain that have been estimated for the food supply of the city of Tabriz will be more than 132,000 *tuman*s. After repayment of their loan the Service's needs have to be met by giving an allotment (*tafavvot*) of two *tuman*s per *kharvar* as a proper net profit.

This 66,000 *kharvar*s of grain is from the government taxes in kind and the grain surplus of landowners and villagers located at a distance of up to 16 *farsakh* from the city and from the villages whose cost of transport of grain from there to Tabriz does not exceed 8 *tuman*s per *kharvar* (e.g., via the railway and boat whose cost is lower than that of other means of transportation) and these quantities may be collected in case of proper management and supervision.

The location of the 66,000 *kharvars* of grain in summary will be as follows:

1. Government grain from villages at up to 16 *farsakh* from the city not transported by tax payers (*gheyr bar kardeh*)	10,000 *kharvar*s
Villages' grain transported by tax payers (*bar kardeh*) from up to 16 *farsakh* from the city	2,000
Total	12,000 **[25]**
2. Transported by tax payers (*bar kardeh*) from villages farther away than 16 *farsakh*	1,000
3. Grain not transported by tax payers (*gheyr bar kardeh*) from villages beyond 16 *farsakh*, but via the railway and boat; their cost should not exceed 8 *tumans*/*kharvar* (80 *qran*s)	2,000
4. Transportable Crown land revenue	3,000
5. Grain of peasants and landlords from above areas after deduction of seed and own food needs estimated at	48,000
Total	66,000 *kharvar*s

Because the above grain is gradually transported and delivered to the Granary, and the Granary office constantly will have outgoing deliveries for the daily needs of the city, the maximum [required] storage of the Granary may be estimated at 40,000 *kharvar*s. It is a basic requirement that the responsibility of the Alimentation Service is: the transport of the above quantity to the central Granary, the adoption of necessary steps for the performance of this task as well as the payment of all transport charges of the grain entered into the Granary to the order of the transporters.

The amount of money for the available grain in the province that the Alimentation Service will buy from the offices of Taxes and Crown lands, it has to pay to the two aforementioned offices, after sale, in accordance with the local price. The local price consists in the official price of grain at which the Alimentation Service buys it in the city of Tabriz and after deduction **[26]** of transportation cost that the abovementioned office pays directly to the transporters for the transport from the local place to the Granary. For the paid transportation cost for the Taxes and Crown land grain the Alimentation Service has to keep special records for the information of the two offices aforementioned (*edareteyn-e mazbureteyn*).

The transportation fees for the grain purchased from landowners and peasants and the price of the grain itself (in accordance with the official market rate) have to be paid in cash to the muleteers themselves.

The current government Granary has a capacity of not more than 8,000 *kharvar*s and when it happens that there is a difference between the stock and that capacity the government has no choice but to rent additional storage space. But as there is no special and sufficient storage space to warehouse grain in the city it is necessary to rent space in places such as cavaravanserais, large stables, etc., which from the point of view of storage of grain is not suitable. Because above the stock was estimated at most at 40,000 *kharvar*s it is to the advantage and interest of the Alimentation Service that it establishes new storage space for 30,000 *kharvar*s of grain.

The funds for these arrangements are estimated as follows:

If we assume the price of bread that will be sold to people at 2 *qran*s and 400 dinars per *man* and grain at 25 *tuman*s per *kharvar*, and if bread is assumed at 2 *qran*s per *man* then grain has to be sold at 20 *tuman*s to the bakers. [**27**] If the Alimentation Service buys the above at prices that are 2 *tuman*s lower per *kharvar* then the price of grain in Tabriz (including the transportation cost to Tabriz) has to be sold at the fixed price of 23 *tuman*s per *kharvar* or 18 *tuman*s. As the fixing of one of the two above prices is uncertain for the time being, we estimate these two prices on average at 20 *tuman*s per *kharvar*. As was mentioned above of the 66,000 *kharvar*s of grain the amount of stock in the Alimentation Service's Granary will be maximum 40,000 *kharvar*s, of which 18,000 *kharvar*s is grain from taxes and Crown land and its local price will be paid after sale, but the price of 28 *hazar* (28,000 dinars), which is left will be bought from various people and the Alimentation Service needs to have cash and the amount should not exceed:

1. 22,000 *kharvar*s x 20 *tuman*s	440,000 *tuman*s
2. Amount of transport cost	15,000 *kharvar*s not transported
by tax payers (*gheyr bar kardeh*) of tax and Crown land grain	90,000
3. Investment granary building for 32,000 *kharvar*s	44,000
4. Investment establishing Alimentation Service and extra staff for the transport of grain	46,000
Total amount of investment necessary	620,000 *tuman*s

Because for some time the establishment of the monopoly is in effect in the capital and under the direction of competent Belgian managers, it is clear that as until now great results have been achieved and have been realized based on experience and practice, [**28**] it is possible to initiate the same method in Azerbaijan and to develop a uniform law for the entire country. Of course, the Alimentation Service has established a suitable central organization with government, municipality, Taxation, Crown lands, and other related local offices and based on the internal regulations the manner of its organization and the limits of its authority. Therefore, this subject has no need for new opinions and the situation of its management structure is not included in the following description and it only provides basic information as to the matter of public food supply. Likewise, it is possible, after acquiring the necessary experience in accordance with the conditions of time and place and of some of the local peculiarities related to the Azerbaijani situation, that the above Service be given permission, with the approval of the authorities, to make part of the improvements and changes in the above regulations as needed.

Secondly. In case the government does not consider the arrangement of the monopoly of sale and purchase of grain necessary then it is possible to improve and carry out the organization and methods that are currently in operation. In this way one may also totally secure the city's food supply. However, in case of adoption of the second method not only will the government forego the benefit of important unrestricted income, nay, it has to spend a capital of 10 to 12,000 *tumans* per year to set up this organization.

The current system of the Alimentation Service comprises two fundamental objectives. [**29**]

One. The importance of collecting the necessary number of the means of transportation for government grain to the city so that by summertime when the delivery of grain to the city markets is lower than in normal times the government can sell to the bakers a quantity from its Granary that it considers necessary. In doing so, it prevents the price of grain from rising so that the business of the bakeries is not disrupted and the opportunity for hoarding by people does not arise.

Two. Supervision of the internal order and method of the city's bakeries so that there are always good and edible loafs of bread of one *man* at new weight in the shops so that it is sold to people at the correct weight and the official price.

Concerning the first part the quantity of grain that the government has to put in reserve is estimated to be as follows:

As in the first part of this Note the amount of total annual needs of this city has been estimated at 66,000 *kharvars*, of which 21,000 *kharvars* are for the consumption of home bakers and unofficial bakeries such as *lavash*, *kukeh*, and other bakers and for animal fodder; 45,000 *kharvar*s is for official bakeries (*sangak-pazi*). Until the end of Jadi (5th month) the bakers may obtain all their needs from outside the city and they have no need for government grain. But, every year, from Dalv [Bahman/Jan-February] until next year's harvest, i.e. in Asad (7th month) [Mordad/July-Aug] bakers for part of their daily baking requirements [**30**] have a need for government grain.

Their requirements in each of the seven above-mention months in normal years are as follows:

Dalv 600 *kharvar*s; Hut 900; Hamal 1,200; Thowr 1,800; Howza 1,800; Saratan 1,800; Asad 1,900, Total: 9,000 *kharvar*s.

In other words if the government in normal years reserves 9,000 *kharvar*s for the baking of *sangak* bakeries in the city it may always control the price of bread and nobody may interfere, but as was indicated, this estimate is for normal years and unless the bakers' need for government grain exceeds the amount and the season is stuck with whatever is that year's output, meaning, in the years that the output is good the baker's need for government grain is smaller and even begins later. In the contrary case, i.e. in a year when the output is abundant it is possible that the government having one-sixth, nay with one-eighth of the amount of baking output of all bakeries the Alimentation Service may act as it sees fit, but in case of shortage of the output by one-fourth, nay, even one-third the above quantity will be contracted at a loss. For the government to be successful in its objective it has to have collected the maximum of requirements of provisions for the city in the central Granary. The difference being only that in case of insufficient government reserves the bread question, nay the development of all [**31**] of the country's business will be endangered. In case there is extra grain in the Granary the government may always sell its grain at a level suitable with the official bread price to the bakers. The government will not suffer a loss in this way. In this manner improving the business and encouraging depends on that the government may at maximum store and stock the need for provisions in the Granary. Based on the above views, it is my opinion, that collecting and transporting a quantity of grain that the government with certainty and without paying attention to whatever annual output there is has to have in stock 15,000 *kharvar*s, i.e. equal to one-third of the annual baking [output] of the official city bakeries. In all this, one has to give importance to the two subjects below:

First. Ensure the storage of grain, so that, in case of need of stocking a quantity of grain of one year for the needs of the next year, grain is not lost and rotten.

Secondly. In sale to the bakers the observance of the above is not ignored so that before the crop arrives the stock of the Granary has not run out. This means that in years that grain is scarce and bakers consume extravagant amounts of government grain it has to prevent with necessary steps even by all means their irregular activities. In years of plenty when the bakers naturally are less interested to buy grain from government stock they have to be obliged by legal contracts to buy government grain, so that an enormous quantity does not remain year after year. [**32**]

Basically, it is proper to see to it that a quantity of grain that from one year to the other is stored does not cause problems in the spring of the following if that coincides with a drought or a bad harvest.

In summary, the first duty of the Alimentation Service consists in: collecting a quantity of 15,000 *kharvar*s of grain and to give sufficient importance to its storage and in its gradual consumption and have a good system for that. In addition, the internal rules and arrangements of the city's bread question have to be strictly observed and implemented.

As was mentioned above with most natural obstacles and especially shortage of means of transportation is the real motor of success in this work:

First. Try to maximally transport the amount of the city's grain.

Two. Reduce as much as possible the consumption of grain.

Third. Establishment of strong and serious supervision concerning the price and quantity of bread.

The maximum transport of the quantity of grain.

First. Depends on having sufficient funds for their transportation cost and,

Two. Having ready the means of conveyance and monitoring, thrift in the use of grain, as well as inspection of bakeries and mills depends on the good judgment in the manager's performance and honesty.

For the Alimentation Service to be successful in the performance of its objectives it is necessary to have the following authority:

1. The above-mentioned officer of the Alimentation Service has to comply with the circumstances of the moment [**33**] and with the decisions of the government, the office of the governor or of the Municipality or of the Taxation office. In that case, the Alimentation Service, taking into account the limits of the budget and the laws passed by the high authorities concerning the regulations of the internal affairs with regard to the different branches of its own office, must have total authority. The Alimentation Service will have to submit its own rules for information and approval in general to the above-mentioned authorities.

2. The Alimentation Service, in particular in related affairs, must have the right to correspond with all city and provincial authorities and offices and have direct contacts.

3. The high authorities have to strongly support the progress of the affairs of the Alimentation Service; there must be especially strong and real cooperation by the taxation office in the execution of its tasks concerning foodstuffs.

4. The country's employment law that has been submitted to the national council has to treat the article of the staff of the Alimentation Service just as other regular government officials.

5. The above-mentioned office has to be free and independent in the pursuance of all violators of its own regulations without paying attention to the authorities and accepting intermediation.

6. It has to have 6,000 *tuman*s in funds to set up the Alimentation Service's organization

7. One *tuman* per *kharvar* of the sale of grain to the bakers has to be allotted as funds for the Alimentation Service to be used for its own necessary activities and also a fund for starting and completing its own organization has to be put at its disposal. [**34**]

8. The Alimentation Service has to have the following sections:

1. Transport of grain and requisition of means of conveyance.

2. Bakeries.

3. Mills and Water, related to the water wheels.

4. Grocers and markets where the city's grain is delivered and sold.

9. It is necessary to have funds equal to 60,000 *tuman*s for the use of the expected transport costs of 15,000 *kharvar*s of grain, which should be transferred to the Alimentation Service.

10. The identification and determination of taxation and Crown land villages, whose government grain will be added to the above amount in cooperation with the office of taxation is one of the task of the Alimentation Service.

11. The Alimentation Service has to make use of the railway, boats, carts, camels and donkeys in identifying the most common means of transportation

12. Also, it is among the Alimentation Service's task to reduce the cost of transportation in cooperation with the provincial Taxation office.

13. The limits of the responsibilities of the taxation staff and agents concerning the establishment of transportation and transfer of grain has to be done in cooperation with the views of the Taxation office and established by the Alimentation Service.

14. The collection of taxes in grain is one of the special tasks of the fiscal agents. [**35**]

But concerning the share of grain that has to go to the city, the Alimentation Service has the responsibility to send special agents into the province for supervision and speeding up of its transportation.

15. The formation and establishment of local granaries in several places in the province is subject to the approval of the Alimentation Service.

16. The Alimentation Service must have the right to correspond and have direct relations with the fiscal agents and of the Crown lands in particular concerning transportation.

17. The Alimentation Service has to have a choice of a special representative either in the local granaries or in the center so that attention is paid to the speed of weighing grain and the peace of mind of the muleteers, to prevent the granary keepers from overcharging and lowering cost without basis, as well as from entering unclean grain into the granary grain and accepting bad instead of good grain. The doors of the granaries have to be sealed with wax seals by the keepers.

18. The Alimentation Service has to have the right in the case of need, especially have means of transportation such as carts, droshkies and camels.

19. It is necessary that the needed storages and warehouses exist with the capacity of 12,000 *kharvar*s of grain at new weight, the necessary storages and ware houses exist and because the current granaries cannot hold more than 8,000 *kharvar*s it is necessary to construct an additional granary of 4,000 *kharvar*s. [**36**]

20. In case the need of transport is more than 15,000 *kharvar*s of grain for the use of the army and others it is required to establish a local extra quantity with the agreement of the Taxation office and it will be one the special duties of the Alimentation Service to determine and select the names of the villages one by one.

21. Requests of the Alimentation Service concerning the security of the roads via which the city's grain is transported have to be given total attention and treated seriously by the provincial governor and other competent authorities.

22. All grain transported to the Granary without exception is allotted to the city's bakeries.

23. Part of the responsibilities of the Alimentation Service is the determination of the date that the sale of grain to the bakers will begin as well as the fixing of the sales price, which has to be in harmony with the official price of bread, and to be in cooperation with the views of the provincial authorities.

24. The relation of the price of bread to that of the market price of grain to the bakers has to be conform the written list on p. 17 of this Note (article 2)

25. Every effort should be made that apart from the provincial authorities, the Taxation office, and the Alimentation Service nobody else will have information about the existing stock in the government Granary.

26. The Alimentation Service has to have strict and complete supervision over the grain that different people bring into the city for sale so that they may prevent the hoarding by uncaring persons [**37**] and may establish the limits of the activities of the grocers and the places of the sale of in the various markets in the city.

27. The Alimentation Service has to have the right to establish government bakeries in an unlimited number.

28. The Alimentation Service needs to be given the authority to permit the sale of numerous pieces of official bread in line with the just and normal market price.

29. The Alimentation Service has to exercise strict supervision over the operation of the mills and the method of grain milling.

30. The rent and the lease of the mills between the millers and landowners has to be concluded with the knowledge of the Alimentation Service.

31. All the waters that are running to operate the mills have to be within the jurisdiction of the Alimentation Service.

32. The Alimentation Service has to have a sufficient quantity of flour in the government granary before unexpected troubles, problems and misfortunes occur, so that shortfalls in the needs of the bakers may be resolved.

33. The Alimentation Service has to have information on the specifics of steam mills and the authorities should not begrudge cooperation and assistance to realize useful projects.

Report of Bread

Referring to my telegram no. 14, sent May 21st, I respectfully submit the following report.

The data as submitted has been obtained from the available records in this office but the greater portion has been secured from the individual reports collected from time to time by an employee who has been in close touch with the bread situation.

From the facts it appears that the question of BREAD has always been and is, at present, a very important factor in the life of Tabriz. It plays a very large role in the political and economic history of the city and is closely allied with the interests of the Government.

The past records of Tabriz show that the riots and coups d'Etat have been started first with the question of bread, this matter being a pretext in the hands of unprincipled elements for exciting the common people, usually resulting in acts of violence, all for the benefit of such unscrupulous persons.

The authorities too have abused the bread question in the same way in order to gain popularity or to attack their personal or political adversaries, all losses resulting from these struggles being for the account of the Government. The records of the Finances show losses to the Government from fifty to one hundred thousand tomans on the price of State grains (taxes in kind transported to city), in the sales at reduced prices, to enable the bakers to sell the bread at a lower price than the current day price of the market. In the famine years the loss reached the astounding figure of five hundred thousand tomans.

According to the fundamental law of the country, the Alimentation Service, to be lawful, must be under control of the Municipality. In the past years, however, it has necessarily been, according to the exigencies, sometimes under Finance, sometimes under Municipality (as it is now) and sometimes independent, having for superior authority, the Governor General.

It consists at present of the following branches:

1. Transport of a sufficient quantity of Government grain (taxes in kind) to the city, to avoid any shortage during the winter when the roads are impassable on account of snow or other adverse weather conditions, or should there be a conspiracy to try and 'corner' the supply and thus control the market price.
2. Control of the bakers to oblige them to always have good bread in abundance and to sell it to the people of the city, in all walks of life, without any shortage in weight and at the same official price to all.

To give an idea of the importance of the task the following facts are enumerated:

i. Tabriz has a population of about 170,000
ii. The yearly consumption is about 66,000 *kharvars* 100 batman of 1000 *mesqals* of grain – 48,000 wheat and 18,000 barley.

3. From the total consumption ¾ is baked in market bakeries and about ¼ in the homes.
4. The quantity of grain deemed necessary to be stored by the Government in normal times is 9,000 to 15,000 kharvars, i.e. about 1/7 to 2/9 of the total consumption of the city and is subordinated to the relative productiviness of the harvest. As much as the harvest is good so much the needs of the bakers for Government grain is small.
5. The taxation in kind in Azerbaidjan accounts, according to the tax rolls, to about 51,500 *kharvars*, excluding the taxation of Public Domains [Crown lands]. From this amount during the past year, It-il, only about 26,000 *kharvars* were considered recoverable and 17,700 transportable (as to the distance to the city) to the grain storehouse of Tabriz. The rent in kind of State Domains [Crown lands] was about 7,000 *kharvars* giving a total of 33,000 *kharvars* recoverable and from which 16,000 *kharvars* (maximum) transportable Government grain to the city.

6. The tax payers were, until last year, allowed in giving their taxes in kind, to have 1/16 of the quantity of grain delivered (or 6.25 *batman* in each 100 batman) as impurities. Since last year this privilege has been reduced to 5% by the order of the Minister of Finances.
7. The taxation in kind consists of 2/3 wheat and 1/3 barley, the mixture is called '*ghalla.*'
8. In the market the weight is expressed in *kharvars* of 106.25 *batmans*, principally the 6.25 *batmans* to be considered impurities.
9. From the quantity mentioned in Art. 3, 3,000 *kharvars* are recoverable taxes in kind, payable f.o.b. Tabriz.
10. The transportation of the balance, i.e. 6,000 to 12,000 *kharvars*, can be collected from taxation in kind from villages situated at 6 to 16 *farsacks* from the city. Approximately within circles, measured by every *farsack* distance from the city, 750 *kharvars* of transportable taxation grain is collected.
11. The transport of 6,000 to 12,000 *kharvars* necessitates respectively 20,000 to 60,000 tomans.
12. The usual method of transportation is by the caravans of donkeys and camels. As a rule every *kharvar* of 100 *batmans* of 1,000 mescals is carried by 7 to 8 donkeys or 3 camels. Only the grain of the districts traversed by the railway is transported by the railroad. About 2,500 *kharvars* is carried by the railroad, 2,000 by camels and the balance of government grain on donkeys. Statistics show that every year about 60,000 camels enter the city of Tabriz. Notwithstanding this fact that they are always under requisition and it is declared to be a law that every camel driver is obliged, after each trip of general merchandise, to then transport Government grain, about 60% of camels are diverted from the grain transportation and instead of 30,000 camels the government profits usually from 6,000 to 7,000. This diversion of the camels in the past was due to bribes offered by the drivers to dishonest Alimentation Chiefs.
13. As a rule the Government receives a reduction in the transport of about 30% to 50% of the current rate charged by the railroad. This also applies to the camels and donkeys,

hence the camel drivers did not wish to transport Government grain when they could carry general merchandise. The average rate of transport during the past years has been, for the Government grain, 5 *krans* per *kharvar* per *farsack*.

14. The storage capacity of the warehouses in Tabriz is for 8,000 *kharvars* and in cases where more storage is required additional caravanserays are rented for temporary storage. These are not suitable for grain storage as they leak from the rains or snows such dampness causing the grain to spoil.

15. Usually the need of the bakers for Government grain begins with the month of Dalve [February-March] and progresses, in the case where the needs are in the limit of 9,000 *kharvars* as follows: *Dalve* 600, *Hut* 900, *Hamal* 1,200, *Sour* 1,800, *Jowza* 1,800, *Saratan* 1,800, Assad 900, total 9,000 *kharvars*.

16. The number of bakeries in Tabriz is about 120, of which 95 are official ('*sangag*') and 35 semi-official ('lavash' and '*kuka*'). The shops of '*sangag*' are considered official, because they are connected only with the Government warehouses for the purchase of grain. The semi-official bakeries are simply controlled by the Alimentation Service. All the bread shops are paying license to the Alimentation Service.

17. Every official shop, to be able to cover its expenses, must bake a minimum of 140 *kharvars* of grain daily, including impurities and every batman of flour produces an increase of 50%. Hence every baker bakes 140 – 7 (impurities) or 133 *batmans* plus 50% (increase) or 199.5 or about 200 *batmans* of bread. The 133 *batmans* of flour are divided into 24 portions bearing the expression of '*parcheh.*'

18. The proportion of mixture of the bread baked is ¾ wheat and ¼ barley.

19. The grinding and baking expenses of every *kharvar* of grain now amounts to 75 *krans*.

20. The proportion between the price of grain and bread must be as follows, considering i. the *kharvar* of 100 *batmans* of 1000 mescals; ii. the impurity of grain 5%; iii. the quantity sold to the bakers being '*ghalla*' (i.e. 2/3 wheat and 1/3 barley);

iv. the bread to be baked to be at the rate of ¾ wheat and ¼ barley; v. securing a reasonable profit for the bakery.

In Krans	Price of one *batman* of *Ghalla*	Price of one *batman* of bread
	1.50	1.60
	2.0	2.00
	2.50	2.40
	3.10	2.80
	3.60	3.20
	4.20	3.60
	4.80	4.00

21. No steam driven or oil burning mills are now operating in Tabriz and the number of water driven mills is about 150.

Considering the above mentioned facts I deem it possible to settle definitely, once and forever, and very easily the bread question of Tabriz and obtain the following advantageous results;

i. Provide a plentiful supply of bread for 175,000 people.
ii. Secure a peaceful life in the city, avoiding trouble, riots, coup d'Etat which have a demoralizing effect on the civic progress of Tabriz.
iii. Avoid financial losses to the Government.
iv. Putting an end to the questionable acts and abuses of dishonest Chiefs of Alimentation all of which has been a charge on the people.
v. Securing the interests of all classes of people (city population, peasants, taxpayers etc.) by the maintenance of a reasonable and stable price of bread.
vi. Enable the Government to combine the grains and needs of good and bad years as to the amount of harvest and avoid famines or at least to facilitate the control of many difficulties occurring in dry and famine years.

There are two ways for the realisation of this project.

1. A monopoly of the Government for the purchase and sale of all grains. This principle will enable the government to realize a net income of about 60,000 tomans yearly if the

> grain is sold at an average increase of 2 tomans a kharvar over the cost price. This will not at all be a burden on the people considering the important fluctuations which have occurred in the past and are still occurring in the price of bread.

This matter has been studied carefully and the plan seems feasible the only difficulty is the amount of capital necessary to be advanced (loaned) in starting the work. This amount is estimated to be about 640,000 tomans, summarized as follows:

1. Price of 22,000 *kharvars*, permanent balance of grain to be purchased from private parties, average price 20 *tomans* per *kharvar*:	440,000
(Note; The permanent balance of the warehouse, considering the continual in and out movement, is estimated 40,000 *kharvars* of which 18,000 *kharvars* is the Government Transportable grain that the price can be paid after the selling)	
2. Construction of permanent grain warehouses in Tabriz – always an asset	50,000
3. Transportation from the villages	100,000
4. Administrative expenses	50,000
Grand total:	640,000

As I understand the monopoly system is now in force in Teheran so you will be in a position to judge the possibility of the adoption of this scheme for Tabriz, from the present workings in Teheran.

2. The other way to handle this question is not less efficient way, only it will deprive the Government from an important income and will require also an allotment of a credit of about 10,000 tomans yearly. This however is not so important considering the advantages that the final settlement of the bread question offers to the Government and the people of Tabriz.

This way consists in the amelioration and perfection of the existing regulations in Alimentation Service giving them a force of law.

The principal task of this service is, as I mentioned in the above report is:

1. Transportation of a sufficient quantity of Government grain to the city to avoid any shortage during the adverse weather conditions or should there be a conspiracy to 'corner' the supply and thus control the price.
2. Control of bakeries in order to force them to always have an abundant supply of bread on hand and to sell to the people without shortage in weight and at an official price to all.

   As to the first above, as I mentioned in Art. 4, the requirements of the official bakeries for Government grain is a minimum of 9,000 kharvars and a maximum of 15,000 kharvars, running in proportion of periods mentioned in Art 15. But in case of the adoption of the minimum quantity the Government runs the risk of danger, when harvest is bad, and, on the contrary, in case of adoption of the maximum, there is no risk of loss for the Government on account of an abnormal decrease in price considering that according to Art. 20 the Government can always oblige the bakers to buy the Government grain at the proportionate prices, stipulated in that article between the grain and the bread and then determination of the price is really in the hands of the Government, consequently the effort of the Alimentation Service considering the lack of transport and the bad roads so the difficulties which are connected with the transport of the necessary quantity must be, for the success and good progress of the work the realisation of the following principles:

1. To transport the maximum quantity of government grain to city
2. To use the strict minimum quantity so far as the bad prospect of the new harvest is concerned.

And as to the second of the above the success in control of the bakers depends simply in the honesty and integrity of the Chief.

Up to the present time the obstacles as to realisation of these principles were as follows:

1. Lack of lawful administrative regulations.

2. Lack of available funds necessary for the transport of grain which has paralyzed the effects of the efforts of the Chief.
3. Delay in the regular payment of the salaries of the employees on account of the lack of funds.
4. And principally the lack of permanent and regular personnel and arbitrary changes in the Chiefs of personnel usually connected with reasons of personal character. This circumstance has had a very bad influence on the morale of the personnel, because the Chief and his assistants considered themselves always temporary objects to be dismissed at any time by superior authority without the right of protest and without the hope of securing other employment, so considered they had the right to 'provide for the future' in every possible way.

And if the natural character of the Chiefs of service and of their acolytes, mostly obscure, and also the extremely large chances of shortage that gives them this administration are considered it will not be at all surprising to see that the bread question has always been the source of fabulous shortages for dishonest Chiefs and always of permanent danger to the civic progress of the city of Tabriz.

To give an idea of the chances of shortage I mention here that the quantity of daily consumption from the official bakeries is 200 *kharvars* of bread or about 73,000 *kharvars* per year; the number of camels entering the city is about 60,000 every year. In cases of conspiracy with the bakers and camel drivers every single *shai* [sic' *shahi*] of shortage per batman of bread and every single toman for every diverted camel will provide the Chief with enormous amounts. And it goes without saying that every *shai* of shortage costs ten times more in sending the Alimentation Service from bad to worse.

It is by favor of this superficial and defective condition of the service that almost every year there is a crisis in bread question and the responsible authorities in the critical moments try and find advisers to help them and to share with them in the appointment of commissions of irresponsible or personally interested undesirables and in the end create panics among the people.

To repair all of these effects and to avoid difficulties in the future the following steps should be taken:

1. To place all of the Alimentation Service under the absolute control of the Finance Administration considering that [it] is closely connected with the Finances for example – Use of Government taxation grain, its collection and transport, the payment of transportation expenses, the care of conservation of the grain in the warehouses in the city of Tabriz and in the Province, etc. etc.
2. To give to the personnel a permanent and official character and to give this branch all the rights of the personnel of other civil administrations by placing them under the Civil Service rules and subject to the regulations of that law.
3. To choose a Chief who will properly carry out the orders deemed necessary by the Finance Administration.
4. An available credit of 60,000 tomans for the transport of grain; an extra credit of 15,000 tomans yearly for administrative expenses, including the income of the [Alimentation] Service which not aggregates 6,000 tomans annually.
5. An allotment of a credit of 6,000 tomans for the construction of a supplementary warehouse for about 4,000 *kharvars* of grain.
6. To place following under the Department of Alimentation under the supervision of the Finance Administration, the following sections:

    a. Requisition of means of transport.

    b. Bakers.

    c. Mills and settlement of the litigation of the waters they use for grinding.

    d. Public place for selling of grain in the city and the right of full control.

7. Certain powers to the Chief of Service as to the changes and permutations in the personnel, the choice of the villages from where the government grain must be transported, decision as to

best means of transport deemed profitable and suitable and in each case fix the rate cost of such transport, fixation of the period of grain to be sold to the bakers with the previous accordance and approval of the Finances, creation of official government bakeries and different kinds of bread to be baked with the different prices, sanitary control of all bakeries with right to fine or close if not up to Government standard, control of good progress of the transportation and the conditions of warehouses, preparation of sufficient supply of flour for the eventual needs in bad weather when some of the water mills cannot run, etc. etc.

8. All grains transported to the warehouses to be sold only to the official bakeries.
9. A system to be arranged so as to keep secret the amount of grain on hand in the warehouses.

Considering the above rights conferred to the Chief of Alimentation Service he must assume with the supervision of the Provincial Director of Finances, who reports to the Administrator General of Finances and the Finance Ministry, the responsibility of the whole bread question of Tabriz.

The three following points must be the object of the principal attention and care of the Chief of the Service:

1. To provide the people of the city with good and an abundant supply of bread during all the year and at a minimum price having always in mind at the sae time the interests of the proprietors and the peasants, i.e. to avoid abnormal decrease in price.
2. To try to increase lawfully the incomes of the administration to a maximum and to decrease the expenses to a minimum.
3. To use all vigilance and energy in watching the acts of the employees and all persons under his control for the best progress of the work.

At the same time, the Chief of Alimentation must study and elaborate a complete instruction for the special use of different sections comprising his Department which will be put in force after the approval by the proper authorities. He must always have in mind the perfectioning of the organization of his Department profiting from the experience acquired from time to time as the work progresses.

The Department of Alimentation must have its special bookkeeping in complete and full order. The expenses must not exceed the limit of the budget approved by the proper authorities. The monthly accounts must be sent to the Provincial Director of Finances for examination and approval to obtain a full discharge and subject at all times to audit and examination by the Finance Department.

Respectfully submitted
[signature]
Provincial Director of Finances.

Tabriz, July 10, 1923.

[in hand writing] This copy for Mr. Jumal [sic: Jamal] with many thanks for his valuable assistance which rendered it possible to prepare this report.

Edmund H. Jones
Provincial Director of Finances
Tabriz, July 10, 1923

This report shows that although the Alimentation Service was still part of the Municipality of Tabriz, it was not a regular and permanent part of the provincial administration, while its funding and operating rules were insufficient, incidental, and casual. There was no formal relationship with other provincial departments that dealt with the supply of grain (Taxation, Crown lands, etc.), while there was no forward planning to prevent food shortages. In short, the Tabriz Alimentation

Service at best reacted to food problems that arose, with uncertain funding and support, with a disinterested and inexperienced staff. It still had not overcome the cultural ills of Iranian society that still asserted themselves and tried to undercut effective government food policy and its implementation for personal gain. Therefore, it is not surprising that both Jamal and Jones insisted that the Alimentation Service be put on a permanent legal footing, with proper funding and objectives, dedicated staff, and rules and procedures to be followed and respected for its activities and relations with other government agencies. Unfortunately, I have been unable to find further information on the activities of the Alimentation Service in Tabriz in the years thereafter.

CHAPTER FIVE

THE SITUATION IN TEHRAN, 1922-1935

When the American Arthur Millspaugh took over the management of Iran's finances as Administrator-General on 18 November 1922, he found the Alimentation Service was working at a loss. Nevertheless, he recognized the importance of government's interference with the price and quality of life necessities in the city, as "the conduct of the Alimentation Service is not merely a symbol of governmental efficiency, but also an indication of the political attitude of a government toward the people."[1] In April 1923, he put Col. Charles McCormack in charge of the offices of Direct Taxes, Crown lands, Alimentation (*edareh-ye arzaq-e `omumi*), and the Taxes of Tehran. Furthermore, Millspaugh had Edmund Jones look into the food supply problems of Tabriz. Mirza Eshaq Khan was the manager (*modir*) of the Alimentation Service during April 1922-23 until McCormack took over. Mohammad Taher Khan Sartip was chief of the Tehran Granary. As both remained

1. Millspaugh 1925, p. 78; Idem, 1926, p. 25; Sheean 1927, p. 129.

in function, this enabled a smooth transfer to McCormack as chief of in Tehran in April 1923.[2]

Fortunately for McCormack, 1301/1922-23 was a normal year and there were no major food supply problems for Tehran. However, that totally changed in 1302/1923-24, when at the beginning of 1302/ March 1923, the amount of grain in stock only sufficed 1-2 days' of consumption, while it was still two months until the harvest. The Alimentation Service was forced to ask the Ministry of War to consume barley from its own reserves rather taking barley from the government Granary. Also, barley that was reserved for the muleteers was given to the bakers. At the time of harvest Tehran's bread situation was in crisis mode and famine threatened.[3]

This bread crisis was due to a combination of factors. The harvest was one month late due to a plague of *senn* (Varamin) and locusts (Damavand), rust (*zank*), storms, violent winds and floods that had reduced the amount of grain harvested and as well as it quality.[4] What made matters worse was that there was an unexpected loss of grain in the Tehran Granary. Apparently, proper management had been neglected and preventive measures against insects (*sheshpesh*) had not been taken, which caused the loss of 15% of 9,000 *kharvar*s of grain. The granary director has asked permission to remove 5,000 *kharvar*s of wheat that had tare (*talkheh*),[5] but this was refused. He resubmitted his request after the arrival of the Millspaugh team, who

2. On 30 Hamal 1302/20 April 1923, McCormack assumed his new function and combined the offices of direct taxes and Crown lands into one service and those of Alimentation and the taxes of Tehran into another one. Government of Iran 1302 a, p. 19; Government of Iran 1302 b, p. 58.

3. Government of Iran 1302 b, p. 58; Government of Iran 1303 a, p. 51.

4. Government of Iran 1302 c, pp. 116-17; Government of Iran 1303 a, p. 52.

5. *Talkheh* is tare or darnel (*Lolium temulentum*) a weed that grows among grain, especially wheat. It is difficult to distinguish its grain from that of wheat and to separate them by sifting. Because of its bitterness (*talkh*) it gave bread baked from flour that had been mixed with tare an unpleasant taste.

approved his proposal. However, by that time the quantity of good wheat was much reduced and most of the bad wheat had to be used to make flour. As a result, the quality of bread was bad and consumers were not pleased. The major landowners of Khamseh wanted to take advantage of the situation; they asked for a higher price for their grain and for the dismissal of the Alimentation Service staff in their area. To avoid that their grain might be confiscated they emptied their warehouses by transporting it to other provinces, where they sold it at high prices, and distributing the unsold part among their peasants. Through intermediaries they informed the Alimentation Service that they were willing to sell grain at a price of 1 or 2 *tuman*s higher than agreed upon. McCormack refused as it would be illegal, because the landowners had agreed to and already sold grain at the lower price. The main culprits were As`ad al-Dowleh[6] and Amir Afshar, each of whom had agreed to sell at least 2,000 *kharvar*s to the government. However, As`ad al-Dowleh only delivered 600 *kharvar*s and Amir Afshar 1,000 *kharvar*s, but did not honor their promise to sell more. As a result, more than half of the grain of Khamseh went to Qazvin and only one-eighth to Tehran, for of the 4,000 *kharvar*s that had been counted on only 500 *kharvar*s came to the capital. The matter was brought to the attention of the authorities and the Minister of War, who issued the necessary orders to collect grain from the landowners. However, by that time their warehouses were empty, and they expressed their regret to be unable to execute the government's orders. Other problems worsened this situation; the harvest was one month later than normal, the incomplete collection of the preceding year's taxes in kind (grain) and the improper fixing of the conversion rate (*tas`ir*) of some of the grain. Gradually good wheat became scarce in the Tehran Granary and the Alimentation Service was forced to mix it with bitter (*talkhehdar*) wheat as well as with 1% of barley.[7] With this grain mix the bakers made *taftun* bread and sold it at low

6. Probably, Hoseyn Qoli Sardar Zanjani As`ad al-Dowleh, a major landowner (d. 1947). Mojtahedi 1327, p. 190; see also Varjavand 1349, vol. 3, pp. 2249.

7. Government of Iran 1302 a, pp. 28-30.

price. Despite all this the quality of bread for Tehran's consumers was considered satisfactory. Nevertheless, only at the last moment famine was prevented. On 1 Saratan 1302/22 June 1923 there was not one *kharvar* of grain in stock so that the Alimentation Service was forced to borrow 54 *kharvar*s to be able to deliver the daily supply to the bakers.[8] Fortunately, one or two days later the bread crisis came to an end. Grain from the new harvest from other provinces came available and the quality of bread improved and was kept at this level for the remainder of the year. To minimize the chance of a recurrence of the *senn* plague in Varamin and the other Tehran districts an area of 250,000 *zar* in the Qarah Aghaj Mountains was burnt.[9]

On 2 July 1923, Eyn al-Saltaneh noted that the quality of bread had been bad for some time, which he ascribed to the activities of the Alimentation Service, from which office Mirza Eshaq Khan the Babi had been removed.[10] On 21 Asad 1302/13 August 1923, Modir al-Molk was appointed deputy-manager (*mo`aven*) of the Alimentation Service. His first act was to develop a food supply program that was in line with the estimated average consumption of the preceding period. He then speeded up operating procedures at the granary. As a result, per 1 Saratan/22 June 1923 this year 43,409 *kharvar*s of wheat and 10,160 *kharvar*s of barley were entered into the granary. On 21 Sonboleh/13 September 1923 there were 31,265 *kharvar*s in the Granary and each day 400 to 400 *kharvar*s are added to it. The purchase of grain was much easier than in 1922, so that in the last quarter of 1923 the food supply situation gradually improved. Table 5.1 shows how much grain was bought from provinces outside of Tehran, how much grain was still available for sale in these provinces and what the estimated

8. Government of Iran 1303 a, p. 52.
9. Government of Iran 1302 a, pp. 30-31, 34; Government of Iran 1302 c, p. 117.
10. Eyn al-Saltaneh 1376, vol. 8, p. 6640, who seems to have been mistaken as in December 1923, Mirza Eshaq Khan is mentioned as still working for the Alimentation Service. Government of Iran 1302 c, p. 116.

available taxes in kind were in Tehran and the provinces from which it obtained its grain.

Table 5.1: Grain bought, available for sale, and available as tax in kind in September 1923 (in *kharvars*)

From	Purchased	Available for sale	Estimated tax in grain available
Tehran and its environing districts	-	20,000	11,000
Barbarud, Khomeyn, Chaplaq, Komreh	7,200	2,000	2,000
Araq	2,000	4,000	7,200
Khamseh	5,800	3,000	3,700
Shahrud	1,595	2,000	1,300
Damghan/Semnan	-	1,000	900
Malayer	-	-	1,000
Qazvin	-	-	4,000
Total	16,595	32,000	31,100

Source: Government of Iran 1302 b, pp. 59-60.

On 22 September 1923, 123,000 *kharvars* of grain were available, while the annual wheat consumption of Tehran was estimated to be 110 to 120,000 *kharvars*. This meant that a grain shortage or a rush to hoarding might not happen.

Table 5.2: Grain situation in September 1923:

Entered into the granary per 1 Sonboleh 1302/22 August 1923	43,409 *kharvar*
Purchased until now (22 September 1923)	16,595
Still available for purchase	32,000
Tax in kind that may be collected	31,100
Total	123,104 *kharvar*

Source: Government of Iran 1302 b, p. 62.

Despite the optimistic outlook as to the quantity of available grain to secure Tehran's demand transport remained a serious problem and therefore, required special attention. In fact, the Alimentation Service staff was ordered to develop good relations with transporters, which had positive effect in view of availability of animals and carts (*`arabeh*) during 1 Saratan/22 June to 25 Sonboleh/17 September 1923:

Table 5.3: Availability of pack animals and carts during Saratan-Sonboleh 1302/ June-September 1923

Month	Camel, mule, donkey	Cart
Saratan 1302/June-July 1923	4,489 head	-
Asad 1302/July-August 1923	9,630	402
Till 25 Sonboleh 1302/17 September	13,867	306
Total	27,867	708

Source: Government of Iran 1302 b, p. 62.

To improve relations with the bakers of Tehran, the Bakery's Office (*sho`beh-ye khabbaz-khaneh*) was transferred to the government Granary and placed under the Granary chief. This was welcomed by both the government and the bakers. This move was more to placate the bakers than that there was a change in policy, prices or procedures. The change was made because the bakers had repeatedly complained about the working of the Bakery's office. However, after investigation it appeared that the losses that the bakers claimed they suffered were in fact profits. As a result, the Alimentation Service several times proposed the complaining bakers who suffered a loss to hand over their bakery to the government, which would easily earn 15 *qran*s each day. Not one baker accepted the proposal, while the chiefs of the bakers' guild even tried to get permission to open additional bakeries. Apart from the loss-profit issue bakers also had complained about the imposition of an illegal tax of 5 *qran*s per day, which was discontinued. Despite the temporary price reduction and abolishment of the illegal fee, expenditures during the first 6 months of 1302 compared with 1301 showed an economy of 36,091 *tuman*s.

Apparently control of the flour mills had been relaxed, because the Alimentation Service reported that it had established supervision over the millers, who had allowed all kinds of dirt into the flour. Also, better control was established over the bakeries. Such a step was really necessary, because in June the quality of wheat was not very good (grain from the new harvest was not yet available) and, therefore, the Alimentation Service gave the bakers a temporary price reduction of 1 *tuman* per *kharvar*. When the grain quality was good again some bakers tried to have the temporary reduction made permanent, but this was rejected and the grain price remained the same at 23 *tuman*s per *kharvar*. Nevertheless that did not stop bakers to constantly pressure the government without good justification to raise the bread price. What did rise was the quality of bread, because not only more grain entered the city and grain stocks increased, but also because the grain from Arak, Shahrud and other provinces was much better than that of Tehran that had suffered from pests.[11]

The better quality of bread by June 1923 was not only because of the better flour available to bakers, but also because McCormack had fired staff of the Bakery Office (*sho`beh-ye khabbazi*), which was in charge of government bakeries, that had underperformed, while those bakers who had stolen money were handed over to the police.[12] Not only the proper performance of the staff of the bakery office improved the quality of the flour, but so did the better sifting of the grain. It had been found that after grinding the grain still was not completely clean. Moreover, because dirt had been mixed with the grain some of it had to be rejected. Some bakers took advantage of this situation and raised the price of bread in Tehran excessively. Modir al-Molk, who was the deputy-chief of the Alimentation Service as well as his successor Mirza Eshaq Khan and Mohammad Taher Khan Sartip, who was director of Granary, effectively addressed this problem. Their investigation found that grain was mixed with pebbles and the like, which the sifting equipment was unable to remove. Therefore, a group of poor village women, who lived near the Granary, were hired

11. Government of Iran 1302 b, pp. 58-64.

12. Government of Iran 1302 a, p. 34.

to clean the grain prior to sifting. This was a win-win situation, for the result was that the grain became cleaner, poor women received an income, and bakers received flour without contamination. Also, henceforth the sifters were paid daily. Another step taken also had a beneficial impact on the quality of the grain. Until then, the sifting in local granaries was done in the open air. This meant that the grain to be sifted was exposed to the harsh sun in summer and to snow and rain in winter. The result was that not much attention was paid to the quality of the final product. As of June 1923 steps were taken to ensure that all sifting was done under a roof, so that the whole operation was protected against outside elements.[13]

To make bakers more accountable and facilitate control, in 1923, and perhaps earlier, bakers had to sign an agreement with the Alimentation Service. In this agreement the baker, who was identified by name and location, undertook to bake unadulterated bread with the flour or grain that he received from the state granary, within a period of 24 hours, and to sell the bread at the weight (four loaves of *sangak* bread were about 3 kg) and at a price fixed by the government. He further undertook not to close his shop without permission and not to sell bread to ambulant sellers (*nan-forushan-e dowreh-gard*).[14] Despite the new rules, they still retained "unsanitary methods and an age-old reputation for skull-duggery."[15]

By December 1923, the Alimentation Service was very positive about next year's food situation in Tehran. The harvest had been good, while there were 40,000 *kharvar*s in the Granary. In fact, Millspaugh reported that since the creation of the Alimentation Service never before so much grain had been in stock. At the end of Oqrab/November there were 73,246 *kharvar*s of wheat in Tehran and districts, when in the previous year it had been 43,132 or 30,114 *kharvar*s more. With the surplus of barley from the previous year in stock and the sufficient amount of wheat from 1923 the intake of barley into the Tehran granary

13. Government of Iran1302 c, pp. 115-18.

14. Rowghani 1385, pp. 41-43.

15. Millspaugh 1926, p. 103.

was stopped. In fact, the Alimentation Service decided to diminish its stock of barley in Tehran and districts to 12,400 *kharvars*, which was 5,400 *kharvars* less than the stock in the preceding year. To stimulate its sale the price of barley was lowered.

The Bakery Office was not the only division of the Alimentation Service, but so was the Transportation Office (*sho`beh haml va naql*), whose work was essential to the Service's success. In fact, Millspaugh was very pleased about its excellent performance. From 1 Saratan/ July 1922 until 9 Qaws/1 December 1922 and again during the same period in 1923 it transported the following amounts of grain to the Tehran districts:

Table 5.4: Number of means of transport used to carry grain to Tehran (July-December 1923-23)

Means of conveyance	1301	1302	Increase
Camels	50,141	60,147	10,006
Other means of transport	415	1,488	2,073
Total increase			11,079

Source: Government of Iran 1302 c, p. 118.

As a result of the good harvest and the steps taken by the Alimentation Service grain in stock in Tehran and its environs increased considerably between on 1 Qaws/22 November 1922 and 1923:

Table 5.5: Changes in grain in stock between 1301 and 1302

In *kharvars*	1301	1302	Increase	Decrease
Wheat Tehran	33,082	38,827	5,745	-
Wheat in districts	10,050	34,419	24,369	-
Subtotal	43,132	73,246	30.114	-
Wheat in Tehran and provinces	17,824	12,408	-	5,416
Total grain	60,956	85,654	24,698	-

Source: Government of Iran 1302 c, p. 119.

Apart from these amounts available at 1 Qaws/22 November 1923 the Alimentation Service also bought another 1,000 *kharvars* of grain. Thus, in December 1923, Tehran had a stock of 40,000 *kharvars* and therefore, there was no fear of a bread crisis. In fact, if there would be no delay in next year's harvest then there was enough grain for two months' consumption.[16]

In Hut 1302/March 1924, there were 39,296 *kharvars* of wheat in the Granary and with the grain stock in the district granaries there were 57,398 *kharvars* available or 114% more than in Hut 1301/March 1923. Because there was a surfeit of grain in the market barley did not sell and thus permission was given to sell 10,146 *kharvars* of barley in stock, leaving some 3,687 *kharvars*. Because of adverse weather conditions (hail, storm, rust) the quality of grain was not good. After a few months, to ensure the quality of bread, 5,000 *kharvars* of the affected wheat was mixed with good wheat resulting in bitter tasting bread. This grain mixture was sold at 10 *tumans* per *kharvar* to *lavashi* bakers. A committee that the bakers had chosen submitted that with such bad wheat they were unable to make a proper living and therefore, they were given a discount of one *tuman* per *kharvar* until the next harvest. The more so since the danger of drought, as had existed in the preceding year, was absent. Better flour was produced when special attention was paid when the grain was milled. From this flour *taftun* bread was made at a fixed price of 6 *shahis* per *man* and made a special kind of cheap and good quality bread available to the poor.[17]

The purchase and transport of wheat depended on the funds and means of transportation available to the Alimentation Service, which from 1919 to 1928 was in the form of a credit from the Imperial Bank of Persia (see Appendix I). In practice there was always a delay in the purchase of grain, because it was mostly bought when winter approached (with its blocked roads), or in spring (when camels needed to graze), which resulted in more delays in transport. In 1924, to resolve this problem, the Alimentation Service decided to buy as

16. Government of Iran 1302 c, pp. 118-19.

17. Government of Iran 1302 d, pp. 69-70 and Table 22.

much grain possible outside Tehran province right after the harvest without wasting time and to transport it before the severity of winter time would create problems. The main problem of buying grain in 2-3 months' time was the lack of funds, therefore the Alimentation Service asked the Imperial Bank of Persia for a credit of 1 million *tumans*. On 1 Hamal 1303/21 March 1924, with these funds 25,875 *kharvars* of wheat was bought, a quantity exceeding the stock in the Granary on that date. Thus famine was prevented. But it was not enough to have enough grain till the next harvest of 1303, but it was also necessary to prevent the occurrence of famine in the future by having a sufficient reserve stock. Therefore, the Alimentation Service decided to buy an additional amount of 20,000 *kharvars* of grain before the harvest of 1303. The *omana-e maliyeh* were ordered to spare no means to buy and transport this amount of grain. As a result, on 1 Saratan 1303/22 June 1924 instead of 20,000 *kharvars* there were 33,979 *kharvars* in the government Granary, which was quite a difference with the situation one year earlier (see above). The Alimentation Service might even have gathered a stock of 45,000 *kharvars* or about 40% of annual consumption, if there had been additional funds. This reserve stock had to be maintained until such time that the problem of quickly transporting grain from Kermanshah, Isfahan, and Sistan had been resolved.[18]

The Alimentation Service felt that in 1924 it had prevented famine in Tehran, because in March 1924, only 23,101 *kharvars* were available in the granary. In fact, the Alimentation Service had not more than 3,941 *kharvars* in stock representing 13 days of Tehran's consumption (see Table 5.6). Deliveries to the Granary were also down (see above). From 1 Hamal/20 March to 30 Qaws 1303/22 December 1924 there was were the following increases in both stock and entries into the Granary: taxes in kind from Tehran province were up by: 3,639 *kharvars* and from Crown lands by 11,819 *kharvars*; purchased grain

18. Government of Iran 1303 a, pp. 51-52. People in Qazvin complained that wheat was bought at 14 *tumans* and sold to bakers at 15 *tumans*, so that good bread sold at 1 *qran* and 8 *shahis* per *man*. This lasted till the harvest of 1303/1924.

by 23,501 *kharvars* or a total increase of 38,951 *kharvars* (see Table 5.7). In December 1924 there were only 23,101 *kharvars* of grain in the Granary, which meant that there was a shortfall of 35% in Tehran's food supply and, therefore, the Alimentation Service had no choice but to buy additional grain in other provinces. Given this serious situation, the export of wheat from the Caspian ports was banned. However, export of wheat from Khorasan and Azerbaijan was allowed. Taking into account the rice needs of Gilan and Mazandaran the government allowed an export of 35,000 *kharvars* of rice from Mazandaran. A total of 118,000 *kharvars* of rice was allowed to be exported from Gilan. By the end of December 1923, the grain situation had much improved, because there was 27,042 *kharvars* in the granary or 90 days' consumption, or more than half of the Tehran's requirements until the next harvest. Nevertheless, the export ban of wheat from the Caspian ports remained in force.

Table 5.6: Summary of grain stored per 1 Jadi 1303/21 December 1924

In stock 1 Hamal 1303/20 March 1924	23,101 *kharvars*	More than in 1302
Received from Tehran province from 1 Hamal to 1 Jadi 1303/21 December 1924	38,951 *kharvars*	Less than in 1302
Received from other provinces	4,942 *kharvars*	More than in 1302

Source: Government of Iran 1303 a, Table 23.

Because in November 1924 much snow had fallen, which halted all traffic, more transport had to be used to get supplies in. Nevertheless, the Alimentation Service was certain that in the next six months it would be able to transport and buy sufficient wheat so that by the next harvest it would have not less than 20,000 *kharvars* in stock. To ensure that the next crop of taxes in kind and of Crown lands would be higher the Alimentation Service intended to give better seed to the Crown land villages and to private landlords willing to sow it and to sell at agreed upon price (*qeymat-e varedeh*) plus the cost of collection and transport. As it seemed likely that in the districts around Tehran a shortage of bread would occur the Alimentation Service opened government bakeries there, where bread at a fixed price and quality was sold. To ensure the supply of wheat and rice to Tehran a commission has been formed consisting of representatives of the Ministries of Foreign Affairs, Interior, Public Welfare, Finance and of the Tehran Municipality.

Because bakers had complained that they lost money due to the prices fixed and rules applied by the Alimentation Service it had allowed the opening of new bakeries. This led to many complaints by bakers arguing that the new bakeries cut into their profits. Therefore, the opening of new bakeries was no longer allowed, unless the bakers themselves would propose it. Despite the low quality of the grain in 1924, the Alimentation Service claimed that neither the quality of bread was lowered nor was the price of bread raised.[19]

Table 5.7: Comparison of grain entries from 1 Hamal/20 March to the end of Qaws/22 December 1302/1923-34 and 1303/1924-25

	1302 *kharvars*	1303 *kharvars*	More *kharvars*	Less *kharvars*
In stock 1 Hamal	18,104	41,205	23,101	-
Wheat tax in kind Tehran	6,566	2,926	-	3,640
Khaleseh wheat Tehran	16,315	4,495	-	11,820
Wheat purchased	54,623	31,132	-	23,491
Wheat from the provinces	21,674	26,616	4,942	-
Total	117,282	106,374	28,043	38,951

Source: Government of Iran 1303 c, Table no. 23.

In 1925 there was a serious grain shortage due to a bad harvest. This was partly due to yet another plague of *senn* in the Varamin area.[20] As a result, Millspaugh team's major task and headache during

19. Government of Iran 1303 c, pp. 87-88.
20. Eyn al-Saltaneh 1376, vol. 9, pp. 7272, 7285 (and due to lack of water).

1304/1925-26 was the grain supply problem, which was worse than ever before. The expected grain deficit was much larger than the one in 1917-18, which was estimated to have caused 150,000 deaths. The Alimentation Service had been able to collect only 20,000 *kharvar*s of wheat and barley for Tehran from its environs, while Varamin had to supply 17,000 *kharvar*s of wheat and 3,000 *kharvar*s of barley. Other districts supplied seed and food for peasants to prevent that they would abandon their villages. The 20,000 *kharvar*s normally sent to Tehran had to be used as seed and food aid for peasants, so that only 1,000 *kharvar*s remained for Tehran's own food consumption.[21] The problems that this caused did not remain without financial and political problems and turmoil

On 22 July 1925, Eyn al-Saltaneh wrote" "it is warm, there is no water, there is no bread. The annual budget of the Alimentation Service is 300,000 *tuman*s. There should be wheat to give bread."[22] On 23 July 1925 he noted that bread had become better since two days, although this did not last long, because one month later the quality of bread was bad again. He further remarked that two officials of the Alimentation Service had wanted to increase its budget by 200,000 *tuman*s, but that Millspaugh had refused to do so.[23] There continued to be criticism of McCormack and the Alimentation Service, because not only was there a grain shortage, but also of fodder. Moreover, both were taken by force from the producers. The Army paid 27 *qran*s per *kharvar* of straw, while the market price was 6 *tuman*s. The Alimentation Service had fixed the price of grain at 20 *tuman*s, but only paid the landowners and peasants 7 *tuman*s; all of that was to the detriment of the producers. Moreover, the Alimentation Service had been operating in this manner for three years already. He added: "The 7 *tuman*s I wrote down is the sum of the price that consists in

---

21. Government of Iran 1304 a, p. 11; Idem 1304 b, p.18 (150,000 deaths). The Alimentation Service was managed by McCormack, assisted by Mirza Mahmud Khan Naseri, Eshaq Khan, and Taher Khan Sartip and their numerous staff. Idem 1304 a, p. 16.

22. Eyn al-Saltaneh 1376, vol. 9, p. 7289.

23. Eyn al-Saltaneh 1376, vol. 9, pp. 7298, 7316.

droppage (*oftha*), losses, cost of milling and storage, transport cost, seal cost, etc. etc,."[24]

On 23 September 1925 the bakers received less flour than they normally would. According to rumors that went around this shortage was due to drought and that there was only for 3-month's grain consumption in stock. This caused much panic and consternation among Tehran's population. Rumors circulated that one or more women and/or children had died because of hunger. A small a-political protest demonstration grew into a major protest. German and British diplomats reported that this demonstration was organized by Prime Minister Reza Khan to create an anti-British mood in Tehran, which would inhibit Ahmad Shah from returning to Iran. Arguments for this explanation are that the bread shortage only lasted one day, that only the first day the demonstrators had easy access to the *Majles*, because the police had allegedly orders not to stop the crowd, and indeed Ahmad Shah never returned to Iran. Also, a large amount of money was said to have been distributed among the crowd. Finally, after the *Majles* deputies had promised to take action to ensure that bread would be available Reza Khan himself went to the Granary and had grain transported by army trucks to the bakeries. It would seem that anti-government forces saw an opportunity to benefit from the situation and piggy-backed on the government-incited protest. A fact is that both pro- and anti-government and pro- and anti-Shah slogans were heard during the march of the demonstrators. Hoseyn Makki relates that in the Chaleh Meydan quarter the developing situation was seen as a political opportunity to agitate against Reza Khan. The women of this quarter got together and spread the rumor that the grain shortage was artificial and had been created by Reza Khan to force people to submit to him. On 24 September 1925 (2 Mehr) a large crowd of mainly women gathered in front of the *Majles* and entered the building. The women vilified the deputies, some of whom, who being afraid fled. Modarres, the deputy for Tehran, was so upset by this that he proposed the *Majles* to ask the government to put an end to this rioting and disperse the crowd. In reaction to this request Reza

---

24. Eyn al-Saltaneh 1376, vol. 9, p. 7315.

Khan ordered a large number of armed soldiers to take position in front of the *Majles*. However, before orders were given to shoot at the crowd Modarres and a group of his partisans went among them urging them to go home.[25]

On 25 September 1925 again a large crowd gathered, but this time in front of the homes of some of the religious leaders, urging them to take action against the government. A group of demonstrators also went to the *Majles*, but they were dispersed. On 26 September thousands of demonstrators went to the house of Hajj Aqa Jamal Esfahani and of the Imam Jom`eh. Allegedly, some 20,000 gathered again in front of the *Majles* and some of them even were able to enter the building. Modarres, who wanted to end the demonstration, and was able to convince a majority of deputies to demand that the government sent armed troops. Reza Khan came in person to the *Majle*s and standing next to Modarres tried to urge the demonstrators to leave. The people shouted: 'We want the Shah, we don't want the Sardar-e Sepah [Reza Khan]'. When the crowd became unruly, Modarres then asked Reza Khan to order the soldiers to shoot in the air. However, some soldiers shot at the crowd as a result of which one person was killed and a few were injured. The troops dispersed the demonstrators and spread out over the streets to make sure they would go home. The same afternoon members of the *Majles* asked the arrest of the inciters of the riot of the attack. Reza Khan told them that he was unable to do so, unless the *Majles* announced martial law. On 26 September 1925, martial law was announced and imposed on Tehran. Reza Khan not only arrested rioters, but also his political opponents, not only in Tehran, but also

25. For different details (e.g., there was a *rowzeh-khvani* session in the *Majles*) and who said what, see Eyn al-Saltaneh 1376, vol. 9, pp. 7337-38, according to whom the first demonstration started on 21 July 1925. The attack on the *Majles*, according to Eyn al-Saltaneh, began on 29 September (7 Mehr). Eyn al-Saltaneh 1376, vol. 9, pp. 7441-45 (with a description of how events developed and what happened and what was said, in particular by the women demonstrators), 7351 (on Friday 2 October the bazaar was closed, and on the preceding Wednesday, the government announced that it was closed for bread), 7357-58 (events on the third day).

in other cities. As a result, some 800 to 900 people were arrested and imprisoned. Later the government announced that the entire bread crisis had been due to an intrigue by staff of the judicial court, which led to the arrest of several high and low officials.[26]

Although martial law allowed the government to prevent demonstrations about the shortage of bread it did not resolve the issue of the grain deficit, because even though the government may have organized the bread demonstration, there was indeed a real serious grain deficit in the country. Therefore, for the government to have organized the bread riot it really took a serious risk, as it played with fire. For the Alimentation Service had to take extraordinary measures to resolve the grain crisis. Money was borrowed from the Imperial Bank of Persia to buy grain domestically and abroad, while all means available were used to ensure that consumers would not die of hunger. The Alimentation Service took strong measures to increase the capacity of the distribution system and the transport sector as well as its control over both systems. To deal more effectively with the famine 52 provincial branches of the Alimentation Service were established throughout the country, which offices were charged with the distribution of grain and bread as well as with the supervision of bakers respecting the price and other regulations.[27] However, this did not happen without great difficulty and in September 1925, the quality of bread remained bad and its price high. Moreover, to save the inhabitants of Tehran the rural population had to suffer as they had to give all their surplus grain, so that they were unable to properly feed their animals.[28]

The Millspaugh team submitted that people didn't realize that the grain output of the province of Tehran's had dropped over the last seven years and this was the reason for the death of thousands of people. In a normal year Tehran's neighboring districts used to supply

---

26. Makki 1357, vol. 3, pp. 370-78; Mahdrad 1976, pp. 93-95; Wilber 1975, p. 105; Najmi 1370, vol. 1, pp. 158-59.

27. Government of Iran 1307 a, p. 20. Most of these branches (*daftar*) probably were just grain collection points with warehouses, such as the ones shown in Table 5.17.

28. Eyn al-Saltaneh 1376, vol. 9, p. 7338.

80,000 *kharvar*s or 70% of Tehran's needs. In 1297/1918-19, which was a hunger year, Tehran's districts supplied 45,000 *kharvar*s of wheat or 45% of 99,000 *kharvar*s equal to the annual consumption. In 1303/1924-25, Tehran received from its districts 35,000 *kharvar*s or 10,000 less. In 1304/1924-25, the Tehran districts only supplied about 1,000 *kharvar*s for Tehran, while the capital's needs were 110,000 *kharvar*s of wheat and 12,000 *kharvar*s of barley, which was less than 1% of Tehran requirements. This reduction in the surplus of the traditional supply centers was due to a variety of factors, but mostly because of disappointing harvests. This meant that some of these same districts were in need of seed and even of food, and this year the productive districts needed their output for their own consumption.[29]

However, the problem was bigger than Tehran, for not only Tehran had been struck by disaster, so had other cities such as Qom and Kashan, which normally imported 4,000 *kharvar*s. Now they needed 10,000 *kharvar*s. Qazvin which normally was self-sufficient needed to import 10,000 *kharvar*s. Semnan and Damghan, which normally had a deficit of 3,000 *kharvar*s, then needed 7,000 *kharvar*s. Hamadan normally imported 5,000 *kharvar*s, but now had to buy 10,000 *kharvar*s. According to the Alimentation Service, these deficits were real, except for Hamadan, where it estimated that the deficit was only 3,000 *kharvar*s, because some landowners and merchants wanted to take advantage of the current situation. They were invited to sell their grain to the government at one *tuman* discount, but they refused, although they admitted that they had an amount of grain equal to Hamadan's needs. Instead of selling, they immediately began a campaign among landowners advising them to hide their grain, so that they might sell it at a higher price. Therefore, grain from Kermanshah and Esfandabad had to be brought to Hamadan. This was but one example to show that many landowners wanted to take advantage of this bad situation. Therefore, the Alimentation Service considered it likely that the price of wheat and the cost of transport would rise, and increased the price of bread in Tehran from 2.20 *qran*s to 2.60 *qran*s per *man* toward the end of 1924.

29. Government of Iran 1304 a, pp. 15-16.

Table 5.8: Grain needs for 1304/1925-26 for selected major cities (in *kharvar*s)

Province	Wheat and barley
Tehran and environs	138,000
Hamadan	15,000
Qazvin	10,000
Kashan	10,000
Qom	10,000
Semnan and Damghan	7,000
Total	190,000

Source: Government of Iran 1304 a, p. 13.

Not only was the sheer quantity of grain imports much different than normal, but so were the places where it had to come from. In a normal year all barley needed for Tehran was supplied by its districts, but this year only 12,000 *kharvar*s was supplied. In a normal year another 30 to 35,000 *kharvar*s had to come from neighboring provinces, but now it had to come from as far away as Kermanshah, Mashhad, and Maku, while the government was also forced to import grain from India and Russia.

Table 5.9: From where and in what quantity grain needs of selected major cities will be supplied in 1304/1925-26

Place of supply	*Kharvar*s
Grain added in Tehran and environs at harvest time	15,000
Tehran districts	20,000
Azerbaijan via Zanjan and Astara	31,000
Maku via Russia	3,500
Zanjan	17,000
Khomeyn etc.	18,000
Malayer, Nehavand and Borujerd	5,800
Kermanshah	17,000
Khorasan	10,000
Esfandabad	7,000

Place of supply	*Kharvar*s
Russia	44,700
India	13,000
Total	202,000

Source: Government of Iran 1304 a, p. 13.

Based on the expected future supply (see Tables 5.8 and 5.9) the Alimentation Service expected to have a surplus in stock of 12,000 *kharvar*s by the next harvest.[30]

In 1925, to facilitate the purchase of the identified grain resources, the Alimentation Service opened many provincial branches whose main task was to buy the local surplus at a fixed price. For example, the Azerbaijan branch had been created with the sole objective to supply grain to the capital. The Zanjan branch also had to supply Tehran (12,000 *kharvar*s per year). These provincial Alimentation agents had the right to confiscate hoarded grain. Of course, the grain needed for local consumption had to remain available for the local population. The latter usually had no problem with this, because price regulation ensured the availability of bread at a fixed price. Until June 1927, the Alimentation Service had more than 52 local purchasing branches that operated throughout much of Iran.[31] For example, offices are mentioned in Kermanshah, Sonqor, Hamadan, Qazvin, Khorasan, but also in smaller jurisdictions such as Sangsar, Khomeyn, and Damavand.[32]

30. Government of Iran 1304 a, pp. 12-13

31. Government of Iran 1307 a, p. 20; Government of Iran 1306 b, p. 31. In 1924, it was reported that there was no branch in Malayer, suggesting that in that year the Service had already established purchasing branches elsewhere, which seems to have been the case in Arak and Shahrud. Government of Iran 1303 a, pp. 88, 90-91. In 1928, there was no Alimentation branch in Kerman. IOR/L/PS/12/3444, Trade Report of Kirman Consulate District for the year ending March 1928, p. 3, which suggests that there never had been one in that city, which given its distance from Tehran and its surplus situation are logical.

32. Government of Iran 1307 a, p. 20; Government of Iran 1306 b, p. 31;

Although sufficient sources of supply had been identified this was only part of the solution to address the food crisis. The other and potentially even a greater challenge was that of transporting all that grain in a timely manner. In normal years, some 46,000 *kharvar*s of grain needed to be transported to Tehran and the other towns, but now this figure was as high as 180,000 *kharvar*s. This meant that the demand for transport was at least four times higher than in a normal year. Moreover, the grain supplies had to come from much more distant places. Normally grain for Tehran came from Khamseh and Khomeyn, in which case the pack animals needed some 30-40 days to return. Now they had to come from Azerbaijan, Kermanshah, Khorasan, and Gilan, so that the return trip instead of 30-40 days was at least 50-60 days. Taking into account distance and bad weather as well as that the animals were also needed for trade and transport of summer (*seyfi*) crops, the Alimentation Service expected to be able to move 10,000 to 15,000 *kharvar*s per month. Although this amount was adequate to meet Tehran's daily consumption, it was not enough for the build-up of stocks in the Granary. Such build-up was necessary, because during winter time transport capacity dropped due to blocked roads, while in spring the animals had to graze. Therefore, it was expected that one had to taken into account that per month 5,000 *kharvar*s less than normal would be transported during those two periods.[33]

Therefore, to avert famine conditions, extraordinary steps had to be taken. The Alimentation Service contracted practically all available animal transport, even from as far as Khorasan and Azerbaijan. Moreover, the import of pack animals was encouraged. Also, all possible transport was sent to Azerbaijan, Kermanshah, Khorasan, Khamseh and Khomeyn to collect and then to transport grain immediately to Tehran or to centralize it at central points from where it might be sent in winter time after the passes closed. The average time of transport from these various locations was twice that from Gilan and twice the number of transport had to be used than if the Russian deliveries had been on time. Because the country's chronic shortage of

Appendix III.

33. Government of Iran 1304 a, p. 14.

transportation, this sudden and major surge in the level of demand on the transportation capacity of the country had a significant impact on commercial traffic. This held in particular for the commercial routes over which the grain was transported.[34]

To reduce the negative impact on commercial traffic Millspaugh argued that modern means of transportation were needed, to wit: 120 trucks, 15 tractors and 60 trailers, which he estimated to require an outlay of 400,000 *tumans*. Moreover, given the scarcity of experienced drivers and mechanics in Iran foreign workers had to be hired.[35] Finally, the Alimentation Service bought 198 motor trucks and 60 trailers, about half of which were in service by December 1925. Millspaugh believed that this increase in transport capacity and speed would allow a rapid return to normal conditions, in particular when a good harvest allowed the Service to make part of its transport fleet available to the demands of normal commercial trade.[36] The Imperial Bank of Persia (IBP) was asked to both facilitate and act as intermediary in the purchase of trucks in India, Iraq and Great Britain. The IBP found that the entire operation was time-consuming and unprofitable. C.F. Warr, one of IBP's staff involved in this car buying operation wrote:

> Night after night the man who was in charge of telegrams and I who was his assistant used to have voluminous telegrams to send all over the Middle East, to Bombay, Calcutta, Beirut, Baghdad, even to France and Belgium: anyone who had a second-hand lorry that was free, would then buy it and then send it back to Persia quickly, and it was quite exciting actually.[37]

34. Government of Iran 1304 b, p. 14.
35. Government of Iran 1304 a, p. 15.
36. Millspaugh 1925, p. 78; Idem, 1926, p. 25; Nielsen 1926, p. 184. On the savings in time and cost due to the use of motorized transport, see Clawson 1993.
37. Jones 1986, vol. 1, p. 198.

To increase the number of cars, in December 1925 the Alimentation Service requisitioned part of the cars of *Auto-Iran*, which then refused to carry the mails any longer, "and the task became incumbent on the Alimentation Service itself."[38] The motorized transport solution ran the risk of running up an extra high fuel bill when a trade dispute broke out between Russia and Iran in February 1926. In that month Russia imposed a trade embargo on exports to Iran, including gasoline. Therefore, to assist the Alimentation Service the APOC made gasoline available at a reasonable price. This assistance helped the Alimentation Service to achieve its food supply objectives.[39]

To incentivize the various types of transporters to improve their performance, the Alimentation Service gave bonuses for prompt delivery and penalties for delays for both animal and motor transport. Military escorts were provided to avoid delays. Arrangements were made to establish bakeries and grain depots to supply bread and barley at the lowest possible price. Thus, the quantity and speed of shipping grain was increased, for both grain and motor transport. Although this effort had a negative impact on the volume of trade, Iranian merchants allegedly supported the Alimentation Service's requisition of the means of transportation, suffering loss without protest to avert a famine.

Because large quantities of grain needed to be transported this strained the capacity of the already inadequate transport system. This problem was aggravated by the fact that grain had to be transported from faraway locations such as Azerbaijan, Khorasan and Kermanshah, but even from Russia and India. Table 5.10 shows the situation at the beginning of 1304/March 1925 and the quantities of grain collected from the various sources of supply until March 1925.

---

38. Auto-Iran was "an offshoot of Soviet Trade Organisation, 'Shark,' which was inaugurated in the spring [of 1925] and which has enjoyed a virtual monopoly of motor transport on the Tehran-Resht road by the simple means of working at a loss, at cut-throat rates." Burrell and Jarman 1997, (vol. 1924-26), p. 417.

39. Ferrier 1982, p. 517. By the end of February 1926 the Russians made gasoline available again. Eyn al-Saltaneh 1376, vol. 9, p. 7438.

Table 5.10: Sources of Grain Supply for 1304 (21 March 1925-20 March 1926)

Available in center and provinces per 1 Farvardin 1304		29,300 *kharvar*s
Iranian grain delivered or ready for transport:		
Azerbaijan	50,000 *kharvar*s	
Khorasan	6,000	
Tehran	17,000	
Khomeyn	23,000	
Khamseh	16,000	
Other provinces	18,000	
Subtotal		130,000 *kharvar*s
Indian grain delivered	14,000	
Russian grain delivered per 1 Dey/22 Dec:		
a. purchase	8,500	
b. exchange	2,220	
c. gift	5,409	
Subtotal		16,143 *kharvar*s
Total grain delivered or ready for transport		
Per 1 Dey/Dec 1304/1925	189,443 *kharvars*	
Russian grain overdue 1 Dey	16,236	
" " due Jan.1926	11,000	
" " due Feb. 1926	4,000	
Total Russian grain due		31,236 *kharvar*s
Grand total on hand and due		220,679 *kharvar*s

Source: Government of Iran 1304 b, p. 17.

Because transport was the structural bottleneck for the supply of grain, it caused serious losses in some cases. For example, there was a delay in executing the agreement between the Russian Commercial Representative and the Director of the Alimentation Service concluded on 28 October 1925 (6 Aban 1304). This agreement covered the sale of 720,000 *pud*s of wheat to be delivered at Enzeli at a price of 1 ruble 64 copecks per *pud*, with the option of payment in *qran*s at a rate of 44.94 per *chernovets*.[40] The agreed upon delivery schedule of Russian grain was as follows:

November 1925 (with grace period of 7 days in December) 150,000 *puds* (825,000 *batmans*)

December 1925	300,000 (1,650,000)
January 1926	200,000 (1,100,000)
February 1926	70,000 (400,000)

No deliveries were made in November. On 4 December 1925, 201,510 *batman*s of Russian wheat were received or a shortage of 621,400 *batman*s for the first period. In December 640,853 *batman*s were received or a shortage of 1,023,637 *batman*s at the end of the month or 65% of the total due on 31 December.[41]

The transport and supply problems, including from Russia, were not unexpected, after all transport had been the structural Achilles heel of food supply in Iran. Therefore, as a precaution, the Alimentation Service had also bought some 14,000 *kharvar*s of wheat in India. This quantity of wheat had been held in reserve in Karachi with the intention to resell it with a profit of >50,000 *tuman*s, had the Russian deliveries arrived on time. Now with half a million lives at stake this wheat was shipped to Iran. However, because this took time, 8,000 *kharvar*s were collected from Hamadan and Kermanshah to replace an equivalent quantity of the Indian grain. The result was a loss of 300,000 *tuman*s due to transport cost of Indian grain as compared with the Russian grain. There also were indirect losses in that people in Hamadan and Kermanshah seeing grain being moved to Tehran

---

40. *Chernovets*, originally the name for a gold coin, was used to denote a banknote since the beginning of the 20th century. One *chernovets* was equal to 10 rubles.

41. Government of Iran 1304 b, pp. 13-14.

increased their efforts to hide their grain, resulting in greater difficulty and cost to supply these two cities.[42]

Table 5.11: A comparison of grain transported per *kharvar-farsakh* between 1302 and 1304

From	To	Dis-tance	*Kharvar* 1302	*Kharvar* 1304	*Farsakh kharvar* 1302	*Farsakh-kharvar* 1304
Tehran	Tehran	10	80,000	17,000	800,000	170,000
Qazvin		20	5,000	-	100,000	-
Khomeyn		60	15,000	23,000	900,000	1,380,000
Zanjan		50	10,000	16,000	500,000	800,000
Arak		50	10,000	-	500,00	-
Total 1302					2,800,000	
Kermanshah		90	-	8,000	-	720,000
Azerbaijan		90		50,000	-	4,500,000
Khorasan		120	-	4,000	-	480,000
Enzeli		60	-	45,000	-	2,700,000
Malayer, eyc.		50	-	6,000	-	300,000
Qasr-e Shirin	Kerman shahan	30	-	14,000	-	420,000
Kermanshah	Hama-dan	30	-	4,000	-	120,000
Total 1304						11,590,000

Source: Government of Iran 1304 b, p. 15.

Table 5.11 shows that in the first six months of fiscal year 1925-26 the movement of grain, expressed in the Persian equivalent of the 'ton-km,' amounted to 11,500,000 *farsakhs-kharvar* as compared with 2,800,000 *farsakhs-kharvar* in 1302/1923-24. This meant that the Alimentation Service had to move 4.1 times more grain than in 1302, which was a 'normal' year.[43] Huge quantities of grain had to be transported over large distances to prevent famine in Tehran and

42. Government of Iran 1304 b, p. 14.
43. Government of Iran 1304 b, p. 16.

elsewhere. During this period the Alimentation Service was able to supply wheat to Tehran and the other large towns in the Service's area regularly, but with great difficulty. Despite this major effort, in February 1926, bread still was in short supply and expensive. In the villages people survived on beets and carrots, because the needs of Tehran received priority. Despite this, poverty was on the increase in the capital.[44]

It is obvious that the action taken by the Alimentation Service increased the shortage of commercial transport. In 1303/1924-25, the normal quantity of goods carried on the Kermanshah-Hamadan-Rasht-Qazvin route was 10,695 *kharvar*s monthly (excluding donkey transport). In 1304/1925-26, in addition 9,000 *kharvar*s of grain/month has to be carried from Rasht to Qazvin alone, in addition to 3,000 *kharvar*s per month to Tehran and 12,000 *kharvar*s per month via other routes. In short, grain demand by Tehran practically absorbed the transport capacity usually available on the Kermanshah-Qazvin and Rasht-Qazvin routes. In addition, there was the demand from other towns such as Hamadan, Qazvin, Qom, etc. which represented another 8,000 *kharvar*s/month. In short:

Table 5.12 Changes in the Movement of Goods in 1304/1925-26

Normal movement of goods between	10,695 *kharvar*s
Kermanshah-Hamadan-Rasht-Qazvin	
Maximum normal movement of grain	4,500
Total	15,195 *kharvar*s /month
Movement in Mehr 1304	6,765
Grain to Tehran	12,000
Grain to other towns 8,000 *kharvar*s less max. 2000 *kharvar*s	
Moved by other local means of transport	6,000

44. Eyn al-Saltaneh 1376, vol. 9, p. 7439. On 16 March 1926, Lambert Molitor wrote that despite good rains the supply of bread was still a serious issue and the crisis continued. MA, Farde 61, 6101, Lambert Molitor to Auguste Molitor, 16/03/1926, p. 4.

Total	24,765 *kharvars* /month
Increase in grain movement 333%	13,500 *kharvars* /month
This is the minimum increase via these routes. The actual increase over all routes was 410%.	
Increase in grain and merchandise movement in 1304	
Equals 37%	9,570
Decrease in merchandise movement in 1304	3,930
(donkey transport not taking into account in the above)	

Source: Government of Iran 1304 b, pp. 16-18.

This means that an increase of grain movement of 410% and an increase on the Kermanshah-Rasht-Qazvin routes of 333% resulted in a drop in transport of goods of only [!!] 37%. Given that practically all transport was used to move grain a fall of one-third in merchandise transport is a noteworthy achievement, or so Millspaugh submitted.

Because of the fixed price of bread as well as the high cost of grain and of grain transport the Alimentation Service suffered a loss of about 1.5 million *tumans* in fiscal year 1304/1925-26 year (see Table 5.13). However, the government defended the additional expenditures by pointing out that that the security of supply of 500,000 people trumped financial considerations, which, after all, amounted only to 3 *tumans* per person in that year.[45]

Table 5.13: Financial statement of the Alimentation Service for 1304/1925-26

	Tumans	*Tumans*
Administrative expenses normal budget	330,000	
Additional staff and cost, excl. motor transport	46,000	
Purchase of motor transport		400,000
Operation of motor transport (staff, material, parts)	450,000	
Cost of garage buildings	35,000	
Cost of tools for garage	5,200	

45. Government of Iran 1304 b, pp. 16-17.

	Tumans	*Tumans*
Cost of Tehran granary offices	24,000	
Total		1,290,200
Grain on hand 1 Farvardin	660,000	
Purchase and transport Iranian grain	3,660,000	
Purchase and transport foreign grain	1,950,000	
Total cost of purchase and transport grain in 1304	6,210,000	
Total expenses of the Alimentation Service for 1304		7,500,200
Revenue during 1304 sale of grain	4,500,00	
Est. value grain on hand in 1304 Tehran and provinces	1,200,000	
Total revenue for 1304		5,700,000
Gross cash deficit for 1304		1,800,200
To be deducted as chargeable to future years		
90% cost garage to be amortized in 10 years	31,500	
66% of motor transport to be amortized in 3 years	266,000	
66% of garage tools to be amortized in 3 years		3,500
50% of spare parts to be amortized in 2 years	6,000	
90% of Tehran granary offices and buildings		
To be amortized in 10 years	21,000	
To be charged against future years and deducted		
From gross deficit for1304		328,600
Net loss for 1304		1,471,600

Source: Government of Iran 1304 b, pp. 18-19.

The 1.5 million *tumans* loss has to be carried into the 1305 budget, because the Alimentation Service had not received authority to fix the price of bread at a level that would have been adequate to cover the cost of wheat supplied to bakers. The expenditures of the Alimentation Service were not carried in the ordinary budget, because they were met by IBP advances repaid from the Alimentation receipts.[46]

Although these additional cost as well as the mismanagement of the purchase of the vehicles and parts led to many negative observations

46. Government of Iran 1304 b, p. 17.

(see below), the investment made by the Alimentation Service also had unintended positive results. The purchase of 198 trucks (about 10% of the total number of cars in Iran in 1925 and 40% of cars not used in the oil industry) encouraged the development of a national road building plan, concessions for car importers and garages and the abolition of all kinds of road fees.[47] The enormous increase in the number of trucks also had another positive impact, viz. a drop in the rate of animal transport as well as the slow disappearance of this kind of transportation. According to E.R. Lingeman, the commercial attaché of the British legation in Tehran, in 1927 "the chief contributory factor [to the drop in the rates of animal transport] has been the introduction of motor transport on a large scale and the realisation of its use for the carriage of merchandise, largely as a result of the operations of the Alimentation Service which itself imported a considerable number of lorries."[48]

However, there also were some down sides to the purchase of the 198 trucks. In 1927, the American Mission was severely criticized by members of the *Majles*, who opposed its role and its continuation. Pointed questions were asked by these deputies about the losses sustained by the Alimentation Service, which became known and somewhat of a scandal after the Budget Commission disclosed the findings of its investigation. The losses were estimated at 1.5 million *tuman*s due to mismanagement, while it would also be difficult to collect the outstanding debts. Deputies pointed out that in 1304/1925-26 the Alimentation Service budget appropriation was 1.5 million *tuman*s only and that the *Majles* had not approved any further addition. The additional funds could only have been made available by the Treasury and only with Millspaugh's and the Cabinet's approval. What was not discussed was the mismanagement of the purchase of the Alimentation Service lorries. According to the British Legation:

---

47. Agah 1958, p. 15; Hadow 1925, p. 34 (A recent rough estimate of the number of motor cars now in use in Persia shows the total to be in the neighbourhood of 2,000, of which 50 per cent. are in use in the oil fields or other districts employed by the Anglo-Persian Oil Company.")

48. Lingeman 1928, p. 26.

This part of the service is the most scandalous of all reason why it was not mentioned. It has absorbed 1.5 million tumans and based on information received this part of the service is riddled with incompetence and corruption.

a. International trucks: selling price, United States, 1,750 dollars – export discount, 25 per cent. –chassis only shipped to Beirut, where the bodies were made up- cost to the Alimentation in Beirut when completed 3,500 dollars.
b. Vulcaniser, cost £120 in England- bought from one Jamil Saab of Beirut second-hand in Tehran- 4,000 tomans.
c. A lot of Dunlop and Goodyear tyres, six months in a wreck off Beirut, brought off and auctioned in Beirut for 1,000-2,000 tomans- brought to Tehran and sold to Alimentation for 22,000 tomans- found rotten and immediately discarded.
d. A number of Alimentation lorries held up for lack of tyres- it was eventually discovered that the needed spares had been ordered by somebody in the service and had been lying seven months in Bagdad – an official was sent to Bagdad to bring them up – the tyres arrived four months later.[49]

---

49. FO 416/81, Memorandum Mismanagement Alimentation Service by E.R. Lingeman. 02/07/1927. Molitor also criticized the American management of the food crisis, although, in my view, he was too pessimistic about the positive impact of the use of transportation by trucks. "Un Colonel (?) le dirige. On saura que cela coûtera! Ces gens se figurent qu'on organise a coup de circulaires et ils prennent si facilement le mot pour la chose, chose dangereuse dans ce pays où rien ne marche que par l'effort continu et personnel du chef. Et puis il est impossible de substituer dans un moment critique les moyens modernes aux moyens traditionnels. Avant que le camion auto ne puisse remplacer la vieille caravane persane pour le transport de blé, il y a quelques étapes à franchir dans le domaine de l'éducation professionnelle des personnes. Javach. Javach [*yavash* - lentement] n'est pas un vain mot. Il faut en tenir compte. "Heile und Weile" [sic; Eile mit Weile - haste makes waste] dit l'allemand c'est ce qui fallait faire en Perse pour le transport des blés. Tandis que "Rien ne sert de courir avec des camions qui restent en rac sur les mauvaises routes. Il fallait partir à temps avec les mulets et les chameaux." MA, Farde 61, 6101, Lambert Molitor to Auguste Molitor, 16/03/1926, p. 4.

Who would get the blame for this scandal soon became clear, for it had an impact on the negotiations about the renewal of Millspaugh's contract, which broke down in July 1927.[50] The revelation of gross mismanagement by the Alimentation Service turned public opinion against Millspaugh. As a result, Millspaugh left the country in August 1927, while Major Hall and Mr. Dunaway were under a cloud and their contracts were allowed to lapse. Mr. Pearson's services were also dispensed with. There remained at the end of the year 1927 one inspector and six provincial directors.[51]

The departure of the Millspaugh mission in 1927 does not seem to have had a negative impact on the performance of the Alimentation Service. Soltan Hoseyn Mirza Rakhshani replaced Richard W. Bonnevalle as chief of the Alimentation Service. The existing staff continued to perform its duties and to execute the policy changes decided upon in 1927. Also, the fact that there was a bumper crop in 1927 was very helpful.[52] The Alimentation Service had feared (12th quarterly report) that the collection of the direct taxes in kind and public domains revenues would experience a reduction, because large tax reductions had been granted due to the general crop failure.[53]

---

50. Initially Millspaugh's contract had been renewed for a period of three years, but changes in certain clauses of the contract proposed by the government were unacceptable to Millspaugh and after three months the negotiations broke down and Millspaugh ended his service on 1 Mordad 1306/22 July 1927. For the hand-over arrangements, see Government of Iran 1306 a, p. 11-12 (Charles McCaskey replaced Millspaugh as Treasurer-General); Idem 1306 b, p. 12 (Major Harry Davis became Treasurer-General and held that function until March 1928).

51. Burrell and Jarman·1997, (1927-1930), p. 127. McCormack remained Chief of the Alimentation Service until March 1927. Government of Iran 1304 c, p. 6. Richard W. Bonnevalle was Chief of General Alimentation and Motor Transport Service as June 1927 until March 1928; Government of Iran 1306 a, p. 7; Idem 1306 b, p. 7; Idem 1306 d, p. vii; Sheean 1927, pp. 128-29.

52. Government of Iran 1307 a, pp. vii, 23.

53. Government of Iran 1304 a, p. 19.

In 1306/1927-28, a total of 1,735 trucks were used to move the large quantities of grain between Tehran and its supply centers (Tehran-Qazvin-Gilan; Tehran-Qom-Isfahan; Tehran-Qom-Arak). In 1305, the trucks were mostly employed by the Alimentation Service and did little merchandise transport. However in 1306, although grain transport still exceeded that of merchandise, 5,683 *kharvar*s of grain and 3,168 *kharvar*s of goods were transported along the above routes. The 1,735 trucks also transported the mail, some 556 *kharvar*s of mail and traveled a total of 411,507 *farsakh*s. The Service's garage was much improved and had become the best in Iran; it had a casting smelter and tire repair workshop that was unique in Iran. During this period 511 cars were repaired, as well as 44 cars of other Ministries.[54]

At the end of Khordad 1306/21 June 1927, there were 61,072 *kharvar*s of wheat and 6,526 *kharvar*s of barley in government stores in Tehran (deduction for monthly grain consumption of Tehran). In addition, there was 6,000 *kharvar*s of wheat in Kermanshah, 6,000 in Azerbaijan and 4,000 *kharvar*s in Malayer, Nehavand, Khomeyn and Arak, which were being shipped to the capital. Also, there were another 7,000 *kharvar*s of wheat in Hamadan, which, if the grain was not needed for local consumption would be sent to Tehran, because the Alimentation Service branch in Hamadan was going to be abolished. Although the Alimentation Service had enough grain in stock, the forecast for the 1306 harvest (Tir-Mordad/June-July) did not look good. This was because there had not been enough rain and snow in 1305/1926-27, which had damaged the crops in many places. Also, locusts had ravaged the crop in Khorasan, Fars and parts of the West. Only the crop of Tehran province, parts of Arak and of the West were somewhat satisfactory. Nevertheless, there was no fear for Tehran's food supply as sufficient stores of grain were available. This optimism was reflected in the closure of the Alimentation Service purchasing branches in Kermanshah, while the ones in Zanjan and Azerbaijan were to be closed after their grain stock had been removed.

---

54. Government of Iran 1306 a, pp. 54-55; for the impact on trade of transport used by the Alimentation Service in 1305/ 1926-27, see Government of Iran 1305 a, p. 21.

The Alimentation Service branch in Hamadan was maintained until harvest time and then closed. Small Alimentation Service branches in Golpeygan, Saveh, Damavand, and Eyvankey had already been closed. The Alimentation Service also had considered closing its branches in Shahrud, Semnan and Damghan, but this decision was delayed after repeated requests from the local population and others. Only in Tehran, Qazvin, Qom, Arak, Khomeyn, Shahrud and Damghan were branches to be maintained. The closure of the branches was not only because of an optimistic outlook, but also as a cost-cutting measure. For since Ordibehesht/22 April 1927, strong steps had been taken to reduce Alimentation Service expenses and unnecessary items were struck from budget and audits of its 1304 and 1305 accounts were ongoing.[55]

As expected, tthe harvest of Tehran province was not too bad, although that of Arak, Khomeyn and Damghan was not as good as in the previous year. Also, the harvest in Khorasan, Zanjan, Azerbaijan and the eastern districts, where there were no Alimentation Service branches, was bad. Nevertheless, no major problems were foreseen for Tehran's food supply. Therefore, the price of bread rose with 50-80% compared with the preceding year. Likewise, there was no fear for famine in Azerbaijan, Zanjan and the eastern provinces, due to steps taken by the Alimentation Service. Shahrud had a shortage of grain, but the chief of the Alimentation Service in that place resolved it by going to Mashhad and getting provincial authorities to help. A shortage at Semnan was covered by supply from Khar. An extraordinary shortage occurred at Qazvin, which normally was supplied from Khamseh. Landlords and grain owners, smelling a profitable opportunity, complained about the existing Alimentation Service's arrangements and asked for change to which the authorities agreed. Consequently, there was not enough stock in Qazvin, while transporting grain from the center, due to the difference between the buying and selling price would result in a loss for the Alimentation Service. For such a loss there was no allocation in the budget, which meant that the local price would rise. To prevent this, the local Alimentation

55. Government of Iran 1306 a, pp. 52-53.

Service branch with support local authorities proposed a purchase price of 14 to 17 *tumans* per *kharvar*. Immediately a quantity from Arak was transported to Qazvin. Also, quantities were bought from Kermanshah and Nehavand. Some of the affected provinces asked for an Alimentation Service branch to be established in their area, but there was no budget for it. As a consequence, the provincial departments had to take care of the problem, the more so, since there was no threat of famine.[56]

Therefore, the Alimentation Service had closed most of its purchasing branches in the various provinces. The Hamadan branch had been closed in Shahrivar 1306/August-September 1927 and its stored grain was shipped to Tehran. The purchase branches of the Alimentation Service in Azerbaijan and Zanjan were closed in respectively, Mordad/July 1927 and Shahrivar/August 1927, as there was enough grain. The Service concluded that if there would be a need to ship grain from Zanjan to Qazvin this year, it sufficed to send a special agent to Zanjan for that purpose, which was a cheaper alternative. Also, if need be, the Zanjan branch could always be reopened at any time. The remaining provincial branches were in Tehran, Qom, Kashan, Arak, Qazvin, Shahrud, Semnan and Damghan, where the Alimentation Service centralized the purchase of grain in provinces where it still had branches.[57]

The local population usually had no problem with the Service's purchasing activities, because price regulation ensured the availability of bread at a fixed price. In fact, as mentioned above, some towns that had no Alimentation branch asked for their establishment when they were being closed down elsewhere. Therefore, it does not come as a surprise that when in 1927 the provincial offices were abolished, this step was not welcomed everywhere. In Damavand, for example, a conflict arose about the problems (the sale of government grain and

56. Government of Iran 1306 b, pp. 31-32; Idem 1306 c, pp. 10-11.

57. Government of Iran 1306 b, pp. 31-32 (As stated in a previous quarterly report a study had been made to cut the cost of the Alimentation Service, while its new budget was under review for approval).

the ending of the fixed bread price) that arose after the closure of the local office of the Alimentation Service. In June 1927, the women of Damavand demonstrated against this development and the local *amin-e maliyeh* called a meeting of all government offices to discuss the problem. Meanwhile, the landowners and hoarders, who were very happy with the closure of the Alimentation Service office, had already begun selling grain at excessive prices. A special commission was appointed to look into the matter.[58]

Of course, landowners opposed the activities of the Alimentation Service as it prevented them from taking advantage of a situation, when there was scarcity of grain in the market. For example, when hoarded grain was confiscated or when grain was transported across a provincial border, as happened in August 1927 in respectively Sonqor and Kermanshah, the landowners and the merchants' union concerned lodged a complaint about this and asked for the closure of the local office of the Alimentation Service.[59] Of course, landowners could not directly oppose the government and therefore, used indirect means to do so. Through various means (use of religious persons; organizing 'spontaneous' demonstrations; petitions) landowners tried to put pressure on the government by showing how unpopular the activities of the Alimentation Service were. To defuse these undermining activities the Alimentation Service, apart from using the forces of law and order, where useful opened one or more bakeries where good low-priced bread was sold. One such case occurred in Hamadan.

At the end of December 1925 Hajj Mirza `Abdol-Vahhab Razavi arrived from Tehran in Hamadan. He formed an association and most local olama and landowners joined him in the Friday mosque. There he declared the eating of bread illegal (*haram*) and tried to arouse people of the city against the Alimentation Service. `Abdol-Vahhab Razavi appointed agents who were sent into the various districts to hide grain. The authorities were able to induce the people gathered in the mosque to leave. Although `Abdol-Vahhab Razavi returned

58. See Appendix III.

59. See letter in Appendix III; Letter dated 15/05/1305 or 07 August 1926.

to Tehran his agents continued to intrigue and mislead the people of Hamadan. As a result, the Alimentation Service allowed the opening of a few bakeries to freely obtain grain, bake and sell *lavash* bread, which was sold at 5 *qran*s to 5 *qran*s 10 *shahi*s per *man*.[60] The landowners began agitating to stop people from buying this bread. On 4 Esfand 1304/23 February 1926, this resulted in a short-lived demonstration by women and children from the Dorudabad quarter in Hamadan, organized by local landowners, who were well-known speculators. As a result, the bazaar was closed for a few hours. After order had been restored the bazaar was reopened and a few days later the police arrested some 30 the women demonstrators and their husbands. Those involved in the intrigue and demonstration received either a flogging or imprisonment.[61]

Also, an attempt had been made to have people sign a petition to close the Alimentation Service in Hamadan. A report about this event was sent to Tehran, in which it was concluded that:

> First, ... the said petition has been prepared and sealed by the actions of one person, Sheikh Hassan, the problem-maker, and the people who sealed it were unaware of its contents and were often children, and each of them had two or three seals. Report no. 146 of the Hamadan Police Commissariat, which is submitted herewith, confirms this. Best of all, at the beginning of his expose, he thanked the government officials for their actions in establishing the Hamadan Alimentation [Service] and limiting the actions of the speculators in the past year, and finally requesting to dissolve the Hamadan Alimentation Service because of this year's good harvest. Second: The Ministry of Finance considers the continuation of Hamadan's Alimentation [Service] necessary to prevent the activities by speculators and to create public welfare, and it does not believe that these statements will have any effect. It has sent the following instructions to the Hamadan Taxation Office:

---

60. The Alimentation Service had also opened bakeries in Damghan, Semnan, Shahrud, Qazvin and Zanjan under similar circumstances in 1920, see above.

61. See letter in Appendix III.

> 1- The Alimentation [Service] of Hamadan has to purchase all the surplus wheat from the owners and farmers according to the prescribed rate that the Hamadan Tax Office has announced to the public by Proclamation no. 3379, dated 5 Tir of 1305/27 June 1926 and a copy of it is sent herewith.
> 2- 295 *man-e* Tabriz of cleaned wheat is accepted in exchange for one *kharvar* and the price [for it] paid.
> 3- They should not impose any burden on the sellers of goods under whatever name or custom.
> 4- Whenever the sellers deliver unsifted wheat grain and object to the droppage that the Alimentation [Service] allows, they may deliver their wheat to the Alimentation warehouse to sift and clean it. In this case, the costs will be borne by the supplier and the waste will belong to the seller of the goods.
> 5- The sellers of wheat and muleteers and all the people who complain about the Alimentation agents may immediately have recourse to the Head of Finance and submit their complaint with the correct documents. In case of non-compliance, they may refer directly to the Central Alimention Service or the Ministry of Finance to proceed with the investigation and realization of their right.
> 6- The Alimentation [Service] at Hamadan has to be extremely serious about the purity and quality of the grain, so that the bread of the city is good and of high quality in every way.
> 7- Bakers should not accept unclean grain.
> 8- All bakers are required to buy the daily needs of their shops according to the price set by the Alimentation office.
> 9- Investigation of fraud by bakers and millers has to be brought to the knowledge of the Police representative, who will always be in the Alimentation office, and will be done and they will be treated according to the provisions of the regulations.

According to the above, it is an urgent matter for the Ministries of Interior and War to issue urgent telegraphic orders to the government, law enforcement and the military administration that as to the actions of such persons in the development of all Alimentation affairs of the Hamadan office to provide full assistance to the Tax and Alimentation Office at any time and take action against persons who seek trouble.

As soon as the Alimentation Service agents were withdrawn from the provincial supply center in mid-1927 landowners and merchants began hoarding grain. The problem was so serious that on 29 September 1927 (06 Mehr 1306), the Minister of Finance wrote a letter to his colleague of Interior stressing the need that the latter's Ministry support the fiscal agents (*omana-ye maliyeh*), who were in charge of collecting government grain in kind as well as of confiscating hoarded grain. The Minister of Finance further emphasized that governors should not automatically offer government grain for sale, because it had to be used as a means to prevent hoarding and grain profiteering. Also, attention should be paid to the export of grain from one province to the other as this usually was for profiteering purposes.[62]

At the time of its conception, the message of the above letter was no longer applicable to the situation of Tehran and, in fact, to most provinces of Iran. The letter was probably written to remind governors of the need to respect certain rules with regards to government grain so as to prevent scarcity problems in the future, for there was then enough grain in the market. On 1 Tir 1306/22 June 1927, there were 69,000 *kharvar*s in the Granary of Tehran. About 10,000 *kharvar*s from the previous year were stored in Azerbaijan, Kermanshah and Hamadan, or a total of 79,000 *kharvar*s. This meant another 81,000 *kharvar*s had to be collected for the center, to which end steps were taken. Because never before had there been so much grain in the Alimentation Service stores private grain owners hurried to transport and sell their grain, as keeping it would be unprofitable. Therefore, the Alimentation Service not only had to rent warehouses outside Tehran, but it also began construction of two new warehouses in the courtyard of its premises.[63]

On 1 Mehr/22 September 1927, there were 130,868 *kharvar*s, and at the end of Adhar/22 December 1927, a quantity of 137,343 *kharvar*s.

---

62. See letter in Appendix III; Circular note dated 1 Tir 1306/23 June 1927.

63. Government of Iran 1306 b, pp. 31-32 (As stated in previous quarterly report study has been made to cut cost of the Alimentation Service; the new budget is under review for approval).

After seven months, until beginning of the next harvest 1307/1928, 60,000 *kharvar*s had been consumed, so that an amount of 77,434 *kharvar*s remained as reserve. This reserve had been constituted in 1305 for use by Tehran. Part of the grain had come from the closed branches of Kermanshah, Hamadan, Azerbaijan and Zanjan. As stated above, the budget of the Alimentation Service and its accounts had been thoroughly audited since 1926 to determine where and how to cut expenditures. The result of this review was that, as of 1 Mehr/24 September 1927, the Alimentation Service had to operate with a smaller budget, while the branches had to submit monthly accounts. For the second half year of 1306/1927-28 the budget allocation was 628,010 *qran*s, while for the first six months of 1306/1927 it had been 938,040 *tuman*s. Thus, in the second half the budget was 310,030 *qran*s lower. Moreover, in 1307/1928-29 the budget would be even lower than in 1306.[64]

At the end of Esfand/21 March 1928, both in Tehran and provinces, a total of 143,456 *kharvar*s were in stock. There was still some grain coming in from Tehran province, which was the remainder of what peasants had set aside the previous year as a reserve for *Nowruz* and was sold thereafter; also some grain was brought by owners from the provinces. Therefore, there was more than enough grain to satisfy Tehran's grain needs. In fact, some grain was even sent to Qazvin, whose needs were covered by supplies from Arak, Kermanshah and Nehavand until the beginning of the harvest.[65]

---

64. Government of Iran 1306 c, pp. 10-11.
65. Government of Iran 1306 d, p. 16.

Table 5.14: Received in the central granary from the provinces during the first 6 months of 1307 (in *kharvars*)

Name of province	Available in cash	Available in kind	Available in kind	Compared with Mordad 1307-23/07/28
		Wheat	Barley	
Kashan	199,747.40	173,755.50	158.75	-
Qazvin	59,293.50	192,415.75	870.00	-
Araq	133,062.55	383,041.50	46.00	-
Shahrud	52,057.05	38,597.00	-	-
Damghan	38,099.45	-	1,649.25	-
Semnan	16,540.90	10,090.75	-	-
Qom	43,019.30	275,135.25	3,386.00	-
Total	1,041,784.45	1,073,035.75	6,110.00	-

Source: Government of Iran 1307 a, p. 20.

The Alimentation Service budget for the first half of 1307/1928-29 was 747,254 *qrans*, which due to the closure of provincial offices, the reduction of the budget and the cost of center was only 515,972 *qrans* for the second half of the year, or a reduction of 231,282 *qrans*. In 1928, because Isfahan had a grain shortage it was supplied from Kashan, Arak, and Qom with a quantity of 300,000 *man* of wheat, as follows:

Arak	150,000 *man*
Qom	120,000 *man*
Kashan	30,000 *man* or a total of 300,000 *man*

Because of the good harvest of 1305/1926-27 as well as a cost-cutting measure the provincial purchasing branches were only maintained where grain was still held in stock. Therefore, the branch in Khomeyn had been closed in early 1928 as there was no further need for it. At each remaining branch only a warehouse keeper (*anbardar*) and a weigher (*qapandar*) were retained, who were dismissed once the stocks were sold. As supplies were also sufficient to satisfy Tehran demand the Alimentation Service reported that in the beginning of 1307/March-April 1928 about 126,000 *kharvar*s of wheat were in stock in the central granary, which was twice the annual needs of the Alimentation Service reserves. Given this quantity, the bumper crop of 1307/1928-29 and the shortage of granaries it was decided to rent granaries near the existing one especially for the imports. The Alimentation Service was also forced to store and buy all grain that entered during first six months of 1307/March-September 1928:

> 1. Ten warehouses were rented near the central granary and outside the city at 3,645 *qran*s.
>
> 2. Six warehouses were established in the districts by order of the Ministry, each with a warehouse man (*anbardar*), a weigher (*qapandar*), a weigh-helper (*mirza-ye pa-ye qapan*), and a droppage gatherer (*oft gir*). This sped up grain collection and alleviated pressure on the Tehran Granary. These warehouses were at: Karimabad Varamin; Kheyrabad Varamin; Yengi Imam Sauj Bolagh; Karaj Sauj Bolagh; Kenargerd Ghar; Raviyeh Fashaquyeh.
>
> 3. As the price of grain and the cost of its transport in the provinces were cheaper than in the central province staff was appointed in Kermanshahan, Khomeyn, Arak and Zanjan to prevent that grain would be transported to Tehran, and to inform people to store it in the provincial centers. If transported 10% of the local transport cost would be levied as preventive measure.
>
> 4. Good clean grain was in stock and it was made known that those who had no land and wanted to prepare bread at home were allowed to buy grain at the Granary for their needs.
>
> 5. At all city gates staff was appointed (permanent and temps) to prevent grain from entering Tehran.[66]

The imports at beginning of 1307/March 1928 as well as entries and departures from the Granary were as follows:

---

66. Government of Iran 1307 a, pp. 20-21; Idem 1306 d, p. 16.

Table 5.15: Overview of entries and departures of food grains in first half of 1307 (in *kharvar*s)

Name	Imports	Imports	Exports	Exports	In stock	In stock
	Wheat	Barley	Wheat	Barley	Wheat	Barley
Available beginning 1307	142,296	1,160	-	-	-	-
Farvardin	5,771	387	10,151	954	-	-
Ordibehesht	3,649	677	11,341	1,047	-	-
Khordad	3,302	714	13,242	1,055	-	-
Tir	16,420	960	9,879	965	-	-
Mordad	28,686	1,014	9,137	861	-	-
Shahrivar	34,128	1,911	9,137	861	-	-
Total	234,252	6,833	61,750	5,958	172,502	875

Source: Government of Iran 1307 a, p. 22.

By March 1929, there was so much grain and of good quality of the 1307/1928 harvest that the remaining provincial branches of the Alimentation Service were closed and the sale and purchase of grain was discontinued, because at the end of Esfand 1307/21 March 1929, the stock available in the provincial warehouses was 231,078 *man* of wheat as shown in Table 5.16. Also, part of the grain was transported to Isfahan for sale. The rest of the grain was employed for local use to which end special agents were sent to Qom, Kashan, Arak, Damghan, and Shahrud, so that at the beginning of the harvest of 1308/1930 all existing stock was sold.

Table 5.16: Grain in stock, entered and exported in 1307/1928-29 (in *man*)

Names	Stock 30 Shahrivar 1307 `	Stock 30 Shahrivar 1307 `	Entered 2nd half year	Entered 2nd half year	Exported 2nd half year	Exported 2nd half year	Sent to Isfahan	Stock by year's end	Stock by year's end
	Wheat	Barley	Wheat	Barley	Wheat	Barley	Wheat	Wheat	Barley
Tehran	16,177,116	81,419	6,171,026	1,9068,211	5682062	628652	-	16666079	520928
Qazvin	183415	870	-	-	52640	-	-	120775	870
Qom	275125	2386	1000	-	-	2311	90914	185775	1074
Kashan	174896	158	-	-	1161	-	29089	143545	158
Arak	429721	46	25174	-	18464	-	111073	225258	46

Names	Stock 30 Shahrivar 1307`	Stock 30 Shahrivar 1307`	Entered 2nd half year	Entered 2nd half year	Exported 2nd half year	Exported 2nd half year	Sent to Isfahan	Stock by year's end	Stock by year's end
Semnan	9575	-	-	-	9575	-	-	-	-
Damghan	-	1649	-	-	-	1649	-	-	-
Shahrud	34840	-	-	-	34840	-	-	-	-
Total	17182601	87529	6197206	1068212	5798745	232612	131078	17350984	523128

Source: Government of Iran 1307 b, p. 15.

As of the end of Dey 1307/20 January 1930, the district stores did not transfer their government grain to the provincial stores any longer. The Alimentation Service bought 467,833 *man* that was sold to the bakers.[67]

Table 5.17: Stock in district granaries second half of the year 1307/1928-29 (in *man*)

Names granaries	Entries	Entries	Exports	Exports	Stock per 30 Esfand 1307	Stock per 30 Esfand 1307
	Wheat	Barley	Wheat	Barley	Wheat	barley
Karimabad	90,906	88,305	-	-	90,906	88,305
Zaviyeh-ye moqaddaseh	102,573	52,807	-	52,807	102,572	-
Kenareh-ye Kord	61,768	28,954	61,768	28,954	-	-
Kheyrabad	52,948	26,474	52,948	26,474	-	-
Karaj	97,401	21,776	-	21,776	97,401	-
Yengi Imam	62,237	18,980	62,237	18,980	-	-
Total	467,823	247,296	176,953	158,992	290,880	88,305

Source: Government of Iran 1307 b, p. 15.

In Farvardin/March 1929, the Tehran Granary was full and there was no need to buy grain. Therefore, in the last two months of 1307 (January-March/1929) and first month of 1308 (March 1929), no grain was bought. The Alimentation Service focused its attention on the sifting of grain and the delivery of flour to the bakers. On 18 Farvardin 1308/7 April 1929, an inspection was done to assess the condition of the Granary's stock and to prevent damage by insects etc. On 21 Khordad 1308/11 June 1929 the inspection ended. It was

67. Government of Iran 1307 b, pp. 15-16.

found that the Granary's stock was: 13,602,820 *man* of wheat and 413,966 *man* of barley or total of 14,016,785 *man* and that 7,000 *kharvar*s of grain had been lost, most likely due to beetles (*shepsheh*) and weevils (*lombeh*).

In 1929, Mirza Hasan Khan Mehr-Avaran was the manager of the Alimentation Service. He decided to stop the purchase of grain until 1 Tir 1308/22 June 1929, because the existing stock was sufficient for one-year of Tehran's consumption. Therefore, he decided he only needed 80,000 *kharvar*s, of which 30,000 *kharvar*s would be obtained from Crown lands and taxes in kind and 50,000 *kharvar*s from landlords, at a price of 22 *tuman*s per *kharvar*. This decision was made public on 15 Mordad 1308/6 August 1929 and this quantity of grain was soon delivered. The government decided to buy an additional 10,000 *kharvar*s of the 1308/1929 surplus at a lower price, so the Alimentation Service bought a total 60,000 *kharvar*s. At the city gates as well as at the borders of Qom, Saveh and Qazvin guards saw to it that grain from outside did not enter the province of Tehran, which had the desired result. The export of grain from Tehran was banned. Sufficient guards were also employed to prevent the transport of grain without a permit as well as the buying and selling of grain not via the Granary. On 24 Esfand 1308/15 March 1930, the price of bread in Tehran dropped from 24 *tuman*s to 20 *tuman*s per *kharvar*. In that same month, to bolster the Granary's position in the market, steps were taken to prevent spoilage of its stock. Because there was not enough Granary capacity at the premises of the Alimentation Service it was forced the use five of the six district granaries (not used was the one at Kenareh-ye Kord).[68]

Table 5.18: Entries and departures from the Granary in 1308/1929-30 (in *man*)

Description	Wheat	Barley
Stock per 01/01/1308	16,666,079	520,979
Crown lands and Taxation entries	3,227,189	1,978,194
Entries of surplus provincial warehouses	34,425	3,026

68. Government of Iran 1308 a, pp. 15-17; Idem 1308 b.

Entries of purchased grain	5,940,165	5,821
Entries received from provinces	-	181
Total	25,867,858	1,608,201
Sales in 1308	10,906,986	870,546
Stock per 01/01/1309	14,960,872	737,655

Source: Government of Iran 1308 b, p. 16.

In 1929, the Alimentation Service was probably renamed the Alimentation and Guild Service (*servis-e arzaq va asnaf*) and was part of the municipality of Tehran. A circular letter by that service to all bakers, dated 23 Mordad 1309/14 August 1930, informed them of new regulations, including the payment of a fee of 10% for the upkeep of the Service. It further contained detailed instructions on how the interior of the bakery had to be arranged, with a tiled oven and walls as well as with a white-washed ceiling. Also, there had to be a separate basin for water, the flour storage areas had to have a white-washed ceiling and cemented walls. The Alimentation Service was in charge of supplying bakers with 60,000 *kharvar*s of flour during the first six months of the year, which it bought at 15 *tuman*s per *kharvar* (300 kg) and resold to the bakers' guild, which had to repay the sum in 12 installments. The bakers' guild was responsible for the internal distribution of the grain among its members and was also responsible for the repayment of the money owed to the Alimentation Service. From this quantity the volume needed for the military and police was deducted. After the 60,000 *kharvar*s had been supplied the bakers were free to buy and sell grain in the market. To prevent hoarding and price increases, bakers had to apply the government's fixed bread prices.[69]

The *sangak*, *lavash* and *taftun* bakers, who formed a guild, were divided into 10 sections or *jowqeh*, and each section was responsible for (i) the purchase of one-tenth of the municipal wheat; (ii) for five percent of the daily wheat consumption of Tehran; and (iii) the rapid daily sale of good quality bread throughout the year. Each section had to appoint a representative. These ten representatives

---

69. Rowghani 1385, pp. 53-55; Baladiyeh-ye Tehran 1310, p. 194.

were jointly responsible to the Alimentation and Guild Service and for their members for one year. Within two weeks all bakers had to sign an undertaking promising to adhere to the various rules. A baker who did not sell good bread, that days' bread would be all given to the orphans and poor. Fuel had to be distributed among members in an equitable manner. The price of bread was fixed at 9 `*abbasi*s per *man*. If they could not bake good bread they had to buy good wheat at whatever cost, while the price of bread remained unchanged.[70] In the following years the operating rules for bakers were refined and reinforced.

Table 5.19: Chiefs of the *Edareh-ye Arzaq-e `Omumi-ye Eyalat-e Tehran* (1918-35)

Name	Dates	Source
Lambert Molitor	September 1918-April 1922	See text
A. Willemsens	October 1920-?1921	See text - acting
Kamal al-Vezareh	?1921-July 1921	See text
Mirza Eshaq Khan	April 1922-1923	See text - acting
Col. Charles McCloskey	April 1923-March 1927	Government of Iran 1305 a, p. 6.
Richard W. Bonnevalle[71]	June 1927-March 1928;	Government of Iran 1306 a, p. 7; Idem 1306 b, p. 7; Idem 1306 d, p. vii
Soltan Hoseyn Mirza Rakhshani	March 1928-1929	Government of Iran 1307 a, p. vii; Idem 1307 b, p. 23
Mirza Ahmad Khan Mahmudi	March-September 1929	Government of Iran 1308 a, p. v
Mirza Hasan Khan Mehr-Avaran	September 1929- March 1931	Government of Iran 1308 b, p. 7
Col. Khodayar Khodayari	March 1931-1935	IOR/L/PS/12/3451, p. 33

70. Rowghani 1385, pp. 56-57.

71. His function was also listed as Chief of the General Alimentation and Motor Transport Service.

The world-wide Depression of 1929 caused problems for, among others, the price-fixing policy of the Alimentation Service. Due to the effects of the Depression, domestic market prices were rising and the price of silver was rock bottom and thus, also that of the silver *qran*, while the government's attempt to control the rate of exchange failed. To deal with many, if not all, of the problems, on 11 March 1931 the *Majles* passed and ratified the Trade Monopolies Act of 25 February 1930. The new law created government monopolies over sugar, opium, tobacco, tea, matches, and cotton piece goods as well as of wheat and rice. Later that year, the rules were relaxed for the last three products. In the case of wheat and rice, Foroughi, the Minister of National Economy sent Parliament the Bill on Exemption of Customs duties on grain exports, which it approved on 9 Shahrivar 1309/30 September 1930. Forughi justified the Bill by arguing that:

> One of the most important means of improving the economic situation is to promote the export of Iranian goods to foreign countries. It may be exported in large quantities, but what has made it most difficult to export grain is the levying of 15 *qran*s per *kharvar* of customs duties. Therefore, in order to eliminate this ban, the following articles are submitted and its approval is requested.
>
> Article 1: From the date of enactment of this law, the export of wheat and barley from Iran will be exempted from paying one *shahi* per *man* of export duties, and two *shahi*s per *man* of road duties.
> Article 2: The Ministry of Finance is in charge of implementing this law.[72]

Although grain export was exempt of paying duties, traders still had to get a special and expensive license to trade in cotton piece goods, wheat, and rice. Henceforth, all foreign trade of the other products was done by the Ministry of Commerce. The law's objective was to

72. *Majalleh-ye Otaq-e Tejarat* no. 11, 1309, p. 11. With thanks to Dr. Shahram Gholami for this reference.

remedy foreign exchange problems and to cushion the economy of Iran against the Depression, to reduce the alleged margin between imports and exports, secure greater exchange stability, increase Iran's bargaining power (especially vis-a vis the Soviet Union) and to stimulate domestic production and industrial development. In theory, the entire foreign trade of Iran had become a government monopoly, but in actual practice imports were subjected to a system of quotas and import licenses and in most cases, made dependent on prior export of Iranian goods. The immediate effect was to disturb trade conditions.[73]

The Alimentation Service continued its activities, while it suffered from various external and internal problems, mostly due to its management by self-interested parties. One not so shining example is that of Col. Khodayar Khodayari, a close friend of Reza Khan in the Cossack Brigade (from which was fired in 1917 for bribery) and his supporter in the coup d'etat in 1921. Thereafter he held several ministerial posts, while in 1931 he became Director of Alimentation Service.[74] The functions of the Alimentation Service were continued by the government in accordance with the law of 1311/1932 approving the construction of a grain elevator. In 1936, the construction of 21 grain elevators was approved, but only the one in Tehran was completed (July 1939) before Reza Shah's abdication. The other grain elevators (Tabriz, Isfahan, Mashhad, Kermanshah, Ahvaz and Shiraz) were unfinished shells lacking the necessary machinery. However, they stood as symbol of the government's realization that, combined with control over distribution and the price of grain, regional granaries were the key to successfully resolve the recurring food crises. Each region with a grain elevator was to be self-sufficient in securing

---

73. Simmonds 1935, p. 1; Administration Report 1931, pp. 9-10 (with details about the working of the law and problems with its implementation).

74. IOR/L/PS/12/3451, p. 33. For more information on Khodayar Khan, see Varjavand 1349, vol. 1, pp. 673-74, which confirms the British assessment of this officer, who stole himself rich and became a major greedy landlord. On the abuses of the bread question, see Floor 2015, pp. 149, 154-55 and Idem 2018, pp. 112-26.

its food supply.[75] Originally, 21 grain-elevators were planned to be built, but only seven were constructed with a capacity of 170,000 tons. By the end of WW II only three had been completed with a storage capacity of 92,000 tons, representing 5% of the annual crop and 10% of urban consumption. The grain elevator in Tehran was among the largest in the world.[76] Its storage capacity was to be used as government leverage in the grain market, for this large concrete grain elevator, "called in Persia the Silo, also housed a flour mill, equipped with modern machinery," was the main source of flour for Tehran.[77] The Alimentation Service's line or supervisory Ministry of Finance set prices for grain, with a view to secure Tehran's food supply and stimulate grain production.[78] In 1932, the British embassy in Tehran reported that due to recurring food supply problems (caused by drought and sub-optimal management), the Alimentation Service was 2.5 million *qrans* in debt.[79]

Although the responsibility of the Alimentation Service was limited to the food supply of Tehran, if need be, its activities also were extended to other cities, as discussed above. It also continued to do so in the years thereafter, when needed. For example, in 1932, the failure of rain and consequently of the crops in the province of Bushehr caused serious problems for its population. Wheat and barley prices soared, until the municipality imposed price control; wheat straw was unobtainable. The governor of Bushehr made real efforts to help the sufferers and after a month of hard work was able to overcome Tehran's apathy by convincing it to exempt wheat and fodder import from trade monopoly restrictions. Wheat from Kerman and aid did not reach Bushehr until October. At Christmas rain fell and next year's crop prospects looked good.[80] There was drought again in 1933 in

75. Avery 1967, pp. 243-44; Yakta'i 1340, pp. 414-15. The construction was already planned in 1928, see Government of Iran 1307 a, p. 22.

76. Agah 1958, pp. 182-83.

77. Millspaugh 1945, p. 100. In fact, eight of these silos were built.

78. Gholami 1396, p. 221.

79. IOR/L/PS/12/3465, p. 3.

80. Administration Report 1932, pp. 4-6, 9.

Bushehr province; consequently animals died by the thousands as the crops had failed. "The Government had sent 5,000 tons of grain from Mohammerah to be used as food and seed, the Governor of Bushire had requisitioned money from the few wealthy of Bushire and had brought 2,000 tons of wheat from Basra, 2,000 tons from Kermanshah, and from other places had come 2,000 tons of wheat and 1,600 tons of barley. Water, too, had been brought down from Mohammerah to be distributed to the people in skins." Nobody died of starvation, but there were many thin people. The Resident commented that "it was pitiful to see the old people and the animals."[81]

In July 1935, the government created a Company for the Stabilization of Prices of Cereals (*Sharekat-e sehami-ye tathbit-e ghalleh-ye Iran*) for buying and selling grain domestically before the harvest, and if need be to sell the surplus abroad. It further fixed grain prices annually with a view to capture more revenues as well as to prevent hoarding and other supply problems.[82] Bakers continued to obtain their grain from the *edareh-ye koll-e ghalleh va nan*, an office of the Price Stabilization Company, which also had the monopoly for the distribution of grain.[83] In its budget for 1314/1935-36, the government allocated 30 million rials for the Company and stated that "with regard to the stabilization of the price of grain, it was stated that this was intended to secure for agricultural producers a fair price for their grain; as a result their prosperity would be increased, and, as a consequence, their ability to purchase the produce of the towns."[84] According to the British, however, because of rising inflation the government price was always too low for the peasants, even though it kept urban bread prices also low.[85] The establishment of the new Price Stabilization

---

81. Administration Report 1932, p. 5; Merritt-Hawkes 1935, p. 4.
82. Gray 1938, p. 17; Gholami 1396, p. 221. It shares were owned by the Ministry of Finance (50%) and the Agricultural Bank (*Bank-e Falahati*) (50%).
83. Yakta'i 1340, pp. 410-14.
84. IOR/L/PS/12/3465, Mr. Knatchbull-Hugessen to Sir John Simon (FO, London), April 23, 1935.
85. Skrine 1962, p. 174. For a discussion of the success or not of the price fixing policy, see Gholami 1396, pp. 220-26.

Company meant the abolishment of the Alimentation Service; Col. Khodayar Khodayari, the head of the Alimentation Service became a director of the Pahlavi Bank in that same year.[86] On 9 September 1936 the export of wheat became a government monopoly, while in 1937 the Company became a department under the Ministry of Finance.[87]

Discussion

Until the second decade of the twentieth century the government of Iran had neither a policy nor an institutional arrangement to effectively deal with the occurrence of famine. Whenever famine happened, government reaction (either local or national) was invariably too little and too late and always was of an isolated and temporary nature. It was only after 1917 that the government created a permanent institution – the Alimentation Service or *edareh-ye arzaq*- that had to prevent the recurrence of famine in Tehran. In Tabriz, a similar organization functioned under the Municipality, but it is unknown until when. Although the government had a regular implementation agency, it had as yet not formulated an official government policy, i.e. one that had been adopted by the *Majles*. The basis or outline of such a policy had been written by Lambert Molitor in 1917, after he had successfully led the effort to combat famine in Tabriz. Although he was given the task to direct the Alimentation Service in Tehran as of June 1918, the guidelines he was given was not a government policy, but rather a set of terms of reference (TOR). Thus, whenever new issues arose that were not covered or clearly spelled out in his TOR Molitor and later his successors had to ask the line Minister to take specific decisions.

At first, the Alimentation Service operated in Tehran and Tabriz. However, after 1923, it apparently only operated in Tehran, because

86. IOR/L/PS/12/3451, p. 33. According to Varjavand 1349, vol. 1, p. 674, Khodayar Khan was for a short period chief of Grain, Bread and Crown lands (*ghalleh, nan va khalesejat*), but he does not mention when.

87. Gray 1938, p. 17; Gholami 1396, p. 221.

there are no data available that indicate that it still was active in Tabriz after that year. This is also clear from the quarterly, and later semi-annual, reports by the Ministry of Finance that detail the activities of the Alimentation Service, which don't mention any activity outside of Tehran. A short-lived exception occurred in 1925, when, due to the severity of a national famine, the Alimentation Service opened temporary purchasing branches in 52 provincial locations. Unfortunately, the available data don't mention the names of all these locations. In mid-1927, all but eight of these provincial purchasing branches were closed.

As of 1918 until 1927 the Alimentation Service was mostly led by foreign officials (Molitor 1918-22 and McCormack 1923-27), who were also in charge of the collection of the direct taxes, which included land taxes in kind, and of the taxes from Crown lands. As of the last quarter of 1927 the Alimentation Service was directed by Iranian officials until the tasks of the Service were taken over by the Company for the Stabilization of the Price of Grain in 1935.

In short, from 1918 to 1929 on average 30,000 tons of flour per year were supplied to bakers in Tehran, excluding the consumption of hight-income private households and the military, who saw to their own needs. The grain was obtained from tax payments in kind, Crown land (*khaleseh*) revenue, and purchases in the market.[88] In doing so the government was able to keep famines like the 1917-18 one within bounds and as such the performance of the Alimentation Service may be called a qualified success. Of course, this success came at a price, because the government had to borrow money (see Appendix I) to finance the large-scale purchases of grain and trucks as well as to pay the expenditure of hiring transporters and staff. The reverse side of this success is that this came at the price of the welfare of the peasantry.[89] Thus, Molitor's and Jamal's premise that the government

---

88. Baladiyeh-ye Tehran 1310, pp. 200-03.

89. This was contrary to the intention of the Millspaugh mission, which stated as it policy that to ensure the food supply of the central cities required control of agriculture, but as much as possible this should not trouble the output of their environing areas. Government of Iran 1305 b,

would be able to make money through proper management of its grain reserves was never realized. In fact, throughout its entire existence the government was forced to subsidize the bread price.

Despite these high cost, neither the Alimentation Service nor the new Company that took over from it in 1935 addressed the underlying causes of the occurrence of famine. Their main interest was to secure the supply of grain to Tehran (initially also to Tabriz), erroneously assuming that the peasants who had to give up their grain had enough left for auto-consumption and seed. This assumption was wrong as indicated by the hordes of peasants that flooded the city when famine was severe (1917-18; 1925-26).[90] In one instance, in 1304/1925-26, the Alimentation Service actually had to make grain and seed available to peasants to prevent them from abandoning their villages, which would have created a shortfall in next year's harvest. However, although advisers pointed out the need for agrarian reform to address the causes of famine, the country's elite was not yet ready for such a revolutionary leap forward. A hesitant step into this direction was the distribution of better seed to peasants on Crown lands and to landowners, who were willing to collaborate, to boost grain production to benefit Tehran, an activity the Alimentation Service pursued in the 1920s. However, providing seed without changing the grain market's other parameters had unexpected consequences that the Service had not foreseen. For example, in 1304/1925-26, the Alimentation Service lent 19,000 *tumans* to the peasants of Tehran province as price support for the purchase of seed to encourage them to produce more grain and prevent a recurrence of the grain shortage that had occurred during that year. However, in 1928 it was reported that the peasants were unable to pay back, because the fixed official

p. 21.

90. "The depopulation of some of the country districts has been mentioned above. In the towns of Tehran, Hamadan, Kazvin and Zinjan, the same famine conditions of course prevailed and were aggravated by the influx of starving rustics. In Hamadan in the spring of 1918 from 160 to 200 persons daily were reckoned to be perishing from hunger, and in Tehran the mortality from famine and disease, chiefly influenza, is said to have totaled 100,000." IOR/L/MIL/17/15/23, p. 168.

price of grain had remained unchanged, while the peasants had made major expenses for seed and other work to achieve a bumper harvest. As their grain surplus would result in a lower price, because the market price was free, or the Ministry of Finance might lower it somewhat, the peasants would suffer a loss. It was expected that this would inhibit them from increasing grain production in the future, thus having the opposite effect than had been intended.[91]

Although as of 1935 the Price Stabilization Company continued the Alimentation Service's activities (grain distribution; price fixing; seed distribution) there was a difference. Whereas the Alimentation Service had been limited to the province of Tehran, the Company had a national task. Not only had it to see to it that Tehran, but also that other cities were supplied with adequate grain supplies. Moreover, the Company had the monopoly of trade in grain, thus having full control over all grain markets in Iran, a remit that the Alimentation Service never had. This monopoly role of the state as a buyer and keeping crop prices artificially low had a negative impact on the rural population. For the peasants were forced to subsidize the urban consumers, and in particular the urban elite, by sacrificing their own desire for better and increased consumption. Peasants were penalized by the (i) difference in the government price of wheat, barley and other grains and those prevailing in the free market and (ii) disregard for the local needs that were considered secondary to that of the big cities.[92]

After the abdication of Reza Shah in August 1941 following the invasion of Iran by the Allies famine broke out in 1942, due to failing rains during the winter of 1941-42. Also, because the old controls, legal and bureaucratic, were not applied any longer hoarding, sales across the border, selling at high prices and bread adulteration became familiar characteristics of Iran's bread supply.[93] It is emblematic that one of those hoarders was the former head of the Alimentation Service, Khodayar Khodayari, who was one of the many major landowners,

91. Government of Iran 1307 a, pp. 20-24.

92. Katouzian 1981, p. 133; Gholami 1397, pp. 318-26.

93. For a discussion of these problems, see Floor 2015, pp. 149, 154-55 and Idem 2018, pp. 112-26.

who misused his position to enrich himself during the famine years of 1941-42. According to the British, Khodayari "attracted notoriety to himself in the autumn of 1942 by being accused, probably with justice, of hoarding large quantities of grain in his villages near Tehran. The Minister of Food, Farrukh, had a public quarrel with him, as a result of which Khudayar threatened to shoot him. An influential man of the old school, and one of Reza Shah's creatures. Has never had any scruples about robbing, thereby accumulating a large fortune."[94] Iran overcame the vagaries of the 1941-42 famine, whose impact lasted well into 1944, with great difficulty, and in the years thereafter was able to effectively address similar outbreaks.[95] Despite the two decades of experience gained by the Alimentation Service, by the Company for the Stabilization of Prices and by the Ministry of Food Supply (*Khvarbar*) during the food shortage years of 1941-44, in 1949 the government of Iran still had no permanent national organization to deal effectively with the results of the outbreak of famine.[96]

94. IOR/L/PS/12/3451, p. 33.
95. See Floor 2015; Idem 2018.
96. Overseas Consultants, vol. 3, p. 99.

APPENDIX I

The Debt Situation of the Alimentation Service

By 1919 the government of Iran had hardly any debts with the IBP. However as of March 1919 it began borrowing money to finance the purchase of grain to supply Tehran. During the next decade the government continued to ask IBP for additional loans, which carried a rate of interest of 6%, 7% or 9%. Initially, the security for these loans were the Customs receipts, while as of 1923 loans were made with 20% of first exploration shares of the APOC as guarantee. The IBP's loans were very important in the fall of 1925, when famine threatened the country and large extra-budgetary expenditures had to be made (see above).[1]

		Cumulative		Balances	
Date	Total advances (krans)	Alimentation advances (krans)	Interest rate	Sterling overdraft (£ Sterling)	Interest rate
March 1919	5,500,000	-	9%	-	-
September 1920	18,189,097	-	9%	-	-
September 1921	8,471,044	1,502,000	9%	402,515	9%
March 1922	4,5761,285	2,252,187	9%	49,929	9%
September 1922	12,025,500	3,495,134	7%	150,000	7%
September 1923	29,270,940	9,785,350	7%	700,000	7%
March 1924	21,460,580	10,465,250	7%	700,000	7%

1. Moody's Analyses of Investments 14 (1923), p. 514; Idem 15 (1924), New York, p. 567 (394,891 *tumans*); 14th report Alimentation Trust Fund (891,247,29 *qrans*).

September 1924	8,307,890	2,147,810	7%	900,000	7%
March 1925	22,131,370	1,078,280	9%	631,732	9%
March 1926	27,581,880	22,418,840	7%	-	-
March 1927	n.a.	18,900,000	6%	-	-
March 1928	8,258,560	5,616,310	6%	-	-

Source: Jones 1986, vol. 1, p. 197.

After the last time that the *Alimentation Service* borrowed money from the Imperial Bank of Persia, its financial situation at the beginning of 1307 till the end of Shahrivar 1307/21 September 1928 was as follows:

	End 1306/20 March 1927		End Shahrivar 1307/21 Sept. 1928	
Description	Loan	Assets	Loan	Assets
IBP loans	5,616,307,20	-	5,770,755.65	-
Loan to Treasurer-general with profits	47,517,335.35	-	46,517,335.35	-
Loans to buy grain	1,988,667.35	-	2,241,251.05	-
Loans to private persons re grain price	-	-	6,479,831.15	-
Loans available in cash in Center and Provinces		3,305,449.55	-	3,610,578.60
Loans for the price of grain on hand in the Center and provinces	-	31,989,061.40	-	39,505,081.35
Loans of collections case that are slowly collected	-	1,845,544.30	-	1,476,055.90
Delinquent loans and part of transport assets	-	16,212,285.00	-	15,935,-4-.25

Non-specified loans due to losses 304	-	1,769,969,60	-	482,408.10
Total	55,122,309.85	55,122,309.85	61,009,173.20	61,009,173.20

Source: Government of Iran 1307 a, p. 22.

After 1928 the IBP no longer provided credit to the Alimentation Service, which as of 1308/1929 received funds to buy grain from the Ministry of Finance, which were given as a loan.[2]

2. Government of Iran 1307 b, p. 16 (with further financial data).

APPENDIX II

Source: MA, Farde 41, 4102.pdf.

یادداشت در باب ارزاق (نان) طهران

مقدمه

مقصود از اطلاعات مفصل ذیل آنست که دولت علیه ایران امنیت امور ارزاقی را در پایتخت و سایر نقاط درک نموده و اساساً برای مسئله نان در آتیه اقدامات لازم را بنماید. هرچند خلاصه ترتیباتی که معمول و مجری گردیده در اینجا نگارش یافته ولی امیدوار است در آتیه نزدیکی بتواند تاریخچهٔ در خصوص ارزاق تدوین و بنظر عموم برساند.

ترتیب نان قبل از تأسیس ارزاق

متأسفانه عمل نان در ایران مخصوصاً در پایتخت، همیشه مسئله سیاسی و دخالت عمده در پلتیک داشته. قبل از آنکه تأسیساتی در این باب بشود، در امر خبازخانه مراقبت و خبازان شخصاً بوسایل مختلفه تهیه گندم دکاکین خود را دیده و دولت نیز غله خود را بقیمت نازلتری بانها میداده است ولی مشارالیهم بدولت هیچگونه فائده از حیث مالیات صنفی یا عوارض دیگر نمی پرداختند و چنانکه در افواه مشهور است مراقبین عمل نان غالباً تطمیع شده و باجحافات و تعدیات خبازان از حیث ازدیاد قیمت و یا خوبی و بدی نان وقع و اهمیّتی نداده و گوش خود را بفریاد این و آن بسته دنیا پس از مرگ، چه دریاچه سراب را شعار خود ساخته بوده اند.

در موقعیکه قانون ۳۲ جوزا از طرف مجلس مقدس دارالشوراء ملی شیّداً ارکانه نسخ گردید قانون تشکیلات مالیه قائم مقام آن چندی بعد شد. مخزنهای اداره انبار در اثر تشکیلات سابقه پر از گندم و جو بود و در زمان وزارت مالیه مرحوم امیر نظام حقوق اغلب وزارتخانها را حواله به غله انبار نموده و از هر طرف حوالجات بدست اعضاء و اجزاء مالیه و از انبار جنس بردند و قیمت گندم را به شش تومان آوردند بطوریکه خریدار برای جنس پیدا نمی شد و تنها علافان بقیمت های خیلی نازل علفه را ابتیاع و در سنهٔ بعد اولین محتکر طهران علافان شدند!!!!! بحران اقتصادی استدامه یافت جنس انبار تمام و محلی جز مصالحی که از فخّارخانه بعنوان عشریه گرفته میشود در میان نماند حقوق یکی از وزارتخانه ها را بمحل آجرهای فخار خانه حواله کردند!!!

انبار خالی شد و بدبختانه حاصل در سنه بعد روی خوشی نشان نداده خشک سالی نیز اضافه گردید لذا خبازان موقع را مغتنم و ملاکین احتکار را پیشهٔ خود ساختند چنانچه چندی بعد در ورامین و خوار انبارهای زیر زمینی کشف گردید که جنس دو سال قبل را در آنجا مخفی داشته بودند پیش آمدهای مزبور قحطی را آورد و جنس نایاب و قیمت آن به یکصد و پنجاه تومان رسید بیست هزار نفر در طهران تلف گردید چند محتکر ثروت خود را چندین برابر نمودند و دولت علیه برای جلوگیری از اتلاف نفوس متوسل بدمپخت شد و جمعی بواسطه بعضی علل از خوردن آن دمپخت معدوم شدند کرورها تومان ضرر دولت گردید که در دفاتر وزارت مالیه ثبت است خباز خانه آن موقع بدون دیناری بدولت رساند و یا آنکه سر و روئي به بامور خبازی دهد مخارج آن در ماه بالغ بر هفتصد الی یکهزار و پانصد تومان بود.

اذهان عموم بقدر مشوّش و پریشان بود که بنظر هیچکس راه چارهٔ نمیرسید علت العلل این مصائب و بدبختی غفلت یا سهل انگاری و یا عدم تشکیلات صحیحه در آنموقع بوده است وبس، و گمان میرود هیچکس نتواند انکار این نقطه نظر را نماید. کابینه آقای وثوق الدوله بروی کار آمد و در آنوقت است که دولت درک نمود اگر مسئله نان اداره شود از اتلاف نفوس و قحطی تا اندازهٔ میتوان جلوگیری نمود و از حیث توسعه فلاحت در سنه بعد بآن خاتمه داد.

مولیتور در اینموقع مانند سایر متفقین بواسطه استیلا قشون عثمانی در آذربایجان بطهران آمده بود نظر باطلاعات و تجاربی که در امور ارزاق تبریز در چند سال قبل (1917-18) بدست آورده بود از طرف دولت وقت برای تأسیس خبازخانه و ا زاق طهران نامزد گشت.

دورهٔ اوّل تصدی

در برج اسد نوبت تأسیسات ارزاق شروع شد در صورتیکه در ادارهٔ انبار غله دولتی فقط برای مصرف دو سه روز جنس موجود بود و خوراک روزانه شهر بالغ بر ۲۵۰ خروار میشد اقداماتیکه در آن دوره با کمک و مساعدت چند نفر از مأمورین قدیمی وزارت مالیه که امانت و صداقت آنها بر همه کس مشهود است بعمل آمده و مساعدتیکه از طرف دولت برای پیش رفت این مسئله شده بقدری کاری و مستحسن است که شرح آن در اینجا بیهوده است زیرا که محققاً یادگار این سال شوم در خاطر عموم طهرانیان مرکوز مانده است آری بحران گذشت حتی جان یکنفر نیز از حیث نان در معرض خطر واقع نشد ادارهٔ بنام اداره ارزاق مشتمل بر دوائر خریداری و حمل و نقل و انبار و خبازخانه تشکیل شد و دولت وملت مسرور شدند امر نان مرتب شد ولی لازم بود اقدامی نمود که منظرهٔ قحطی تجدید نگردد موقعیت مشکل اینجاست زیرا زیرا از یک طرف پیدا کردن جنس برای تغذیه افراد لازم بود و از طرف دیگر بذر و کشت.

خالصجات طهران و مالیات جنس مؤدیان این ایالت باید نصف خوراک سالیانه طهران را بدهد ولی تا آن تاریخ در این زمینه فکری نیندیشیده بودند. مولیتور با مساعدت مأمورین قدیمی ارزاق خالصجات را در تحت وقت درآورده ذرهٔ از بذر و کشت کوتاهی نورزید و مالیات جنسی مؤدیان تا آن اندازه که ممکن میشد از قبل مالیات شعاع السلطنه ها و غیره وصول نمود بذر با کمال خوشی خاتمه یافت و در اینموقع پس از هفت سال جدائی از وطن مألوف از دولت وقت استرخاص نموده بوطن خود حرکت و کفیلی بجای خود گماشت.

در سنه بعد بواسطه جدیت های مذکوره از محصول خود طهران هشتاد هزار خروار از مالیات و خالصه خریداری در انبار تهیه شد و عایدی سالیانه خبازخانه به چهل و پنج هزار تومان رسید از خالصجات ورامین چهارده هزار خروار جنس درصورتیکه در زمان قبل از آن ثلث مزبور از آنجا بانبار وارد نمی شد.

موقعیت ادارهٔ ارزاق در اوّل اشد هذه سنه یا دورهٔ دوم تصدی

اولاً فقدان غله نظر به بدی محصول بواسطه زمستان سخت سنه ماضیه و برف و بارانهای متوالی که یک مقدار بذر را در کلیه نقاط مخصوصاً در بلوکات طهران سوزانده و سن خوارگی در ورامین و زرند. محصول خالصجات بلوکات طهران که بایستی سهم دولتی آن در هذه السنه مطابق بذز کاشته شده

گندم و جو بشود و در سنوات خوبی محصول

گندم و جو بوده و در هذه السنه فقط

گندم و جو بیشتر نداده است و از این بابت تا ۱۵ جدی مقدار ۱۴۴۰۰ خروار گندم و ۶۸۸۰ خروار جو وارد انبار شده است.

ثانیاً انحصار خرید گندم کما فی السابق با دولت و بی قیمت خریداری گندم در انبار بموجب حکم دولت وقت از قرار خرواری بیست تومان و فروش آن بخبّازان از قرار خرواری نوزده تومان معین شده بود و چون بر روساء سابق اداره ارزاق محقق گردیده بود در هذه السنه در بلوکات طهران برای مصرف سال جنس خریدار ی پیدا نخواهد شد آقای حاج فطن الملک رئیس سابق اداره انبار غله دولتی دو فقره قرارداد برای خریداری برای بیست هزار خروار گندم در عراق و بیست هزار خروار در خط خراسان با دو نفر نموده و اداره فعلی بالطبع قراردادهای مزبور را محترم شمرده و حتی به خریدار خط خراسان اجازه داد که تا پنجهزار خروار گندم علاوه بر مقدار قراردادی نیز تهیه نماید. این دو مأمور به ثوب مأموریت خود حرکت کرده و دجار اشکالاتی شدند که در ذیل این یادداشت مشروح خواهد شد.

ثالثاً- کارگران خبازخانه اتحادیه تشکیل داده و از روساء اداره رسمیت آنرا تقاضاء می نمودند و چون این عمل منوط باداره نبود اعتصاب نموده بحضرت عبدالعظیم متحصن گردیده دکاکین را تعطیل نمودند خبازان نیز شکایت از ضرر وارد بخود نموده در بعضی مقامات متنفذ اجتماع کردند که عوارض معمولی خبازخانه را نپردازند.

رابعاً- مسئله جو باعث شکایت کاروانسرا داران و درشکه چیان و صاحبان دواب بود و هر روزه برای بردن جو از میدان، کار بمنازعه و مجادله می کشید.

خامساً- مطابق راپرت های واصلی از مأمورین قزوین و خمسه محقق گردیده بود که در هذه السنه بواسطه نقصان جنس در دو ناحیه مزبوره حمل پنجهزار خروار گندم مالیاتی آنجا برای مصرف طهران غیر ممکن است این بود موقعیّت اداره ارزاق در اول برج اسد هذه السنه تخاقوی ئیل

اقدامات

ادارهٔ فعلی ارزاق

اولاً- اداره فعلی پس از ملاحظه موقعیت مزبوره فوراً صادرات و واردات انبار را تا آن تاریخ تعیین و برآورد مصرف گندم را تا رأس خرمن آتیه یعنی تا اوّل برج اسد ایت ئیل بترتیب ذیل یعنی از قرار ماهی ده هزار خروار تقریباً که یکصد وبیست هزار خروار در سال میشود معین نمود در بادی نظر این عدد اغراق بنظر میآید ولی چون به صورتهای ادارهٔ انبار غله دولتی از اول اسد تا ۱۵ جدی مراجعه شود و صورت آن نیز در ذیل است ملاحظه خواهد گردید که در ظرف پنج ماه و نیم ۵۲۷۰۰ خروار جنس مصرف شده و از این رو مصرف سالیانه ۱۱۴۹۶۰ یا ۱۱۵۰۰۰ خروار می گردد(رجوع بدو صورت ذیل شود)

برای شش ماه و نیمی که باقی میماند یعنی از ۱۵ جدی تا آخر سرطان ایت ئیل تقریباً ۶۵۰۰۰ خروار گندم لازم است که هشت هزار خروار آن فعلاً موجود و ما بقی که ۵۷۰۰۰ خروار است و در نقاط معینه در صورت، تهیه گردیده باید حمل و وارد اداره انبار غله دولتی شود.

صورت برآورد

نمره ترتیبی	شرح	گندم خروار	ملاحظات
۱	موجودی انبار در اول برج اسد	۲۰۰۰	
۲	غلات جنس مالیاتی و خالصه بلوکات طهران	۲۰۰۰۰	
۳	خریداری در ایالت طهران	۴۰۰۰۰	
۴	از جنس مالیاتی عراق	۴۵۰۰	
۵	از جنس مالیاتی ملایر	۱۰۰۰	
۶	از جنس مالیاتی دامغان و شاهرود و سبزوار و نیشابور	۳۰۰۰	پنجهزار بوه ولی دو هزار آن بمصرف خبازخانهای سمنان و دامغان و شاهرود میرسد
۷	از بابت خریداری در عراق	۲۰۰۰	
۸	از بابت خریداری در خط خراسان	۲۵۰۰۰	
۹	از بابت مالیاتی خمسه (۳۰۰۰ خروار)	–	
۱۰	از بابت مالیاتی قزوین (۲۰۰۰ خروار)	–	
جمع		۱۱۵۵۰۰ خروار	

واردی انبار از اوّل اسد تا ۱۵ جدی

نمره ترتیبی	شرح	گندم از قرار من		جو از قرار من	
		سیر		سیر	
۱	موجودی در اول اسد		۲۴۰۰۰۲		۲۳۱۷۸۴
۲	واردی از خالصجات طهران	۲۵	۱۴۴۰۰۲۰	۷۵	۶۸۸۰۳۱
۳	واردی از مالیات طهران	۵۰	۴۳۰۴۵۳	۵۰	۴۳۹۸۷۵
۴	واردی خریداری از طهران	–	۳۷۰۷۰۹۷	۲۵	۶۳۴۳۶۰
۵	واردی مالیات عراق	۲۵	۲۳۲۰۶۷	۷۵	۲۰۵۵۷

۶	واردی مالیات خراسان	۷۵	۳۰۷۹۰	—	۱۹۳۸۰
۷	واردی قزوین	۷۵	۴۵۵۳	۷۵	۳۵۳۱
۸	واردی خریداری عراق	۵۰	۳۵۲۹۹		—
۹	واردی خریداری خراسان		—		
جمع کل واردی		—	۶۰۸۱۳۲۴	—	۲۰۳۷۵۲۱
واردی انبار تا ۱۵ جدی			۶۰۸۱۳۲۴	—	۲۰۳۷۵۲۱
خروج از انبار تا ۱۵ جدی			۵۲۶۸۹۲۴	—	۱۲۲۱۵۲۹
موجودی انبار در ۱۵ جدی			۸۱۲۴۰۰	—	۸۱۵۹۹۲

قیمت فروش گندم بخبازان را ۲۳ تومان یعنی چهار تومان اضافه بر نرخ سابق قرار داد تا ضرری از بابت جنس و تهیه آن بدولت وارد نیاید.

ثانیاً- چون انحصار جو از اول برج عقرب با دولت شد پس از ملاحظهٔ احصائیه نواقل و تدقیق در مصرف جو چران شهری معلوم گردید که مصارف نظامیان ماهی یکهزار و پانصد خروار و مصارف شهری ۳۰۰۰ خروار میباشد و برای هشت ماه یعنی از اول عقرب تا آخر جوزاء ایت ئیل ۳۶۰۰۰ خروار جو نیز باید تهیه گردد.

موجودی در انبار در اوّل عقرب	۹۰۰۰	خروار
خریداری در ایالت طهران	۱۲۰۰۰	خروار
در ولایات	۱۵۰۰۰	خروار
جمع	۳۶۰۰۰	خروار

ثالثاً- بدسائس خبازان و شکایات آنها خاتمه داد یعنی بر آنها اعلام نمود که دولت پش از این همه زحمت حاضر نیست دستخوش چند نفر گردیده و نان سیصد هزار جمعیت پایتختی بواسطه حرکات ناهنجار جمعی خراب گردد و بنابراین هرکس حاضر باطاعت اوامر اداری و قیمتی که دولت معین نموده نمی باشد دولت دکانش را اداره خواهد کرد و بهمین ترتیب تا این تاریخ دولت ئارای ۱۵ باب دکان خبازی است.

رابعاً- برای تأمین ارزاق پایتخت با نهایت صرفه جوئی یعنی با ملاحظه پریشانی و افلاس فرد فرد مملکت اداره ارزاق مجبور شد از ترقی قیمت جنس در عراق جلوگیری کند چه بواسطه تجارت جنس برای همدان و قزوین روزبروز قیمت جنس در ازدیاد بود و از نه تومان به شانزده تومان رسید و بیم آن میرفت جنس مازاد آنجا را برای طهران نتوان تهیه نمود لذا مأمورینی بدانجا اعزام و و پس از جلسه مشورت با متنفذین آن ناحیه از ملاک و غیره قیمت جنس در سلطان آباد به ۱۳ تومان و یازده تومان نه قران و ده تومان تعیین گردید و خط زنجیری برای منع خروج جنس تأسیس گشت.

برای تحکیم کار عراق نانواخانه سلطان آباد و قم نیز اداره شده قیمت عادلانه برای نان این دو ناحیه قرارداد تا مسئله نان را ملاکین و مجتکرین وسیله ننمایند. خبازخانه گم نهایت لزوم را داشت چه بدون آن ممکن بود مقداری جنس عراق باسم نان قم بآنجا حمل و و از آن نقطه بجاهای دیگر یعنی قزوین و کاشان و غیره برای تجارت خارج گردد

۱-نظر بجهات فوق الذکر یعنی برای تأمین خریداری جنس خط خراسان و حمل آن بطهران اداره ارزاق مجبور شد خبازخانهای سمنان و دامغان و شاهرود را نیز تأسیس و دو هزار خروار از جنس مالیاتی آن حدود را که برای طهران تخصیص داده شده بود صرف خبازخانهای آنجا نماید.

ب-خبازخانهای قزوین بخود حکمران نظامی آنجا محول و جنس مالیاتی قزوین و یک قسمت از جنس مالیاتی زنجان که هر ساله بطهران حمل میگردید باختیار حکمران قزوین گذارده شد.

اگر حقیقهً اشکالاتی که در این تأسیسات پیش آمده انسان بخواهد تماماً بنگارد مجلّداتی چند خواهد گردید اشخاصیکه امروز با نهایت راحتی از دکاکین نان میخرند نمیدانند کارکنان این اداره چه زحماتی را برای راحتی آنان متحمل شده و میشوند بر اولیاء مملکت است که زحمات کارکنان این ادره را تقدیر نموده اظهار رضایت و خوشنودی از آنان نمایند تا آن دلسردی که بواسطه انتشارات موهن در جرائد در آنها تولید شده زائل شود.

حمل جنس

خامساً- مسئله که فعلاً از هر جهت اهمیّت دارد مسئله حمل جنس است که اداره هّم خود را در تأسیس و تنظیم آن گماشته و یک شعبه حمل و نقل در عراق و شعبهٔ دیگری در در شاهرود تأسیس کرده است در حوزه ایالت طهران فعلاً جنسی که مانده عبارت از مقدار کمی بقایای خالصجات و مقدار کمی از ملاکین است که نظر بپارهٔ جهات انبار نموده و آنهم توسط مأمورین مخصوص ضبط(توقیف) تماماً پس از وضع خوراک و بذر و مساعدهٔ رعیت خریداری و بانبار غله دولتی حمل خواهد شد.

واردات انبار بواسطهٔ تنظیم عمل حمل و نقل از ۱۵ جدی زیاد شده چه از ۱۵ قوس تا ۱۵ جدی ۱۰۳۶۳ شتر برای عراق و خط خراسان فرستاده شد و نفرات زیادی از آن فعلاً در مراجعت می باشند. با این اشکالات و موانع و زحمات فوق العاده کارکنان، این اداره گرفتار تهمت و بهتان های غیر قابل تحمل این و آن که از نقطه نظر اغراض یا منافع شخصی مخالف این نوع پیشرفت ها میباشند لا ینقطع می شوند این قبیل سنت ها سلب مسئولیت را فراهم می آورد و این اداره تکلیف و وظیفه خود را تا آخرین نقطه بانجام رسانیده

واقعهٔ که برای رئیس ابار جندی قبل پیش آمد فقط برای این بود که ترتیب حمل جنس بهم خورد (چه رئیس مزبور در عمل حمل و نقل نهایت خبرگی و بصیرت را داشت و از زور کفالت مشارالیه است که ترتیب حمل جنس برشته نظم درآمده هزارها نفر شتر باینطرف و آنطرف اعزام گردید) و شهر از حیث نان در مضیقه افتاده استفاده چیان موقع را غنیمت شمرده بآمال و آرزوی دیرینه خود برسند

دسائس و دسته بندیها و تحریکاتی که در عراق و قم و شاهرود شد چند فقره راپرت آن ضمیمه این یادداشت گشته (تماماً بعرض مقامات عالیه رسیده) و شاهد این عمل است و همین حرکات ناپسند ملاکین و محتکرین عمل حمل را خیلی بتأخیر انداخته چنانکه در حوزهٔ عراق عاقبت امر دولت مجبور شد انبارهای محتکرین و ملاکین را بدواً توقیف و پس از آن پیشنهاد فروش بگیرد که بوسائل دیگری نتواند تشبّث کند.

انقلاب خراسان چهارماه تمام عمل مأمورین این اداره را بتأخیر انداخت و مشارالیهم مجبور شدند در این مدت در دامغان توقف نمایند تا رفع غائله شود و فقط از ۱۵ ربیع الاوّل داخل در انجام مأموریت خود شدند.

خاتمه

تنها مقصودی که در این جا دارد اینست که باطلاع عموم برساند اداره ارزاق بوظائف خود کاملاً عمل کرده و از عهده مسئولیت سنگین خود تابحال برآمده است و توانسته است آنهائی که حاضر شده بودند برای منافع شخصی اوضاع سنه مجاعه در طهران تجدید و کرورها ضرر به دولت و ملت وارد آورند بدون دیناری ضرر و بدون اینکه به بذر و کشت و مساعده و خوراک رعایا و صاحبان آنها لطمه وارد سازد بجای خود نشانیده است ولی اکر تحریکات و دسائسیراجع بامور ارزاق شود یقین است که اولاً مسؤلیت این اداره سلب گردیده و ثانیاً به حمل جنس سکته وارد آمده نان پایتخت تأمین نخواهد گردید

اما از نقطه نظر اقتصادی اداره ارزاق بودجهای خود را بمقامات عالیه تقدیم داشته و مخارج تأسیسات ارزاقی از عایدات خود آن مصرف می گردد و امیدوار است در این سنه از این بابت ضرری متوجه دولت نشود.

تذکّر و یاداوری

۱-دولت باید کشت و زرع یعنی فلاحت را اساساً توسعه دهد و بمؤدیان مالیاتی برای عمل جنسی آنها از دادن هرگونه تخفیفی خودداری کند و در قزوین و زنجان و عراق و دامغان هیچوقت اجازه تغییر ندهد

۲-قانونی در موضوع منع احتکار اغذیه باید از طرف مجلس مقدس وضع گردد

۳-نظارت دولت در عمل خبازان در کلیه ایالات و ولایات اجراء شود

۴-تعمیر راه ورامین و راه قم و عراق و تعمیر پل رودخانه شور و سد بندی رودخانهای خوار و ورامین از طرف وزارت فوائد عامه باسرع وقت

۵-معمول نمودن گاو آهن های اسبی در اینموقع که گاوسیری شیوع یافته

۶-تهیه ده اتومبیل بزرگ (گاری) از طرف دولت فقط برای حمل جنس

۷-امانی عمل شدن کل خالصجات مخصوصاً خالصجات طهران و احتراز از اجاره

APPENDIX III

Letters concerning various Alimentation Service branches

Ministry of Finance

Report no. 166, 01 Tir 1305 [23 June 1926][3]

At 12 noon, the Commissariat was informed that Sheikh Hasan Va`ez had gathered a group at the Friday Mosque and had written a detailed petition on a white cloth (*chelvar*) petitioning His Majesty Reza Shah Pahlavi, may god illuminate his reign and realm, for bread to be free and the Alimentation Service to be abolished, on which they want to the people put [their] seal. I, immediately sent Hoseyn Khan *vakil-bashi* (1st sergeant) to the Friday Mosque with two officers, and after making a phone call to my head office, quickly went to the mosque. After investigating the case, it became clear that when Hazrat Hojjatoleslam Agha Sayyed Mohammad Mojtahed Jolani came to the mosque for prayer, that before starting [his] prayer, Sheikh Hasan went to the pulpit and said: O Hojjatoleslam, as we reported to your blessed presence a few days ago, the people of Hamadan are in trouble because of the Alimentation Service, and they want to submit their petitions to His Imperial Highness for bread to be free and the Alimentation Service to be abolished. Now the petition of the people has been written on white cloth (*chelvar*). After having it sealed by the people, it was decided that, through one person, who is provided with 20 *tuman*s for expenses, the petition should be transmitted via Sayyed Hassan Modarres to His Imperial Majesty or be sent by telegram to His Majesty, which costs 10 to 15 *tuman*s. Then he [Sheikh Hasan Va`ez] begins to read the content of the petition

---

3. Sazman-e Asnad-e Melli-ye Iran, no. 310/2239, p. 3; National Library no. 4740548.

and asks Agha Mirza Mohammad for permission that both of them do not go to the pulpit until the petition is submitted for the people's seals. Agha Mirza Mohammad does not pay any attention to it at all and he prays as usual and leaves the mosque. Sheikh Hasan delivers rousing speeches and encourages people to put [their] seal on and sign the petition.

After a quarter of an hour, he came out of the forty column *shabestan* (underground nave) and brought the petition to the large nave (*shabestan*) and placed it on the mat and began to make it available for sealing and signing. At that time the honored chief arrives and observes that under the supervision of police officers with complete courtesy people in groups gave their seals to Sheikh Hasan without asking what for, and he put the seal on [the sheet for] them. Several people, especially when giving the seal, asked Sheikh Hasan what is this about? He replied, "What do you want to do, believer? Go." Most of those who sealed were from the fourth and fifth class. From the artisans it is thought that not more than 100 people have sealed it. [Some] parents had given their seals to small children to give it to Sheikh Hassan and some gave three seals in stead of one. This continued in this way until 4 p.m. when the honored chief arrived. Sheikh Hasan had become tired, and the famous Sayyed Hasan Va`ez, who lives in Mir Ghazab Square, helped Sheikh Hasan, and sealed the sheet of *chelvar* until the bottom of the page in the above manner. After the first page was finished, no one was willing to put [their] seal on the back of this page. Sheikh Hasan took the sheet and together with Sayyed Hasan left the mosque. In accordance with the order of the chief, I followed Sheikh Hassan to bring the paper with him to the government office. On the way, because talking with Sheikh Hasan [failed], the chief himself, contemptuously took the sheet from Sheikh Hasan and brought it to the government office. After official formalities the chief and his agents returned and were patrolling in the bazaar. The artisans were working safely and there was and is complete order. Finally, [I have to say that] the Commissariat is suspicious about the people who were around Sheykh Hassan during the sealing of the petition (*chelvar*). These people seem to have been the instigators of this case. Their identities and particulars will be investigated and a report will be sent.

وزارت مالیه

سواد راپورت نمره ۱۴۶ مورخه اول تیر ۱۳۰۵

بعد العنوان

در ساعت ۲۱ ظهر و کمیساریا راپورت دادند که در مسجد جامع، آقا شیخ حسن واعظ، جمعی را جمع، و عریضه مفصلی بر روی چلواری راجع به آزاد بودن نان و موقوف داشتن اداره ارزاق به اعلیحضرت قدر قدرت شاهنشاه رضاشاه پهلوی خلد الله و ملکه و سلطانه، تهیه [کرده] و می‌خواهند به مهر عامه برسانند. فوری حسین خان وکیل باشی را با دو نفر آژدان به مسجد جامع فرستاده و پس از عرض مراتب با تلفون به حضرت ریاست جلیله، خودِ چاکر نیز فوری در مسجد حاضر شده و تحقیقات اطراف قضیه معلوم شد موقعی که حضرت حجت الاسلام آقای آقا سید محمد مجتهد جولانی جهت نماز به مسجد تشریف می آورند، قبل از شروع به نماز، آقا شیخ حسن بالای منبر رفته اظهار میکنند: حجت الاسلاما؛ چنانچه چند روز قبل هم به حضور مبارک رساندیم و اهالی همدان از جهت بودن اداره ارزاق در مضیقه هستند و می‌خواهند عرایض خود را جهت آزاد بودن نان و برداشتن اداره ارزاق به اعلیحضرت همایونی ارواحنا فدا عرضه بدارند. و اینک عریضه ملت روی ورقه چلوار نوشته و تهیه شده پس از رسانیدن به مهر ملل تصمیم گرفته شد که توسط یک نفر که ۰۲ تومان مخارج او منظور شده، عریضه توسط آقای آقا سید حسن مدرس به استماع اعلیحضرت مقدس همایونی ارواحنا فدا رسانده شود و یا اینکه به وسیله تلگراف آنهم ۰۱ تا ۵۱ تومان مخارج بازدید شده به عرض اعلیحضرت برساند. بعد شروع می کند به قرائت مضمون عریضه و اجازه از حضرت آقای آقا میرزا محمد میخواهد که هر دو کس به منبر نرود تا ورقه را به مهره اهالی برسانند. از طرف حضرت آقا میرزا محمد ابداً اظهار تکلیفی نمیشود و حضرت معظمله به عادت معمولی نماز را خوانده از مسجد تشریف می برند. آقا شیخ شروع میکند به دعوت مردم . نطقهای مهیج که اهالی را برای مهر و امضاء ورقه ترغیب می نموده است.

پس از ربع ساعت از شبستان چهل ستون بیرون آمده و ورقه را به شبستان بزرگ آورده روی حصیر می گذارند و شروع به رسانیدن مهر و امضا می نمایند در این اثنا حضرت ریاست جلیله تشریف آورده ملاحظه فرمودند اهالی در تحت مراقبت های آژدانها با کمال نزاکت دست به دست آمده مهر های خود را بدون اینکه بپرسند موضوع چیست، به دست آقا شیخ حسن می‌دادند و ایشان مهر می‌کردند. چند نفر مخصوصاً موقع دادن مهر از آقا شیخ حسن پرسیدند که مطلب چیست؟ جواب دادند که مومن می خواهی چه کنی؟ برو. و اکثر مُهر کنندگان از طبقه چهارم و پنجم بودند از کسبه بازار تصور نمی رود بیش از ۰۰۱ نفر ورقه را مهر کرده باشند. [برخی ها] از والدین اطفال خورد بیشتر مهر آورده به آقا شیخ حسن می‌دادند و بعضی ها هم مخصوصاً عوضِ یک مهر سه مهر می دادند. قضیه به این طریق تا ۴ بعد از ظهر با تشریف فرمایی حضرت ریاست جلیله ادامه داشت. شیخ حسن شخصاً خسته شده، مقداری هم آقا سید حسن واعظ معروف که ساکن میدان میرغضب است، با آقای شیخ حسن همراهی کرده و ورقه چلوار را تا

آخر صفحه به طریق معروض فوق به مهر رسانیده. پس از اتمام صفحه اول دیگر کسی حاضر نشد در وراء آن را مهر کند. آقا شیخ حسن ورقه را برداشته به اتفاق آقا سید حسن از مسجد بیرون آمده بر حسب دستور ریاست جلیله عقب سر آقا شیخ حسن رفته که ورقه را با خود معظماله در اداره جلیله حکومتی حاضر نمایم. در بین راه چون صحبت و مذاکره با آقا شیخ حسن [به نتیجه نرسید]، خود ریاست حضرت جلیله رسیده به اهانت اخلاق از شیخ ورقه را گرفته با اداره حکومتی بردند. پس از تشریف فرمایی رسمی، ریاست جلیله با مامورین بازگشت و در بازار مشغول گشت بوده اهالی و کسبه در کمال امنیت بر سر کسب و کار خود مشغول و نحیه نهایت انتظام داشت و دارد. و در خاتمه، در اطراف [شیخ] حسن موقع رسانیدن ورقه چلوار به مهر، [برخی] اشخاص بودند که به نظر متحرک و طرف سوءظن کمیساریا واقع، پس از تحقیق از حالات آن‌ها اشخاص را با اسم و رسم تعیین و راپورت عرضه خواهد شد.

امضا کفیل کمیساریا

Ministry of Finance

Office of the Alimentation Service

15 Khordad 1305 [06 June 1926][4]

H.E. the Prime Minister

Regarding the complaint of Mr. Bozorg and Hajji Ali Sonqori, about the confiscating of their wheat by the Amin-e Maliyeh of Sonqor, to His Imperial Majesty registered as no. 179, and which had been submitted to the Ministry of Finance for investigation; I report that according to the results of local fact-finding and documents sent by the Kermanshah tax representative, their complaint [Hajj Ali Songhari and Agha Bozorg] is incorrect and unreasonable. Because as a result of the inspection carried out by the officers of the Alimenation Service, 180 *man* of wheat was discovered in their house and taken to the warehouse. On the same date, the *Amin-e Maliyeh* left 2 *kharvar*s and 40 *man* (30 *man* per head) in their house for their food consumption and a receipt as certification endorsed by one cloth-dealer (*bazzaz*) was taken from them. According to what we learnt, their complaint against us, was only incited by Hajji E`temad Sonqori, because the mentioned Hajji is one of the landlords and speculators there, and some wheat was found in his house. Therefore, Hajj Ali Sonqori has incited Aqa Bozorg to complain about the *Amin-e Maliyeh*. According to letter no. 981, the tax office has requested that such complaints should not be considered, because in the past year the Kermanshah branch of the Alimentation had to collect grain, and landlords were not ready to deliver the surplus of their grain.

The Ministry of Finance.

A copy of the above report was sent to the esteemed Imperial Office.

---

4. Sazman-e Asnad-e Melli-ye Iran, no. 310/2260, p. 1; National Bibliography no. 4744916.

اداره سرویس ارزاق

تاریخ ۱۵ برج ۳ سال ۱۳۰۵

مقام منیع ریاست وزرا عظام

راجع به شکایت آقا بزرگ و حاجی علی سنقری از اقدام امین مالیه سنقر در موضوع ضبط گندمِ مشارالیها به پیشگاه اعلیحضرت همایون شاهنشاهی که طی نمره ۱۷۹ به ثبت و برای رسیدگی به وزارت مالیه احاله فرموده بودند، معروض می دارد، از قرار نتیجه تحقیقات محلی و مدارکی که پیشکار مالیه کرمانشاهان ارسال داشته اظهارات مشارالیهما بی اساس می باشد. زیرا در نتیجه تفتیشی که مأمورین ارزاق می نمایند، مقدار ۱۸۰ من گندم از منزل آنها کشف و تحویل انبار می شود. در همان تاریخ، امین مالیه سنقر برای خوراک عائلهٔ مشارالیهما مقدار دو خروار و ۴۰ من، (از قرار سری سی من) در منزل آنها باقی گذاشته و قبض رسید به تصدیق یک نفر بزاز از آنها می‌گیرد. و مطابق اطلاع به شکایت مشارالیها فقط به تحریک حاجی اعتماد سنقری بوده است. چون حاجی مزبور از ملاکین و محتکرین آنجاست و از منزل مشارالیه مقداری جنس کشف کرده اند. بنابراین آقا بزرگ و حاج علی سنقری را تحریک نموده است از امین مالی شکایت نمایند. اداره مشارالیهما در ضمن مراسله نمره ۱۸۹ درخواست کرده است که به این قبیل شکایات توجهی نشود. زیرا در سنه ماضیه شعبه ارزاق کرمانشاهان مجبور به جمع آوری جنس بوده و ملاکین برای تحویل مازاد اجناس خود حاضر حاضر نبوده اند.

وزارت مالیه

سواد شرح فوق به دفتر محترم مخصوص شاهنشاهی ارسال شد.

Ministry of Finance

03 Bahman 1306 [24 January 1928][5]

To H.E. the Prime Minister

Letter no. 7780 dated 19 Dey 1306/10 January 1928, which includes a copy of the Qazvin Police report regarding the shortage of the crop and the hardship of the peoples' livelihood, was received. In response to this report, it informs the esteemed authorities that the Alimentation Service, as before, is active in Qazvin and has taken and is taking the necessary steps to provide comfort and food for the people. It is obvious that in all places where there is an Alimentation Service, it takes all kinds of possible measures to supply food for the residents there. In other places, the Ministry of Finance basically has followed the same procedure to provide food for the people, i.e. in places where there is a shortage of food, the Taxation Office sells government grain at a fixed fair rate via a commission composed of the provincial or local governor, the financial executive (*pishkar*), the mayor and representatives of the landowners to provide possible relief for residents. The relevant tax authorities have also been ordered to observe the above principle as much as possible to provide food to the people. The report by the police of Qazvin as you may have observed states the same, but in other places, where there is no food shortage, the Taxation offices will sell government grain, as before, at a higher price by auction. Of course, you acknowledge that in this way, the Ministry of Finance will provide the necessary assistance as much as possible to provide relief to different parts of the country. As at the end of letter it is mentioned that permission to export grain from Kermanshah has been given, it is assumed that you have not been properly informed about this, because the Ministry of Finance has not given such permission any way and completely denies the news (marginal handwritten note).

---

5. Sazman-e Asnad-e Melli-ye Iran no. 310/2324, p. 5; National Library no. 4742280.

Preceding [reports] were referenced. Instructions had been given to the Kermanshah [tax office], and as usual, the Ministry of Finance has signed off that to take into account the food situation of the city and the neighboring provinces.

وزارت مالیه

تاریخ ۳ برج ۱۱ سال ۱۳۰۶ نمره ۳۸

مقام منیع ریاست وزرای عظام

مرقومه نمره ۰۸۷۷ در مورخه ۱۹ دی ۱۳۰۶ متضمن سواد راپورت نظمیه قزوین راجع به قلت محصول و سختی معیشت اهالی زیارت گردید. جواباً به استحضار آن مقام منیع می رساند که سرویس ارزاق کما فی سابق در قزوین دائر، و اقدامات لازمه را از برای آسایش اهالی و تأمین ارزاق آنها به عمل آورده و می آورد. در کلیه نقاطی که سرویس ارزاق وجود دارد، بدیهی است حسب الوظیفه جمیع اقدامات ممکنه را برای تأمین آذوقه اهالی به عمل آورده و میآورد. راجع به سایر نقاط نیز وزارت مالیه برای تأمین ارزاق اهالی اساساً این رویه را اتخاذ نموده که در جاهایی که مضیقه ارزاقی هست، اداره مالیه جنس دولتی را به نرخ عادله معینه توسط کمیسیون مرکب از ایالات یا حکمران محل و پیشکار مالیه و رئیس بلدیه و نمایندگان مالکین به فروش برساند تا از این حیث گشایش ممکنه برای اهالی فراهم گردد. و به ادارات مالیه ذی مدخل نیز دستور داده شده است با رعایت اصل فوق، هر قدر ممکن باشد برای تأمین آذوقه اهالی کوشش نمایند. راپرت نظمیه قزوین نیز چنانچه ملاحظه فرموده باشند، مشعر بر همین مراتب است. ولی در سایر نقاط که مضیقهٔ ارزاقی وجود ندارد، ادارات مالیه کما فی سابق جنس دولتی را به اعلی قیمت ممکنه با رعایت اصول مزایده خواهند فروخت. البته تصدیق می فرمایید که به این ترتیب وزارت مالیه لازمه مساعدت را تا سرحد امکان برای گشایش امر ارزاق نقاط مختلفهٔ مملکت به عمل آورده و می آورد. ولی این که در خاتمه مرقومه اشاره شده است که اجازه صدور جنس از کرمانشاهان به خارج صادر گردیده تصور می رود ماوقع را به عرض آن مقام منیع نرسانده اند. زیرا وزارت مالی به هیچ وجه چنین اجازه را نداده و خبر مزبور را کاملاً تکذیب می نماید.

وزارت مالی.

(حاشیه نامه)

سابقه ملاحظه شد. تعلیمی که به کرمانشاهان داده شد، و علی القاعده وزارت مالیه هم امضا فرمودهاند که رعایت ارزاق شهر و ولایات مجاور را بنمایند.

Ministry of the Interior[6]

Chief Office of the National Police Administration

Copy of the report by the police of Qazvin dated 15 Azar 1306/ 07 December 1927, no. 2415, page 1.

Due to the fact that the current year's harvest in Qazvin was not produced due to the three-year war, the Central Alimentation Service has allocated the wheat of Qazvin and Zanjan districts especially to the food supply of Qazvin and fixed its price at 14 *tuman*s per *kharvar*. However, recently the Central Service [in Tehran] informed that the Zanjan wheat should be dispensed with and that the rest of Qazvin's needs will be provided from Kermanshah and Arak, etc. and imported at a price of 17 *tuman*s per *kharvar*. In these last days, due to snow and ice, some mills have stopped working as did the production of flour, so that grain was not supplied to nine bakery shops and caused crowds at the other bakery shops. As a result of this office's notification to the Tax office, the provincial finance manager (*pishkar*), entered into negotiations with the Central Alimentation Service, because no grain was transported from Zanjan and the mills there are not responsible for providing daily flour, it should make a decision to supply the needs of the Qazvin Alimentation Office. In reply, [Central Alimentation] had ordered that, because [grain] must be supplied from other places and will not enter to Qazvin at less than 17 *tuman*s, therefore, the issue of increasing bread prices, in such a way that it does not cause losses to the government, was examined in the provincial Council and its result must be reported. Then, in yesterday's meeting, the council discussed the issue and found out that the wheat in the warehouse is 2,600 *kharvar*s and 5,500 *kharvar*s more are needed to supply

---

6. Sazman-e Asnad-e Melli-ye Iran no. 310/ 2324; pp. 9-10; National Library no. 4742280

the city's bread until the harvest. But because the water mills do not provide enough daily flour supplies, it is necessary to use the carpentry mills, whose rent is more expensive, and for this reason, the price of bread should not be less than one *qran* and 800 dinars per Tabriz *man*, because the price of wheat is 17 *tuman*s and the difference in rent of the mills is fixed at one *tuman*, so that the Taxation office and Alimentation Service have the responsibility of securing the supply of bread until the beginning of the harvest. Therefore, it was approved by the majority that one *`abbasi* per Tabrizi *man* should be added to the price of bread so that the Alimentation Service may quickly supply wheat and dearness can be eliminated. Therefore, it was decided to report the result of the council's decision via the Taxation Office to the Ministry of Finance and the Central Alimentation Service and after approval should be implemented in a timely manner, because [part of] the wheat is supplied from the outside there has been an improvement in bread and its abundance since yesterday.

Place of signature of the chief of police of Qazvin.

وزارت داخله

اداره کل تشکیلات نظمیه مملکتی

سواد راپورت نظمیه قزوین مورخه ۱۵ آذر ماه ۱۳۰۶

نظر به اینکه محصول هذه السنه قزوین به واسطه جنگ سه سالی [است که] عمل نیامده، موسسه ارزاق مرکزی، گندم دولتی بلوک قزوین و زنجان را اختصاص به ارزاق قزوین داده و نرخ را خرواری ۴۱ تومان مقرر داشته بودند. ولی اخیراً از مرکز اطلاع داده‌اند که از گندم زنجان باید صرف نظر نمایید. و بقیه احتیاجات قزوین از کرمانشاهان و عراق و غیره تهیه شود و خرواری ۷۱ تومان وارد خواهد شد. در این چند روز هم به واسطه باریدن برف و یخبندان بعضی آسیابها از کار افتاده اند و در تهیه آرد نکث حاصل شده و به نُه باب از دکاکین خبازی جنسن نرسیده و باعث ازدحام مردم در سایر دکاکین گردیده. در نتیجهٔ تذکر این اداره به اداره مالیه، پیشکار مالی با مراکز داخل مراکز مذاکره شد که چون از جنس زنجان حمله می شود و آسیاب های آنجا هم جوابگوی تدارک آرد یومیه نیست، تضمینی برای تأمین احتیاجات اداره ارزاق قزوین اتخاذ نمایند. [در] جواب، دستور داده بودند چون [گندم] باید از نقاط دیگر تهیه شود و کمتر از خرواری ۷۱ تومان وارد قزوین نخواهد شد، [بنابراین باید] موضوع را در شورای ولایتی مطرح شده، و راجع به ترقی قیمت نان به میزانی که به دولت ضرری متوجه نشود، تصمیم مقتضی اتخاذ، و راپورت دهند. لذا در جلسه دیروز شورا این مسئله مورد بحث و معلوم شد که گندم موجودی در انبار ارزاق ۰۰۶۲ خروار است و ۰۰۵۵ خروبار دیگر احتیاج دارند که تا موقع خرمن نان شهر را تأمین نماید و چون آسیابهای آبی کفاف تدارکات آرد یومیه را نمیدهد، لازم است از آسیاب‌های نجاری هم که اُجرت آن گرانتر است، استفاده نموده و به این جهت نرخ نان را از قرار یک من تبریز یک تومان و ۰۰۸ دینار نمی توان کمتر قرار داد. [به این صورت] که خرواری ۷۱ تومان قیمت گندم و خرواری یک تومان هم تفاوت اجرت آسیاب تعیین شود تا اداره مالیه و [ادارهٔ] ارزاقِ محل، تأمین نان را تا سر خرمن عهدهدار شود. بنابراین با [رأی] اکثریت تصویب شد که [در ازای] یک من تبریز، یک عباسی به قیمت نان علاوه شود تا اداره ارزاق بتواند معجلاً به تهیه گندم اقدام نموده، رفع نگرانی شود. علی هذا مقرر گردید نتیجه تصمیم شورا به وزارت جلیله مالیه و موسسه ارزاق مرکز از طرف اداره مالی راپورت [داده شود] و پس از تصویب به موقع اجرا گذاشته شود. عجالتاً چون مقداری آرد از خارج تهیه شده، از دیروز بهبودی در امر نان و فراوانی آن حاصل شده [است]

محل و امضای رئیس نظمیه قزوین

Ministry of Finance, Correspondence Office[7]

12 Mehr 1306 [05 October 1927], no. 28182

Ministry of the Interior

In this year, in which in some areas the harvest is not satisfactory, while the Alimentation Service branches in part of the provinces have been abolished, landlords and some other people are taking measures that will cause a shortage of bread and hardship. Because it is very important and may have negative effects, this Ministry [Finance Ministry] considers it necessary that a general order be issued by the [Interior] Ministry to the regions and provinces, especially Khorasan, Hamedan and Zanjan, etc., to prevent [such] activities by wheat speculators and as to the collection of taxes by tax officials to provide all help and assistance so that all government grain is collected in the government warehouses. It should be pressed upon the governors that they should not constantly offer government grain for sale, because government grain should be used mainly at the last moment, as it is the only means of preventing and control the operations of speculators. If the government sells its grain in the beginning and when it is finished, the speculators will not see a competitor facing them and will increase the price [of grain], the population will be more and more distressed as a result. Another point in this regard that governors and officials of the Ministry should consider is to keep in mind that the export of grain from one province to another is for [its] sale at exorbitant prices. Under these circumstances the speculators in these times always enjoy two great benefits: one is selling in other provinces and the other is reducing the [amount of] grain in the place of origin and its [consequent] rise in price. By taking note of the above information, it is expected that the necessary orders are issued and that the result is sent to this Ministry.

---

7. Sazman-e Asnad-e Melli-ye Iran no. 310/2329, p. 1; National Library no.7472433.

A copy of the above letter will be sent for the information to the Prime Minister's office.
Ministry of Finance.

وزارت مالیه اداره مراسلات

به تاریخ ۱۲ برج ۷ سال ۱۳۰۶ نمره ۲۸۱۸۲

وزارت جلیله داخله

در حال حاضر سنه که تا اندازه‌ای درباره نقاط وضع محصول رضایت بخش نیست و دوایر ارزاقی در یک قسمت ولایات منحل شده ملاکین و بعضی اشخاص دیگر اقداماتی می نمایند که در نتیجه باعث مضیقه نان و عصر تا حالی از این بابت خواهد شد و چون این مسئله بسیار مهم و ممکن است نتایج سوی داشته باشد این وزارتخانه لازم می‌داند که دستور متحد الشکل از طرف آن وزارت جلیله به ایالات و ولایات مخصوصاً خراسان و زنجان و غیره صادر شود که از اقدامات و مامورین مالیه و معادن را نمایند تا کلیه مالیات جنس دولتی در انبارهای دولتی جمع آوری گردد و ضمن لازم است با حکم تاکید شود که نباید دائماً برای فروش جنس دیوانی پیشنهاد دهند زیرا جنس دولتی اساساً در آخرین موقع باید به مصرف برسانید تا تنها وسیله جلوگیری و تعدیل از عملیات محتکرین باشد و اگر در بدو امر دولت جنس خود را بفروشد و تمام گردد محتکرین رقیبی در مقابل خود نخواهند دید و بر قیمت خواهند افزود و روزبه‌روز مضیقه اهالی از این حیث بیشتر خواهد شد نکته دیگری که حکام و مامورین آن وزارت جلیله باید در این باب در نظر داشته باشند خروج جنس یک ولایت به ولایت دیگر برای فروش به قیمت گزاف است که همیشه در این مواقع محتکرین از دو فایده بزرگ متمتع می شوند یکی از فروش در ولایات دیگر و دیگر کم شدن جنس در محل اولی و ازدیاد قیمت آن با تذکر اطلاعات فوق انتظار دارد که دستور لازم را صادر و نتیجه را به این وزارتخانه ارسال دهند سواد مراسله فوق برای اطلاع مقام محترم ریاست وزرای اعزام ارسال می گردد. وزارت مالیه

Ministry of Finance[8]

Office of the Alimentation Service

08 Mordad 1306 [31 July 1927] no. 23219

His Excellency the Prime Minister

Letter no. 2707, dated 06/04/1306 (22 June 1927), concerning the disturbance about the price [of wheat] in places where the Alimentation [Service] has been dissolved, was received. In reply it is brought to Y.E.'s notice that the Ministry of Finance agrees with the establishment of a commission. At the time of constituting the commission it is required to inform [us] as the representative of this Ministry should also be present.

Regarding the sale of the Damavand grain, it appears that the result of the auction was to the detriment of the Alimentation Service; orders were given to transport it to the Center. In addition, please write us what effect the sale of the grain by auction had on the price, and whether the report received from Damavand is based on some evidence or not.

8. Sazman-e Asnad-e Melli-ye Iran no. 310/2329, p. 4; National Library no.7472433.

وزارت مالیه

اداره سرویس ارزاق

تاریخ ۸ مرداد سال ۱۳۰۶ نمره ۱۳۲۱۹

مقام منیع ریاست وزرای عظام

مرقومه نمره ۷۰۷۲ تاریخ ۶۰۳۱/۴/۶ راجع به اختلال نرخ [گندم] در نقاطی که ارزاق منحل گردیده است، وصول گشته[!]، جواباً به استحضار خاطر مبارک میرساند، وزارت مالیه با تشکیل کمیسیون موافقت دارد. مستدعیست در موقع انعقاد کمیسیون اطلاع فرمایند تا نماینده این وزارتخانه نیز حضور به هم رساند.

راجع به فروش جنس ارزاقی دماوند نظر به اینکه نتیجه مزایده به ضرر سرویس ارزاق بوده، دستور داده شد که حمله به مرکز شود. ضمناً مستدعی است مرقوم فرمایند که فروش جنس به طور مزایده چه تاثیری در نرخ خواهد داشت و آیا راپورت واصله از دماوند متکی به دلایلی بوده است یا خیر.

Prime Minister[9]

Date of record 12 Tir 1306 [04 July 1927]

Ministry of Finance

In places where the Alimentation Service branches were and recently have been dissolved, there will naturally be a disruption of the price of food stuffs. To prevent this from happening, we must think about fixing the price at places where the Alimentation office has been closed. I think a commission needs to be formed. The sale of grain by auction, which, according to information received, is contemplated by the *Amin-e Maliyeh* of Damavand, is not the right way. In any case, the matter has been carefully considered and resolved in an appropriate manner.

9. Sazman-e Asnad-e Melli-ye Iran no. 310/2329, p. 6; National Library no.7472433.

ریاست وزرا

تاریخ ثبت ۱۲ تیرماه ۱۳۰۶

وزارت جلیله مالیه

در نقاطی که اداره ارزاق بوده و اخیراً منحل شده یا می‌شود.، طبعاً نسبت به نرخ ارزاق اختلال حاصل خواهد شد. و برای جلوگیری از این پیش آمد برای تعیین نرخ نقاطی که اداره ارزاق از آنجا برداشته می‌شود باید فکری نمود. و تصور می‌کنم محتاج به تشکیل کمیسیونی باشد. فروش جنس به طور مزایده که از قرار اطلاع واصله امین مالیه دماوند در نظر گرفته است، مورد ندارد و به هر حال موضوع وکیل مد نظر دقت قرار داده به ترتیبی که مناسب باشد اقدام نمایند.

Internal Information[10]

01 Tir 1306/ 23 June 1927

From Damavand.

Due to the dissolution of the Damavand Alimentation [Service], the poor people [are] extremely worried and express their concern. The *Amin-e Maliyeh* held a meeting in his own house where all classes were invited and was attended by the governor and the heads of the government departments. In particular, he reassured the people not to worry about transgressions by speculators and landowners, because the relevant authorities would prevent this. Since the Alimentation [Service] has grain in stock, the Taxation office is not worried about the auction of [grain]. In this meeting only the poor people were worried, but the speculators and landowners [were] quiet. They [were] pleased with the dissolution of the Alimentation [Service] so that they could sell their grain freely at excessive prices. In any case, the governor, the *Amin-e Maliyeh* and the heads of the [government] departments assured them not to be worried. Especially, Hajji Mirza Yahya Khan, the governor, would provide for the well-being of the people.

Marginal note

It should be written to the [Ministry of] Finance that concerning the price [of wheat] in the places where the Alimentation Service is discontinued, a solution must be found and a commission must be formed. The sale of grain by auction is a mistake.

10. Sazman-e Asnad-e Melli-ye Iran no. 310/2329, p.7; National Library no.7472433.

اخبار داخله

اول تیر ۱۳۰۶

از دماوند نظر به انحلال ارزاق دماوند، ضعفا فوق‌العاده در تشویش و اظهار نگرانی می نماید امین دماوند مجلسی در منزل شخصی خود تشکیل و عموم طبقات را با حضور حکومت و روسای ادارات دولتی دعوت نموده [بود]. مخصوصاً به اهالی اطمینان داده شد مظطرب نباشند از تجاوزات محتکرین و مالکین. و مقامات مربوطه جلوگیری میکنند، و چون جنسهای ارزاقی در انبار موجود است، [هر چند که ادارهٔ] مالیه [گندم را] به مزایده گذارده، [اما جای] نگرانی نیست. در این مجلس فوران ضعفا و فقرا متاثر [شدند] ولی مالکین و محتکرین ساکت [ماندن] و از انحلال ارزاق خوشوقت [شدند. چرا] که آزادانه [میتوانستند] جنسهای خودشان را به قیمتهای گزاف بفروشند. به هر حال، از طرف آقایان حکومت و امین مالیه و رؤسای دوایر [به] اهالی اطمینان داده شد [که] مظطرب نباشند. خصوصا آقای حاجی میرزا یحیی خان حکمران که رفاهیت حال اهالی را فراهم می نمایند

حاشیه نامه

به مالیه نوشته شود برای نرخ [گندم در] محالی که [ادارهٔ] ارزاق از آنجا برداشته میشود، فکری باید کرده، و کمیسیونی بخواهید. فروش جنس هم به مزایده غلط است.

BIBLIOGRAPHY

Archives

Molitor Achive, quoted as MA.

The documents were kindly made available to me by the Molitor family, before they became available at the end of January 2021 at: http://belgesenperse.be/

Lambert Molitor's documents concerning the Alimentation Service consisting in (i) letters and (ii) the following reports:

Lambert Molitor: *Mémoires 26 ans en Perse* [numbered typescript] in: Documents, Lambert Molitor: Cliquez ici.

Delcorde, R and Molitor, L. n.d. *L'oeuvre des fonctionnaires belges en Perse. D'apres les souvenirs de quelques-uns d'entre-eux*. [numbered typescript] in: Documents, Lambert Molitor: Cliquez ici.

Farde 38, 3801.pdf. Alimentation. Notes de M. Robinson journaliste americain (de mes interviews).

Farde 38, 3802.pdf. Note-Resumé de mes tribulations dans mes functions a Tauris, 1917-18 (redaction de mon frère Camille Molitor). Décembre 1919 [handwritten note].

Farde 38, 3803.pdf. Jones 1923 Report.

Farde 36, 3617.pdf. Note concernant le service d'Alimentation 20/03/1918 [numbered typescript].

Farde 41, 4102.pdf. Memorandum – Observations de M. Cordonnier.

Farde 41, 4102.pdf. *Yaddasht dar bab-e arzaq-e (nan) Tehran* (see Appendix II). Farde 41, 4101.pdf. Notice concernant l'Arzaghe (pain) de Téhéran (French translation of *Yaddasht*).

Farde 36, 3605.pdf. Zhozef Jamal, *`Ettela`at dar bab-e `amal-e nan-e shahr-e Tabriz va nazariyat dar eslah-e asasi-ye an*. 15 Saratan 1302/7 July 1923 (see chapter III).

Ransquin Papers, quoted as RP.

Privates papers of Emile Ransquin, directeur of Customs at Jolfa, provincial director of Customs and Finance of Azerbaijan, and provincial director of Customs of Gilan (1908-1914), were kindly made available by his descendants Philippe Uyttebroek and Mireille Colette. The documents from this archive are now also available at: http://belgesenperse.be/ .(in:Documents, Emile Ransquin, Documents: Cliquez ici.)

Dossier 1: Journal extraits de correspondence.docx.

Dossier 2: Extraits de presse et divers.docx.

India Office (British Library, London)

IOR/L/PS/10/450, 'Persia - Policy Anglo-Russian relations', Consul Shipley to Sir Walter Townley, Tabriz 10/06/1914.

IOR/L/PS/10/451/1, Persia – Policy. British Interests in the South. Russian Policy.'

IOR/L/PS/10/550/2, 'Persia: The "Moratorium."'

IOR/L/PS/10/646, Persia: famine relief.

IOR/L/PS/12/3444, Trade Report of Kirman Consulate District for the year ending March 1928.

IOR/L/PS/12/3451, 'Persia. Who's Who, and Leading Personalities.

IOR/L/PS/12/3465, 'Persia. Financial Situation, Budget for the year 1311 (March 21, 1932-March 20, 1933).

IOR/L/PS/12/3465, Persia. Financial Situation.'

IOR/L/PS/20/C188, 'Persia. Handbooks prepared under the direction of the Historical Section of the Foreign Office - no 80.

IOR/L/MIL/17/15/11/3, Who's Who in Persia (Volume II) [1923].

IOR/L/MIL/17/15/23, Military report on Tehran and adjacent Provinces of North-West Persia (including the Caspian Littoral).

IOR/L/MIL/17/15/28, History of the Great War based on Official Documents: Operations in Persia 1914-1919.

National Archives (London-Kew Gardens)

FO 416/81, Memorandum Mismanagement Alimentation Service by E.R. Lingeman. 02/07/1927.

Books and Articles

Adhari, `Ali 1354/1975. *Sheikh Mohammad Khiyabani*. Tehran: Bongah-e Matbu`at.

Administration Report = *Administration Report of the Persian Gulf Political Residency for the year (1873 to 1935)* in Government of India. *The Persian Gulf Administration Reports 1873-1947*, 10 vols., Gerrards Cross, Archives Editions, 1986.

Afshar, Iraj 1389/2010. *Daftar-e Tarikh, majmu`eh-ye asnad va manabe`-ye tarikhi*, daftar chaharom. Tehran, Bonyad-e Mahmud Afshar, pp. 489-91.

Agah, Manuchehr 1958. *Some Aspects of Economic Development of Modern Iran*. unpublished thesis Oxford University.

Aghasi, Mahdi 1350/1981. *Tarikh-e Khuy*. Tabriz.

Amir Khizi, Esma`il 1339/1960. *Qiyam-e Azarbaijan va Sattar Khan*. Tehran.

`Aqeli, Baqer 1370. *Nakhust-vaziran-e Iran. Az Moshir al-Dowleh ta Bakhtiyari*. Tehran: Javidan.

Avery, Peter 1967. *Modern Iran*, London: Ernest Benn.

Bahrami, Abdollah 1344/1965. *Khaterat az Saltanat-e Naser al-Din Shah to Avval-e Ku deta*. Tehran.

Baladiyeh-ye Tehran, *Servis-e ma`aref, dayereh-ye ehsa'iyeh*. Tehran: Baladiyeh 1310/1931.

Barton, James L. 1930. *Story of Near East Relief 1915-1930*. New York: MacMillan, 1930 (chapter 8 deals with Iran).

Bast, Olivier ed. 2002. *La Perse et la Grande Guerre*. Paris/Tehran.

Browne, E.G. 1914. *Press and Poetry of Modern Persia*. Cambridge: Cambridge UP.

Burrell, Robert Michael and Jarman, Robert L. eds. *Iran: Political Diaries 1881-1965*. 14 vols. Archive Editions, 1997.

Chaqueri, C. ed. 1978. *The Condition of the Working Class*. Florence: Mazdak.

Clawson, Patrick 1993. "Knitting Iran Together: The Land Transport Revolution, 1920-1940," *Iranian Studies* 26/3-4, pp. 236-50.

Curzon, G.N. 1892. *Persia and the Persian Question* 2 vols. London.

DCR or Diplomatic and Consular Reports, Government of Great Britain:

DCR 423, "Report on the Agricultural Resources of the Province of Azerbaijan, District of Tabreez by K. Abbott," pp. 1-4.

De Lorey, Eustace & Sladen, Douglas 1910. *The Moon of the Fourteenth Night*. London: Hurst & Blackett.

Demorgny, G. 1913. *Essai sur l'Administration de la Perse*. Paris.

___1916. *La question persane et la guerre*, Paris.

Destrée, Annette 1976. *Les fonctionnaires belges au service de la Perse 1898-1915*. Tehran-Liege: E.J. Brill.

Dunsterville, K.C. 1932. *The Adventures of the Dunsterforce*. London: Edward Arnold.

\`Emad al-Kottab 1384/2005. *Komiteh-ye mojazat va khaterat-e \`Emad al-Kottab*. ed. Mohammad Javad Moradi-niya. Tehran: Asatir.

Eyn al-Saltaneh, Qahraman Mirza Salur 1376/1997. *Ruznameh-ye Khaterat*. 10 vols. eds. Mas\`ud Salur and Iraj Afshar. Tehran: Asatir.

Fateh, M.K. 1926. *The Economic Position of Persia*. London.

Ferrier, Ronald W. 1982. *The History of the British Petroleum Company*. Cambridge: CUP.

Floor, Willem 1998. *The Fiscal History of Iran in the Safavid and Qajar Periods*. New York: Bibliotheca Persia.

___2003. *Agriculture in Qajar Iran*. Washington DC: MAGE.

___2005. "Review of Mohammad Gholi Majd, The Great Famine and Genocide in Persia, 1917-1919," in *Iranian Studies* 31, pp. 192-96.

___2015. *History of Bread in Iran*. Washington DC: MAGE.

___2018. *Studies in Medical History of Iran*. Washington DC: MAGE.

___2021. *History of Hospitals in Iran 550-1950*. Washington DC: MAGE.

Forbes-Leith, F.A.C. 1927. *Checkmate, Fighting Tradition in Central Persia*. New York: Robert M. McBride & Company.

___, 2022. "Plague in Sistan – 1905-06" (awaiting publication)

Gholami, Sharam 1396/2017. *Eqtesad-e Keshavarzi-ye Iran*. Tehran: Donya-ye Eqtesad.

Government of Great Britain 1914. *Persia no. 1 (1914) Further Correspondence respecting the Affairs of Persia*. London: HMSO.

Government of Iran n.d. *Majmu\`eh-ye Qavanin. \`Ahdnamehha, Kontratha, Kholaseh-ye Tasmimat-e Mataleb-e Motafarreqeh*. Tehran.

___ 1302 a/1923. *Sevvomin raport seh-maheh-ye ra'is-e koll-e maliyeh-ye*

Iran 21 June 1923/21 Juza 1302. Tehran.

___1302 b/1923-24. *Chaharomin raport-e seh maheh-ye ra'is-e koll-e maliyeh-ye Iran -1 Mizan 1302 /24 December 1923*. Tehran.

___ 1302 c/1923. *Panjomin raport-e seh maheh-ye ra'is-e koll-e maliyeh-ye Iran 1 Jadi 1302/23 December 1923*. Tehran.

___1302 d/1923. *Sheshomin raport-e seh maheh-ye ra'is-e koll-e maliyeh-ye Iran –Jadi-Hut 1302/22 December 1923-20March 1924*. Tehran.

___ 1303 a/1924. *Haftomin raport-e seh maheh-ye ra'is-e koll-e maliyeh-ye Iran rajeb-e seh-maheh-ye Hamal-Juza 1303/21 March-20 June 1924*. Tehran.

___ 1303 b/1924. *Hashtomin raport-e seh maheh-ye ra'is-e koll-e maliyeh-ye Iran rajeb-e seh-maheh-ye Saratan-Sonboleh 1303/21 June-22 September 1924*. Tehran.

___ 1303 c/1924. *Nohomin raport-e ra'is-e maliyeh-ye Ira rajeb-e, seh-maheh-ye Mizan-Qods 1303 (22 Sept-21 Dec. 1924)*. Tehran.

___ 1304 a/1925. *Davazdahomin raport-e ra'is-e maliyeh-ye Iran rajeb-e seh maheh-ye Tir-Shahrivar 1304/22 June-22 Sept. 1925*. Tehran.

___ 1304 b/1925. *Sizdahomin raport-e ra'is-e maliyeh-ye Iran rajeb-e seh maheh-ye Mehr-Adhar 1304/23 Sept. -21 December 1925*. Tehran.

___ 1304 c/1925-26. *Chahardahomin raport-e ra'is-e koll-e maliyeh-ye Iran rajeb-e seh maheh-ye Mehr-Esfand 1304/22 December- 21 March 1926*. Tehran.

___ 1305 a/1926. *Panzdahommin raport-e ra'is-e koll-e maliyeh-ye Iran rajeb-e seh maheh-ye Farvardin-Khordad 1305/22 March-22 June 1926.*

___ 1305 b/1926-27. *Hijdahommin raport-e ra'is-e koll-e maliyeh-ye Iran rajeb-e seh maheh-ye Dey-Esfand 1305/23 December 1926-22 March 1927*. Tehran.

___ 1306 a/1927. *Nineteenth Quarterly Report for the three months Farvardin-Khordad 1306/22 March-22 June 1927*. Tehran.

___ 1306 b/1927. *Twentieth Quarterly Report for the three months Tir-Shahrivar 1306/23June-23 September 1927*. Tehran.

___ 1306 c/1927. *Bist o yekomin raport rajeb-e seh-maheh-ye Mehr-Adhar 1306/24 September-22 December 1927*. Tehran.

___ 1306 d/1927-28. *Bist o dovvomin raport rajeb-e seh-maheh-ye Dey-Esfand 1306/22 December 1927-20 March 1928*. Tehran.

___ 1307 a/1928. *Bist o sevvomin raport-e vezarat-e maliyeh – rajeb-e shesh maheh-ye Farvardin to Shahrivar 1307/21 March-22 Sept. 1928.*

Tehran.

___ 1307 b/1928-29. *Bist o chaharomin raport rajeb-e shesh maheh-ye Mehr-Esfand 1307/23 December 1928-20 March 1929*. Tehran.

___ 1308 a/1929. *Bist o panjomin raport rajeb-e shesh maheh-ye Farvardin-Shahrivar 1308/21 March-22 September 1929*. Tehran.

___ 1308 b/1929-30. *Bist o sheshomin raport rajeb-e shesh-maheh-ye Mehr-Esfand 1308/23September 1929-20 March 1930*. Tehran.

Gray, F.A.G. 1938. *Report on Economic and Commercial Conditions in Iran during 1937*. London: HMSO.

Hadow, R.H. 1925. *Report on the Trade and Industry of Persia*. London: HMSO.

Hellot-Bellier, Florence 2002. "La Premiere Guerrre mondiale a l'ouest du lac d'Urumiye," in Bast 2002, pp. 329-52.

Issawi, Charles 1971. *The Economic History of Persia*. Chicago: Chicago UP.

Jackson, Kate 1920. *Around the World to Persia- letters written while on the journey as a member of the American Persian Relief Commission in 1918*. New York.

Jones, Geoffrey 1986. *Banking and Empire in Iran*. 2 vols. London: Cambridge UP.

Kasravi, Ahmad 1319/1940. *Tarikh-e Mashruteh-ye Iran*. 3 vols. Tehran.

___, 1350/1971. *Tarikh-e Hejdeh Saleh-ye Azerbaijan*. Tehran: Amir Kabir,

Katouzian, Homa 1981. *The Political Economy of Modern Iran 1926-1979*. New York: NY UP.

Kosogovski, V.A. 1344/1965. *Iz Tegenrankovo Dnevnika*, translated into Persian by Abbas Qoli Jali, *Khaterat-e kulunel Kasakufski*. Tehran: Jibi.

Kuhestani-nezhad, Mas`ud 1381/2002. "Sal-e dampokhtak; qahti-ye sal-e 1296 sh." *Faslnameh-ye ganjineh-ye asnad*, 12/1-2, pp. 40-52.

Laureys, Eric. 1996. *Belgen in Perzië 1915-1941, verwezenlijkingen, verhoudingen en attitudes*. Leuven: Peeters.

Lingeman, E.R. 1928. *Report on the Finance and Commerce of Persia, 1925-27* London: HMSO.

Mahdrad, Ahmad 1976. *Iran auf dem Weg zur Diktatur-Militarisierung und Widerstand 1919-1925*. Hannover: SOAK.

Majd, Mohammad Gholi 2003. *The Great Famine and Genocide in Per-*

sia, 1917-1919. Lanham, MD: University Press of America.

Makki, Hoseyn 1357/1978. *Tarikh-e Bist Saleh-ye Iran.* 10 vols. Tehran: Amir Kabir.

Merritt-Hawkes, O. A. *Persia – Romance & Reality* (London: Nicholson & Watson, 1935).

Millspaugh, A.C. 1925. *The American Task in Persia.* New York.

___, 1926. *The Financial and Economic Situation of Persia.* New York, 1926.

Mojtahedi, Mehdi 1327/1958. *Rejal-e Azerbaijan dar `asr-e mashrutiyat.* Tehran: Naqsh-e Jahan.

Molkara, 1325/1946. *Sharh-e Hal* ed. Abbas Eqbal. Tehran.

Mostashar al-Dowleh Sadeq, *Khatera va Asnad. Raportha-ye Polis-e Makhfi az Shaye`at-e Shahri (salha-ye 1333 va 1335 qamari).* ed. Iraj Afshar. Tehran: Talayeh, 1367

Mostowfi, Abdollah 1324/1945. *Sharh-e Zendegani-ye Man* 3 vols. Tehran: Zavvar.

Najmi, Naser 1370/1991. *Az Sayyed Ziya ta Bazargan.* 2 vols. Tehran.

Nazem, Hossein 1975. *Russia and Great Britain in Iran (1900-1914).* Tehran: author.

Nielsen, Oren N. "Near East. Persian Economic Developments, Second Quarter of 1926," in: *Commerce Reports* No. 42, 18 October 1926 (Washington DC: Department of Commerce), pp. 184-85.

Shoko Okazaki, "The great Persian famine of 1870-71," *BSOAS* XLIX 1 (1986) pp. 183-192.

Overseas Consultants, Inc. 1949. *Report on the Seven Year Development Plan for the Plan Organization of the Imperial Government of Iran.* 5 vols. New York.

Polak, J.E. 1865. *Persien, das Land und seine Bewohner.* 2 vols. Leipzig: F.A. Brockhaus.

RMM or *Revue du Monde Musulmane*.

Qodsi, Hasan A`zam 1342/1963. *Ketab-e Khaterat-e Man.* 2 vols. Tehran:

Rockwell, William Walker 1916. *The Pityful Plight of the Assyrian Christians in Persia and Kurdistan.* New York, American Committee for Armenian and Assyrian Relief.

Rowghani, Sayyed Da'ud 1385/2006. *Nan-e Sangak.* ed. and intr. by Javad Safi-nezhad. Tehran.

Ruznameh-ye Majles 1376/1997. 4 vols. Tehran: Ketabkhaneh-ye Muzeh va Markaz-e Asnad-e Majles-e Shura-ye Eslami.

Sadr, Mohsen 1364/1985. *Khaterat-e Sadr al-Ashraf.* Tehran: Vahid.

Sani` al-Dowleh 1306/1889. *Ketab al-Ma'ather va'l-Athar*. Tehran (lithograph).

Shahri, Ja`far 1368/1989. *Tarikh-e ejtema`i-ye Tehran dar qarn-e sizdahhom*. 6 vols. Tehran: Rasa.

___, 1371/1992. *Tehran-e Qadim*. 5 vols. Tehran: Mo`in.

Sharaf al-Dowleh, Mirza Ebrahim Khan Kalantari-ye Baghmiseh 1377/1998. *Ruznameh-ye Khaterat*. ed. Yahya Dhoka'. Tehran, Fekr-e Ruz.

Shedd, Mary Lewis 1922. *The Measure of a Man. The Life of William Ambrose Shedd Missionary to Persia*. New York: George H. Doran.

Sheean, Vincent 1927. *New Persia*. New York: The New Century.

Shuster, W.M. 1912. *The Strangling of Persia*. New York: The Century.

Siassi, Ali Akbar 1931. *La Perse au contact de l'Occident*. Paris: Ernest Leroux.

Simmonds, S. 1935. *Economic Conditions in Iran (Persia)*. London: HMSO.

Skrine, Sir Clarmont 1960. *World War in Iran*. London: Constable & Company.

Tafazzoli, Mahmud, 1340/1961 "Yaddashtha-ye chap nashodeh-ye Sepahsalar-e Tonkabuni," *Rahnama-ye Ketab* 4/5-6, pp. 530-38.

Torabi, Soheyla. "Negahi beh vazi`at-e arzaq dar Iran dar salha-ye jang-e jahani-y avval," *Faslnameh-ye ganjineh-ye asnad*, pp. 24-33.

Wilber, Donald D. 1975. *Riza Shah Pahlavi. The Resurrection and Reconstruction of iran 1878-1944*. Hicksville, NY: Exposition Press.

Wilbraham, Richard 1839. *Travels in the Transcaucasian Provinces of Russia*. London: John Murray.

Yakta'i, Majid 1340/1961. *Tarikh-e Dara'i-ye Iran*. Tehran.

Zirinsky, Michael 2002. "American Presbyterian Missionaries at Urmia during the Great War," in Bast 2002, pp. 353-74.

INDEX

C

D

E

F

G

H

I

J

K

L

M

N

O

P

Q

R

S

T

Other Willem Floor Titles

THE PERSIAN GULF SERIES

A Political and Economic History of 5 Port Cities, 1500–1750

The Rise of the Gulf Arabs, The Politics of Trade on the Persian Littoral, 1747–1792

The Rise and Fall of Bandar-e Lengeh, The Distribution Center for the Arabian Coast, 1750–1930

Bandar Abbas: The Natural Trade Gateway of Southeast Iran

Links with the Hinterland: Bushehr, Borazjan, Kazerun, Banu Ka'b, & Bandar Abbas

The Hula Arabs of The Shibkuh Coast of Iran

Dutch-Omani Relations: A Political History, 1651–1806

Muscat: City, Society and Trade

Karkh: The Island's Untold Story (with D.T. Potts)

The Persian Gulf: Bushehr: City, Society, & Trade, 1797-1947

The Rebel Bandits of Tangestan

IRANIAN HISTORY

Agriculture in Qajar Iran

Public Health in Qajar Iran

The History of Theater in Iran

A Social History of Sexual Relations in Iran

Guilds, Merchants, and Ulama in Nineteenth-Century Iran

Labor & Industry in Iran 1850 -1941

The Rise and Fall of Nader Shah: Dutch East India Company Reports 1730-1747

Games Persians Play: A History of Games and Pastimes in Iran from Hide-and-Seek to Hunting

History of Bread in Iran

Studies in the History of Medicine in Iran

Salar al-Dowleh: A Delusional Prince and Wannabe Shah

Kermanshah: City and Province, 1800-1945

History of Hospitals in Iran, 550–1950

The Beginnings of Modern Medicine in Iran

ANNOTATED TRANSLATIONS

German Sources on Safavid Persia

Exotic Attractions in Persia, 1684–1688: Travels & Observations
Engelbert Kaempfer:

A Man of Two Worlds: Pedros Bedik in Iran, 1670–1675
translated with Colette Ouahes from the Latin

Astrakhan Anno 1770
Samuel Gottlieb Gmelin

Travels Through Northern Persia 1770–1774
Samuel Gottlieb Gmelin

Titles and Emoluments in Safavid Iran: A Third Manual of Safavid Administration
Mirza Naqi Nasiri

Persia: An Area Study, 1633
Joannes de Laet

translated with Colette Ouahes from the Latin

IN COLLABORATION WITH HASAN JAVADI

Persian Pleasures
How Iranians Relaxed Through the Centuries with Food, Drink and Drugs

Awake: A Moslem Woman's Rare Memoir of Her Life and Partnership with the Editor of Molla Nasreddin, the Most Influential Satirical Journal of the Caucasus and Iran, 1907–1931

The Heavenly Rose-Garden: A History of Shirvan & Daghestan
Abbas Qoli Aqa Bakikhanov

Travels in Iran and the Caucasus, 1652 and 1655
Evliya Chelebi

Other Mage Titles

Poetry

Faces of Love: Hafez and the Poets of Shiraz – Bilingual Edition
Translated by Dick Davis

The Mirror Of My Heart:
A Thousand Years of Persian Poetry by Women, Bilingual Edition
Translated by Dick Davis

Layli and Majnun
Nezami Ganjavi / Translated by Dick Davis

Shahnameh: the Persian Book of Kings
Abolqasem Ferdowsi / Translated by Dick Davis

Rostam: Tales of Love and War from Persia's Book of Kings
Abolqasem Ferdowsi / Translated by Dick Davis

Borrowed Ware: Medieval Persian Epigrams
Introduced and Translated by Dick Davis

At Home and Far from Home
Poems on Iran and Persian Culture
Dick Davis

They Broke Down the Door: Poems
Fatemeh Shams / Introduction and translations by Dick Davis

The Layered Heart: Essays on Persian Poetry
In Celebration of Dick Davis
Edited by Ali-Asghar Seyyed Ghorab

Another Birth and Other Poems
By Forugh Farrokhzad, translated by Hasan Javadi and Susan Sallée
Bilingual edition

Obeyd-e Zakani: Ethics of Aristocrats and other Satirical Works
translated by Hasan Javadi

Persia Observed Series

The Strangling of Persia:
A Story of European Diplomacy and Oriental Intrigue
Morgan Shuster

The Persian Revolution of 1905-1909
Edward Brown / Introduction by Abbas Amanat

In the Land of the Lion & Sun:
Experiences of Life in Persia from 1866-1881
C. J. Wills / Introduction by Abbas Amanat

A Man of Many Worlds:
The Diaries and Memoirs of Dr. Ghasem Ghani
Ghasem Ghani / Edited by Cyrus Ghani

Fiction

My Uncle Napoleon
Iraj Pezeshkzad / Translated by Dick Davis

Savushun: A Novel about Modern Iran
Simin Daneshvar / Translated by M.R. Ghanoonparvar

Daneshvar's Playhouse: A Collection of Stories
Simin Daneshvar / Translated by Maryam Mafi

Sutra and Other Stories
Simin Daneshvar / Translated by Hasan Javadi & Amin Neshati

Stories from Iran: A Chicago Anthology 1921-1991
Edited by Heshmat Moayyad

Garden of the Brave in War
Terence O'Donnell

King of the Benighted
Houshang Golshiri / Translated by Abbas Milani

Black Parrot, Green Crow: A Collection of Short Fiction
Houshang Golshiri / Translated by Heshmat Moayyad et al.

Seven Shades of Memory: Stories of Old Iran
Terence O'Donnell

Memoir and History

The Persian Sphinx:
Amir Abbas Hoveyda and the Iranian Revolution
Abbas Milani

Discovering Cyrus: The Persian Conqueror
Astride the Ancient World
Reza Zarghamee

Tarikh-e Azodi, Life at the Court of the Early Qajar Shahs
Soltan Ahmad Mirza Azod al-Dowleh,
Edited and Translated Manoutchehr M. Eskandari-Qajar

Crowning Anguish: Taj al-Saltana
Memoirs of a Persian Princess
Introduction by Abbas Amanat / Translated by Anna Vanzan

Tales of Two Cities:
A Persian Memoir
Abbas Milani

Lost Wisdom:
Rethinking Modernity in Iran
Abbas Milani

French Hats in Iran
Heydar Radjavi

Father Takes a Drink and Other Memories of Iran
Heydar Radjavi

The Persian Garden: Echoes of Paradise
Mehdi Khansari / M. R. Moghtader / Minouch Yavari

Closed Circuit History
Ardeshir Mohassess, foreword by Ramsey Clark

Mosaddegh: Ahead of Their Time, Book 1
Nicolas Gorjestani

Zviad: Ahead of Their Time, Book 2
Nicolas Gorjestani

Cookbooks

Food of Life: Ancient Persian and Modern Iranian Cooking and Ceremonies
Najmieh Batmanglij

Joon: Persian Cooking Made Simple
Najmieh Batmanglij

Cooking in Iran: Regional Recipes and Kitchen Secrets
Najmieh Batmanglij

Silk Road Cooking: A Vegetarian Journey
Najmieh Batmanglij

From Persia to Napa: Wine at the Persian Table
Najmieh Batmanglij, Dick Davis, Burke Owens

Cinema

The Films of Makhmalbaf: Cinema, Politics, and Culture in Iran
Eric Egan

Masters & Masterpieces of Iranian Cinema
Hamid Dabashi

My Favorite Films
Cyrus Ghani

Lightning Source UK Ltd.
Milton Keynes UK
UKHW012234021121
393274UK00002B/36

9 781949 445374